RE-GIFTERS

Published by DC Comics.

1700 Broadway, New York, NY 10019.

Printed in Canada.

DC Comics, a Warner Bros.

Entertainment Company.

ISBN: 1-4012-0371-X
ISBN: 978-1-4012-0371-9

COVER BY SONNY LIEW AND MARC HEMPEL

Re-Gifters

Written by **Mike Carey**

Art by **Sonny Liew and Marc Hempel**

Graytones by **Jesse Hamm**

Lettering by **John J. Hill**

re-gift (rē-**gift**)
—*verb*
1. to give an unwanted gift to someone else; to give as a gift something one previously received as a gift; also written *regift*

Example: *We have a neighbor who we know re-gifts, and we think that is very low class.*

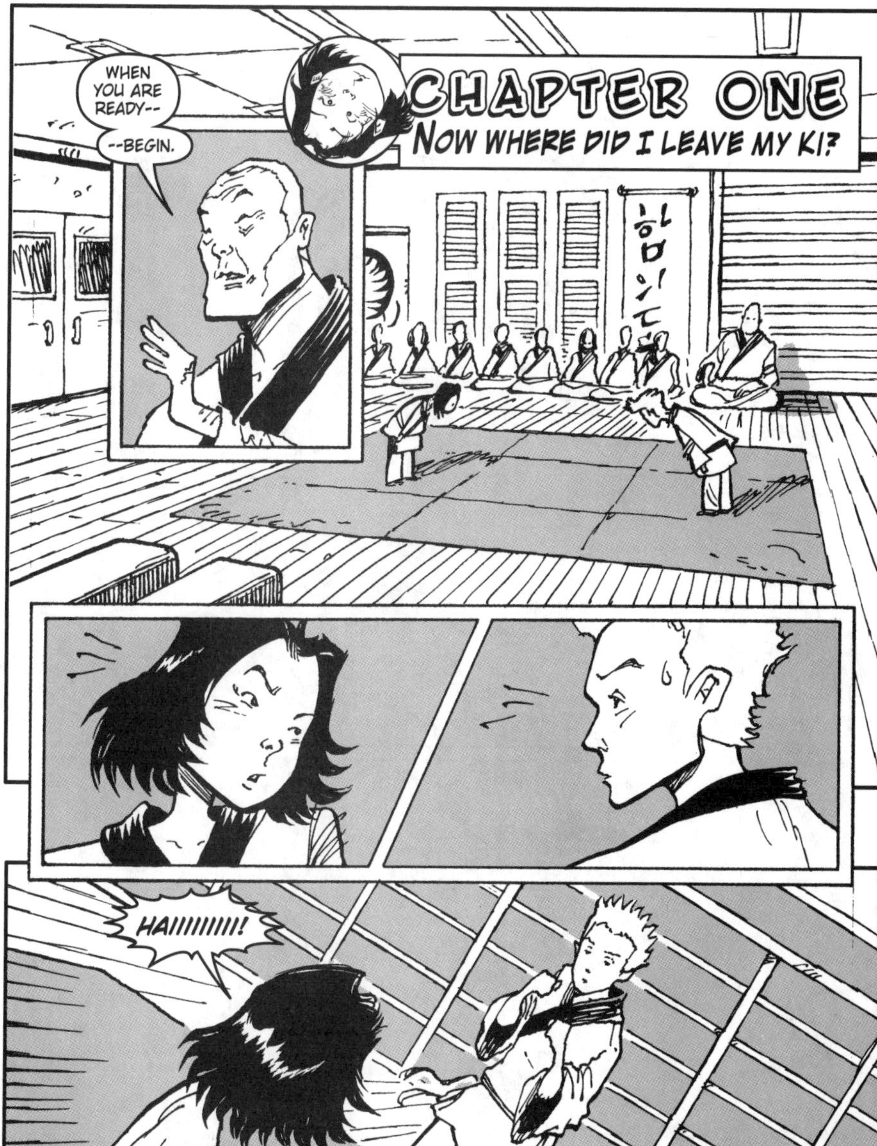
WHEN YOU ARE READY--
--BEGIN.
CHAPTER ONE
NOW WHERE DID I LEAVE MY KI?
HAIIIIIIIII!

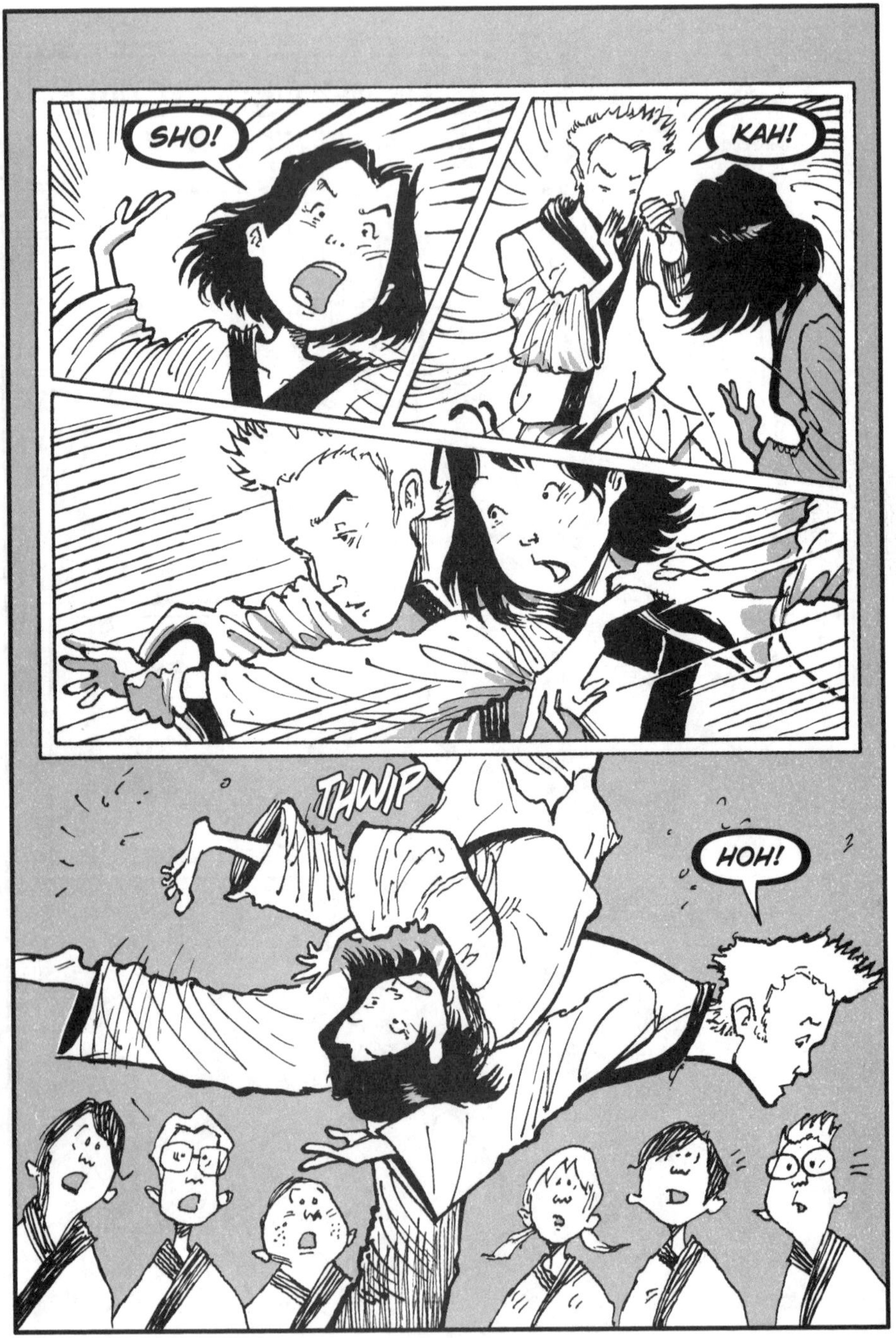
SHO!
KAH!
THWIP
HOH!

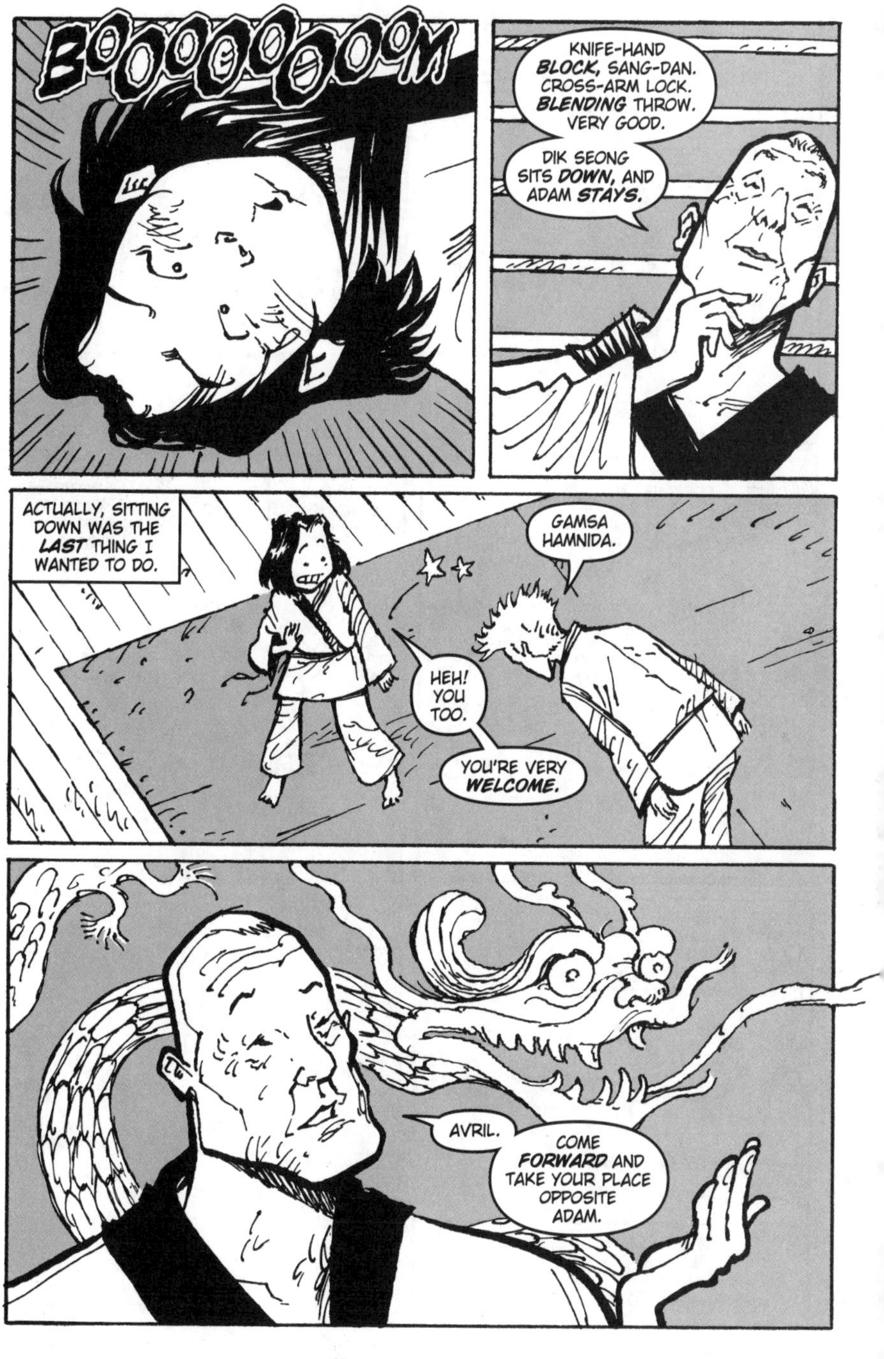
BOOOOOOOOOM
KNIFE-HAND BLOCK, SANG-DAN. CROSS-ARM LOCK. BLENDING THROW. VERY GOOD.
DIK SEONG SITS DOWN, AND ADAM STAYS.
ACTUALLY, SITTING DOWN WAS THE LAST THING I WANTED TO DO.
GAMSA HAMNIDA.
HEH! YOU TOO.
YOU'RE VERY WELCOME.
AVRIL.
COME FORWARD AND TAKE YOUR PLACE OPPOSITE ADAM.

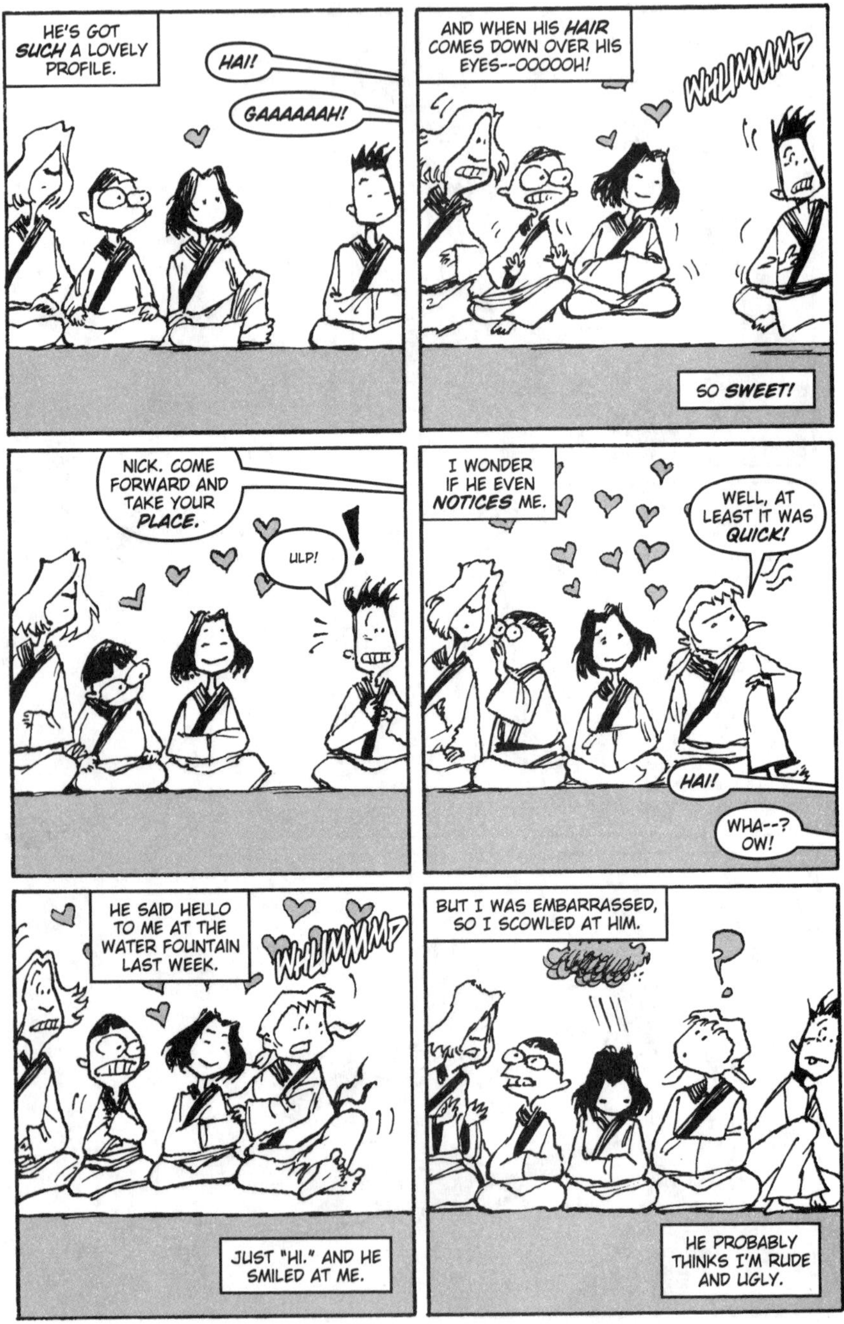
HE'S GOT SUCH A LOVELY PROFILE.
HAI!
GAAAAAAH!
AND WHEN HIS HAIR COMES DOWN OVER HIS EYES--OOOOOH!
WHUMMMP
SO SWEET!
NICK. COME FORWARD AND TAKE YOUR PLACE.
ULP!
!
I WONDER IF HE EVEN NOTICES ME.
WELL, AT LEAST IT WAS QUICK!
HAI!
WHA--? OW!
HE SAID HELLO TO ME AT THE WATER FOUNTAIN LAST WEEK.
WHUMMMP
JUST "HI." AND HE SMILED AT ME.
BUT I WAS EMBARRASSED, SO I SCOWLED AT HIM.
?
HE PROBABLY THINKS I'M RUDE AND UGLY.

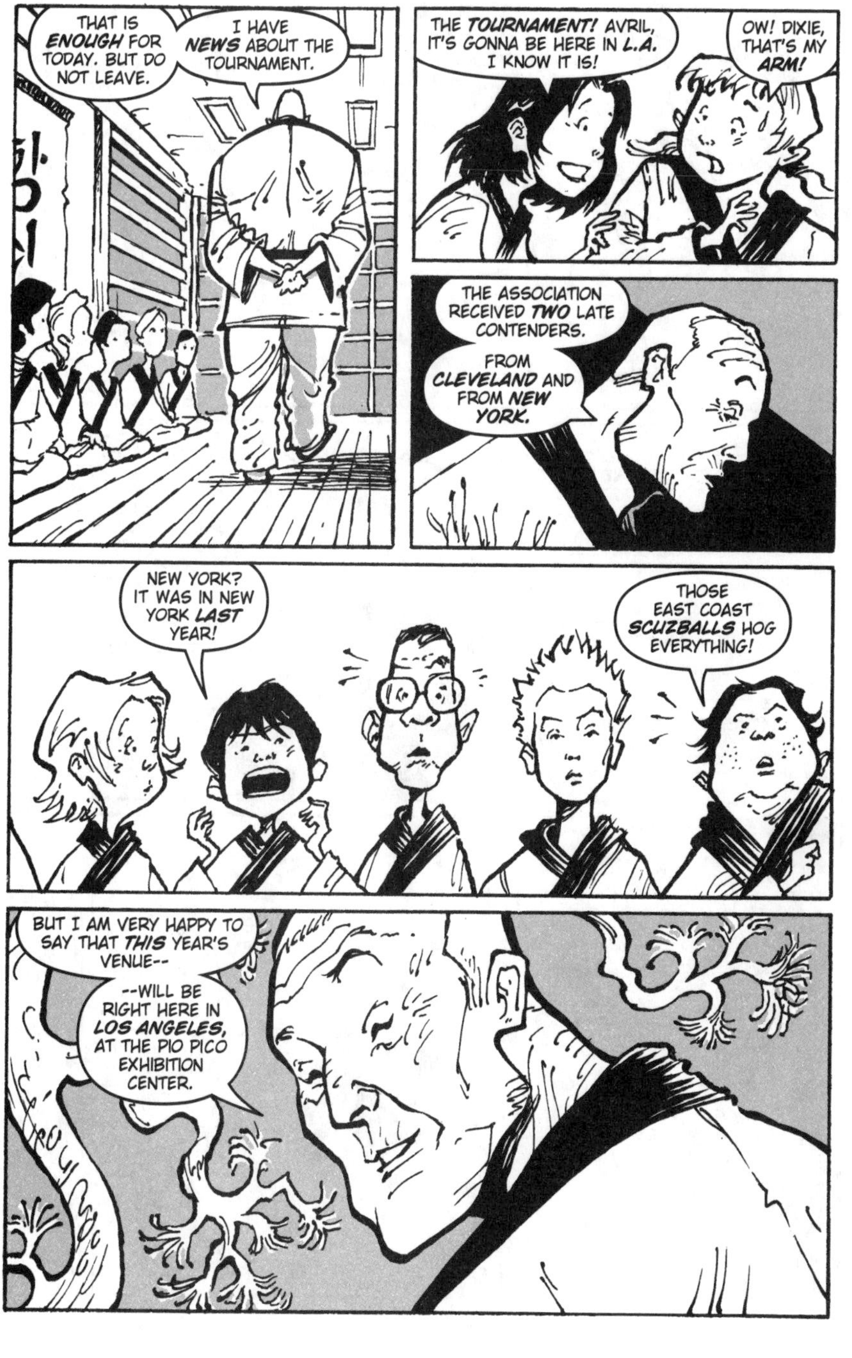
THAT IS ENOUGH FOR TODAY. BUT DO NOT LEAVE.
I HAVE NEWS ABOUT THE TOURNAMENT.
THE TOURNAMENT! AVRIL, IT'S GONNA BE HERE IN L.A. I KNOW IT IS!
OW! DIXIE, THAT'S MY ARM!
THE ASSOCIATION RECEIVED TWO LATE CONTENDERS.
FROM CLEVELAND AND FROM NEW YORK.
NEW YORK? IT WAS IN NEW YORK LAST YEAR!
THOSE EAST COAST SCUZBALLS HOG EVERYTHING!
BUT I AM VERY HAPPY TO SAY THAT THIS YEAR'S VENUE--
--WILL BE RIGHT HERE IN LOS ANGELES, AT THE PIO PICO EXHIBITION CENTER.

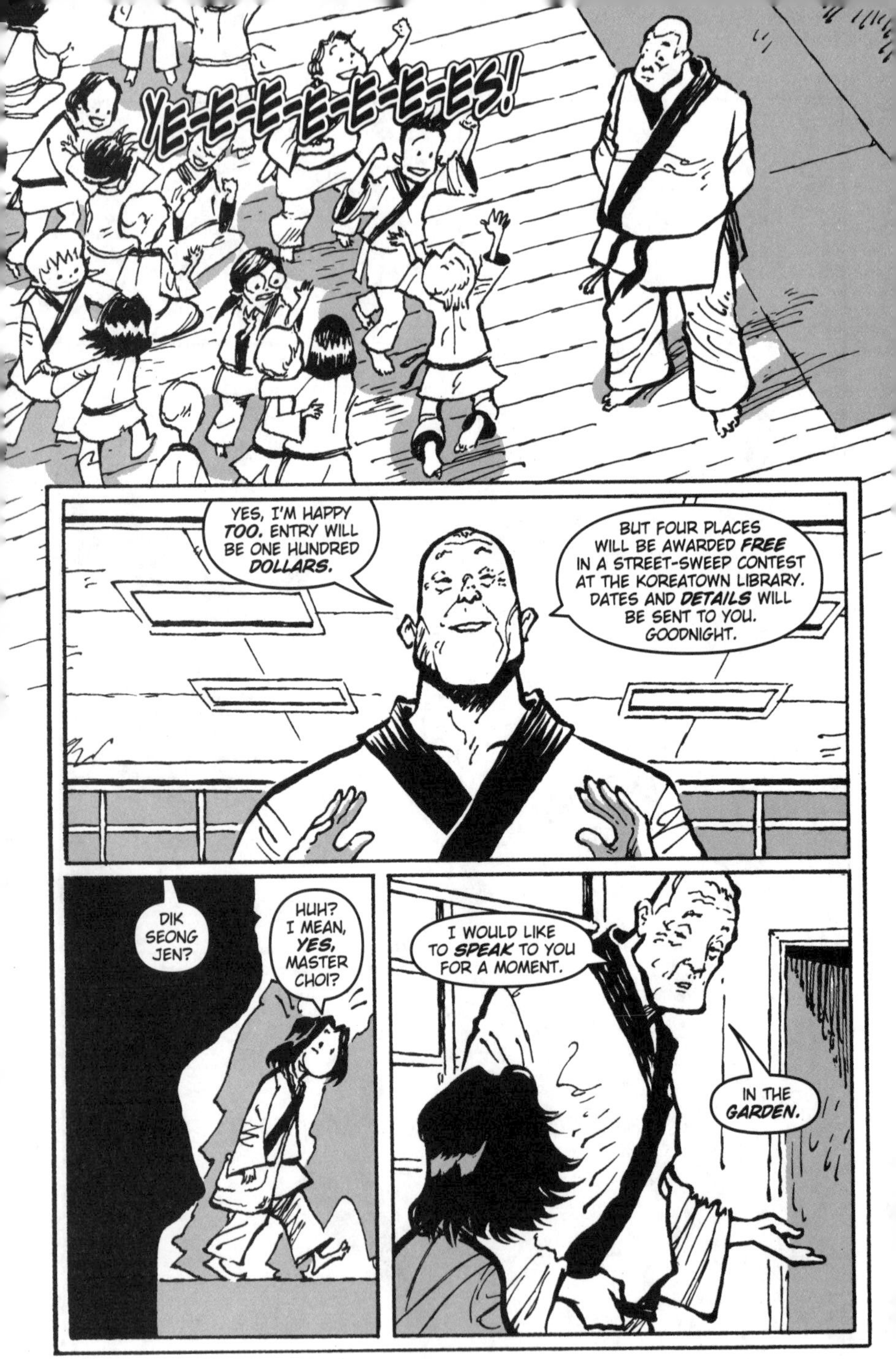
YE-E-E-E-E-E-E-ES!
YES, I'M HAPPY TOO. ENTRY WILL BE ONE HUNDRED DOLLARS.
BUT FOUR PLACES WILL BE AWARDED FREE IN A STREET-SWEEP CONTEST AT THE KOREATOWN LIBRARY. DATES AND DETAILS WILL BE SENT TO YOU. GOODNIGHT.
DIK SEONG JEN?
HUH? I MEAN, YES, MASTER CHOI?
I WOULD LIKE TO SPEAK TO YOU FOR A MOMENT.
IN THE GARDEN.

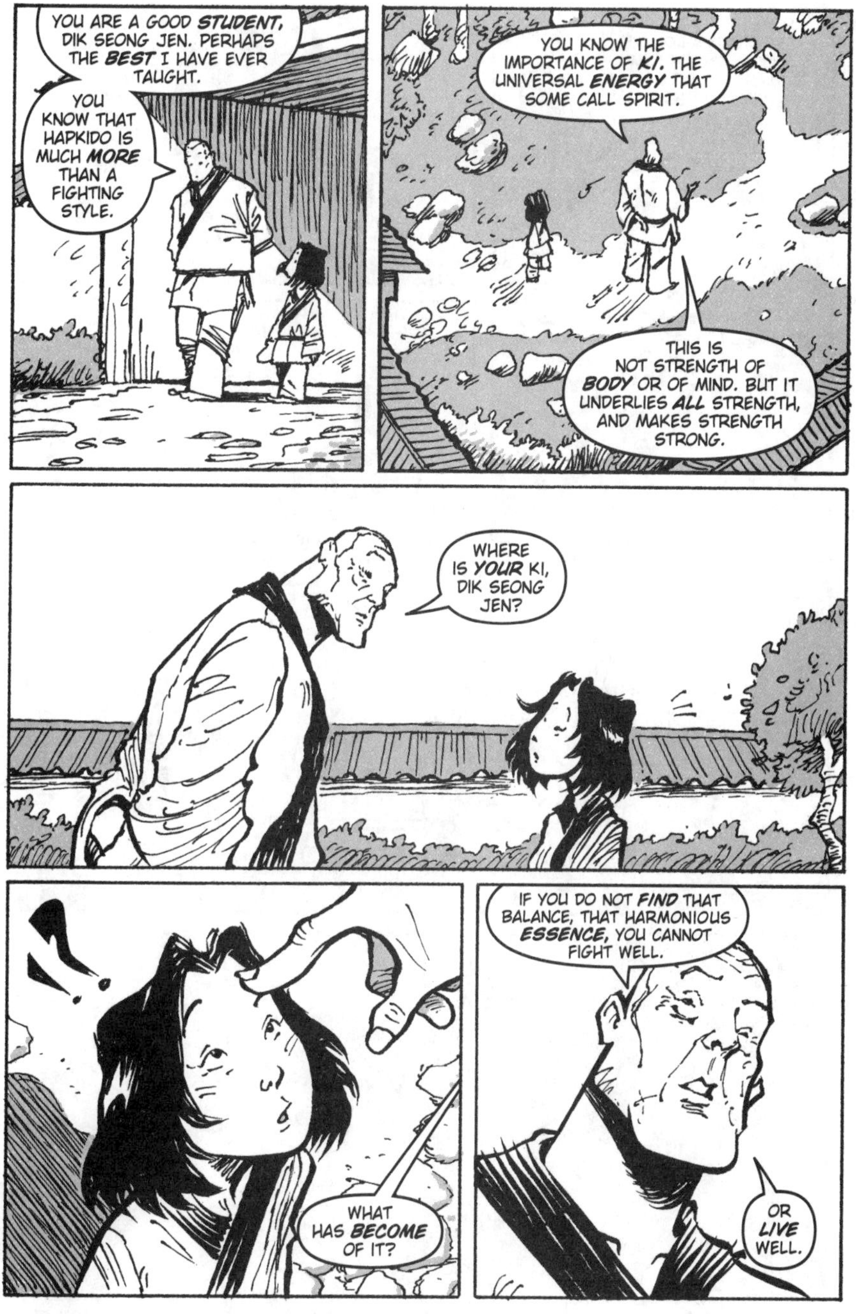
YOU ARE A GOOD STUDENT, DIK SEONG JEN. PERHAPS THE BEST I HAVE EVER TAUGHT.
YOU KNOW THAT HAPKIDO IS MUCH MORE THAN A FIGHTING STYLE.
YOU KNOW THE IMPORTANCE OF KI. THE UNIVERSAL ENERGY THAT SOME CALL SPIRIT.
THIS IS NOT STRENGTH OF BODY OR OF MIND. BUT IT UNDERLIES ALL STRENGTH, AND MAKES STRENGTH STRONG.
WHERE IS YOUR KI, DIK SEONG JEN?
WHAT HAS BECOME OF IT?
IF YOU DO NOT FIND THAT BALANCE, THAT HARMONIOUS ESSENCE, YOU CANNOT FIGHT WELL.
OR LIVE WELL.

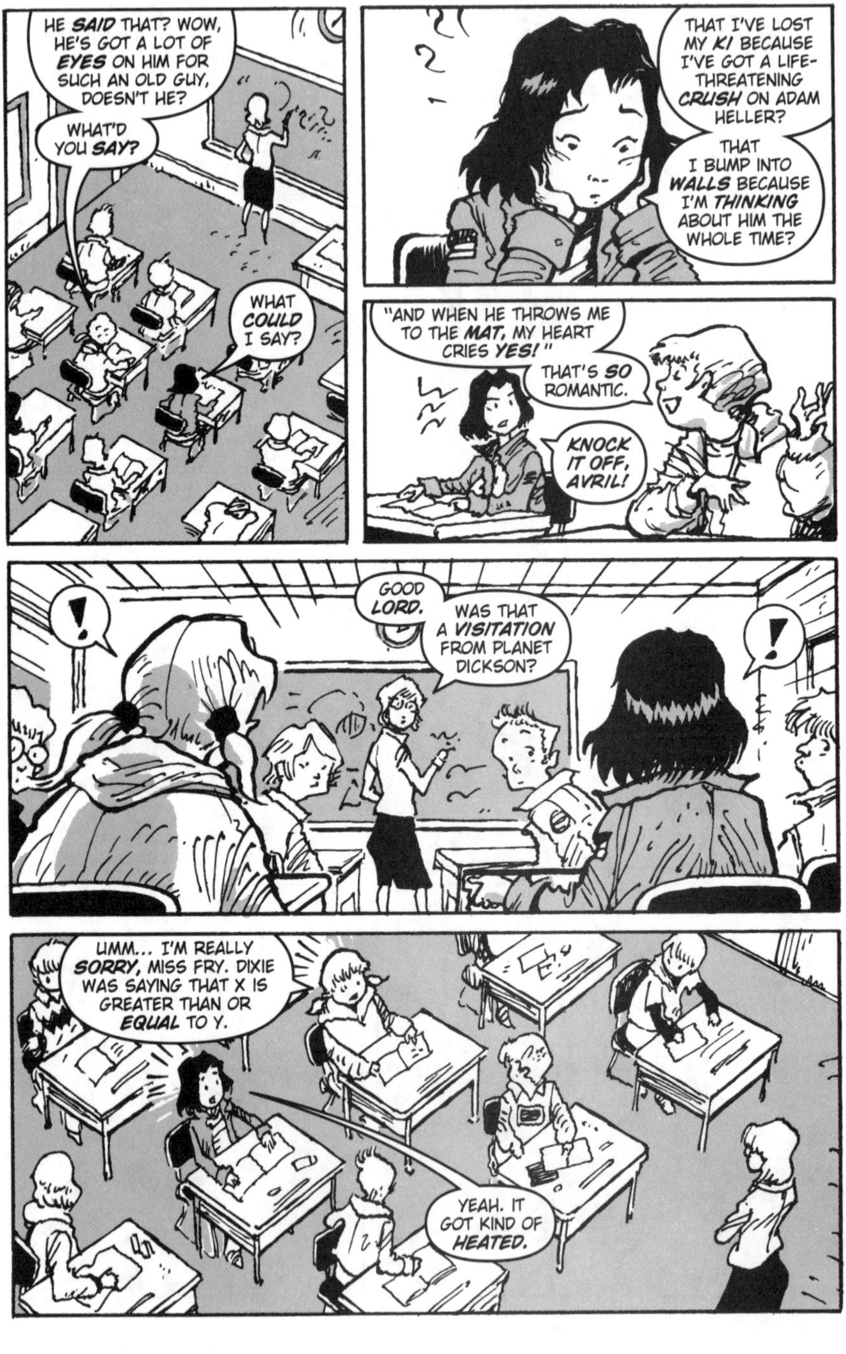

HE SAID THAT? WOW, HE'S GOT A LOT OF EYES ON HIM FOR SUCH AN OLD GUY, DOESN'T HE?
WHAT'D YOU SAY?
WHAT COULD I SAY?
THAT I'VE LOST MY KI BECAUSE I'VE GOT A LIFE-THREATENING CRUSH ON ADAM HELLER?
THAT I BUMP INTO WALLS BECAUSE I'M THINKING ABOUT HIM THE WHOLE TIME?
"AND WHEN HE THROWS ME TO THE MAT, MY HEART CRIES YES!"
THAT'S SO ROMANTIC.
KNOCK IT OFF, AVRIL!
!
GOOD LORD.
WAS THAT A VISITATION FROM PLANET DICKSON?
!
UMM... I'M REALLY SORRY, MISS FRY. DIXIE WAS SAYING THAT X IS GREATER THAN OR EQUAL TO Y.
YEAH. IT GOT KIND OF HEATED.

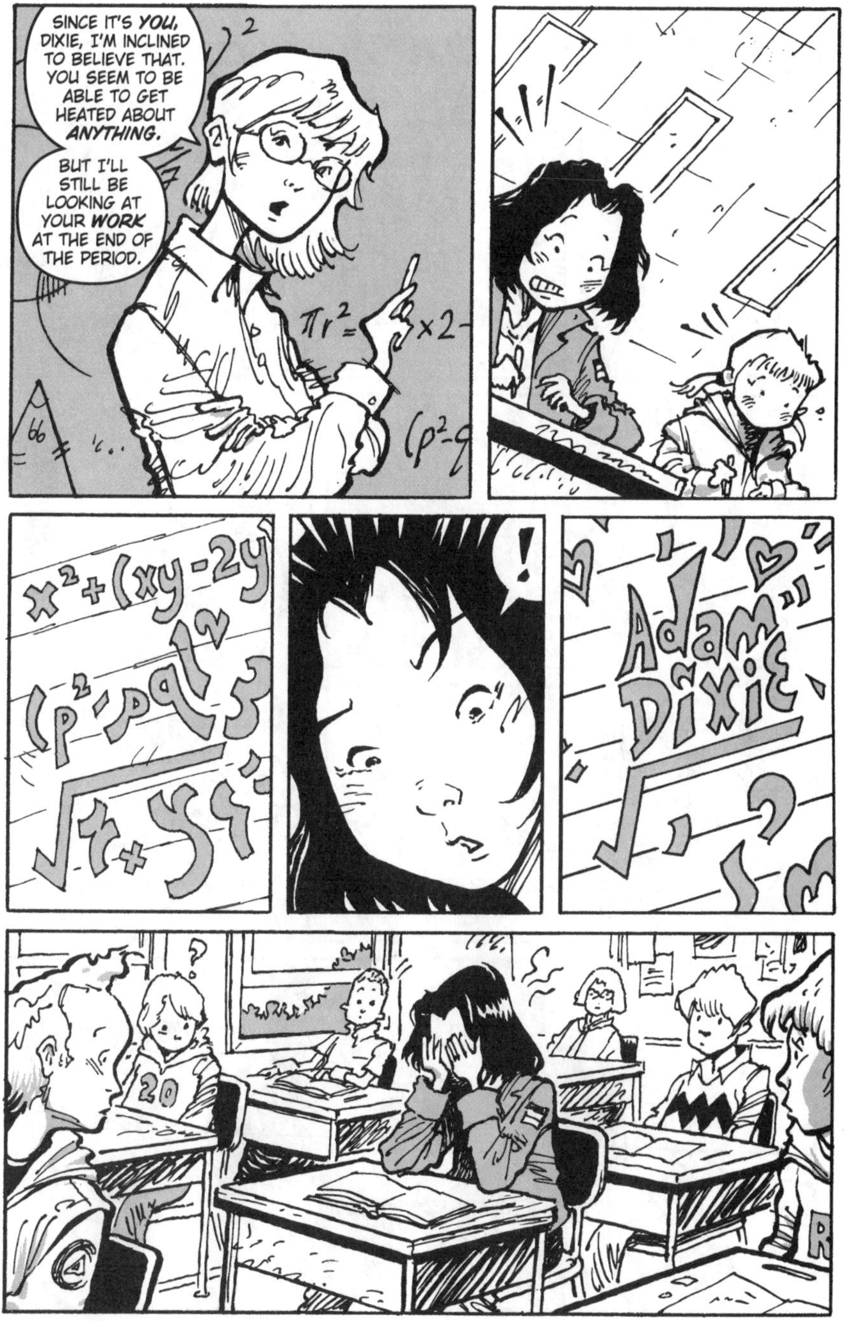

SINCE IT'S ***YOU,*** DIXIE, I'M INCLINED TO BELIEVE THAT. YOU SEEM TO BE ABLE TO GET HEATED ABOUT ***ANYTHING.***
BUT I'LL STILL BE LOOKING AT YOUR ***WORK*** AT THE END OF THE PERIOD.
!
Adam
Dixie

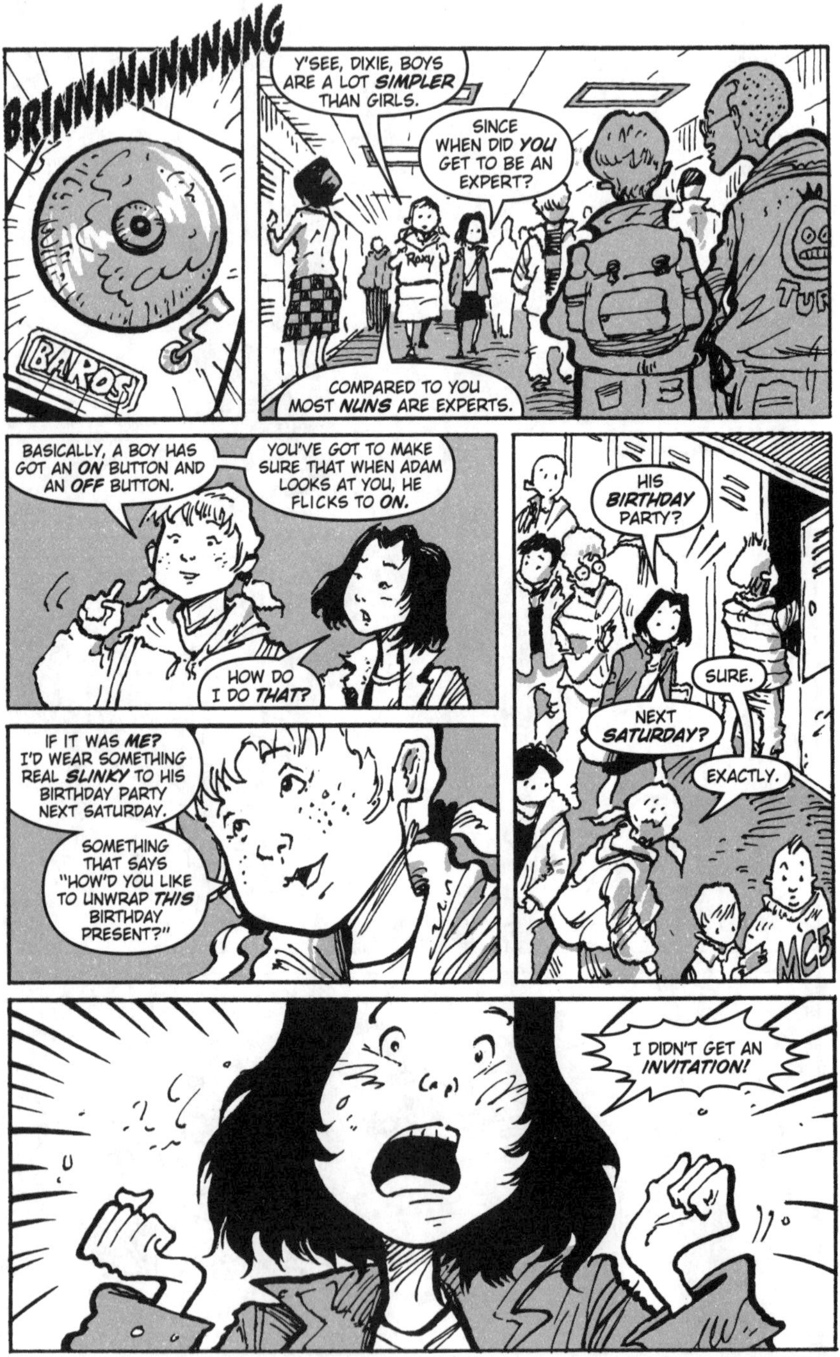
BRINNNNNNNNNNG
BAROS
Y'SEE, DIXIE, BOYS ARE A LOT SIMPLER THAN GIRLS.
SINCE WHEN DID YOU GET TO BE AN EXPERT?
COMPARED TO YOU MOST NUNS ARE EXPERTS.
BASICALLY, A BOY HAS GOT AN ON BUTTON AND AN OFF BUTTON.
YOU'VE GOT TO MAKE SURE THAT WHEN ADAM LOOKS AT YOU, HE FLICKS TO ON.
HOW DO I DO THAT?
HIS BIRTHDAY PARTY?
SURE.
NEXT SATURDAY?
EXACTLY.
IF IT WAS ME? I'D WEAR SOMETHING REAL SLINKY TO HIS BIRTHDAY PARTY NEXT SATURDAY.
SOMETHING THAT SAYS "HOW'D YOU LIKE TO UNWRAP THIS BIRTHDAY PRESENT?"
I DIDN'T GET AN INVITATION!

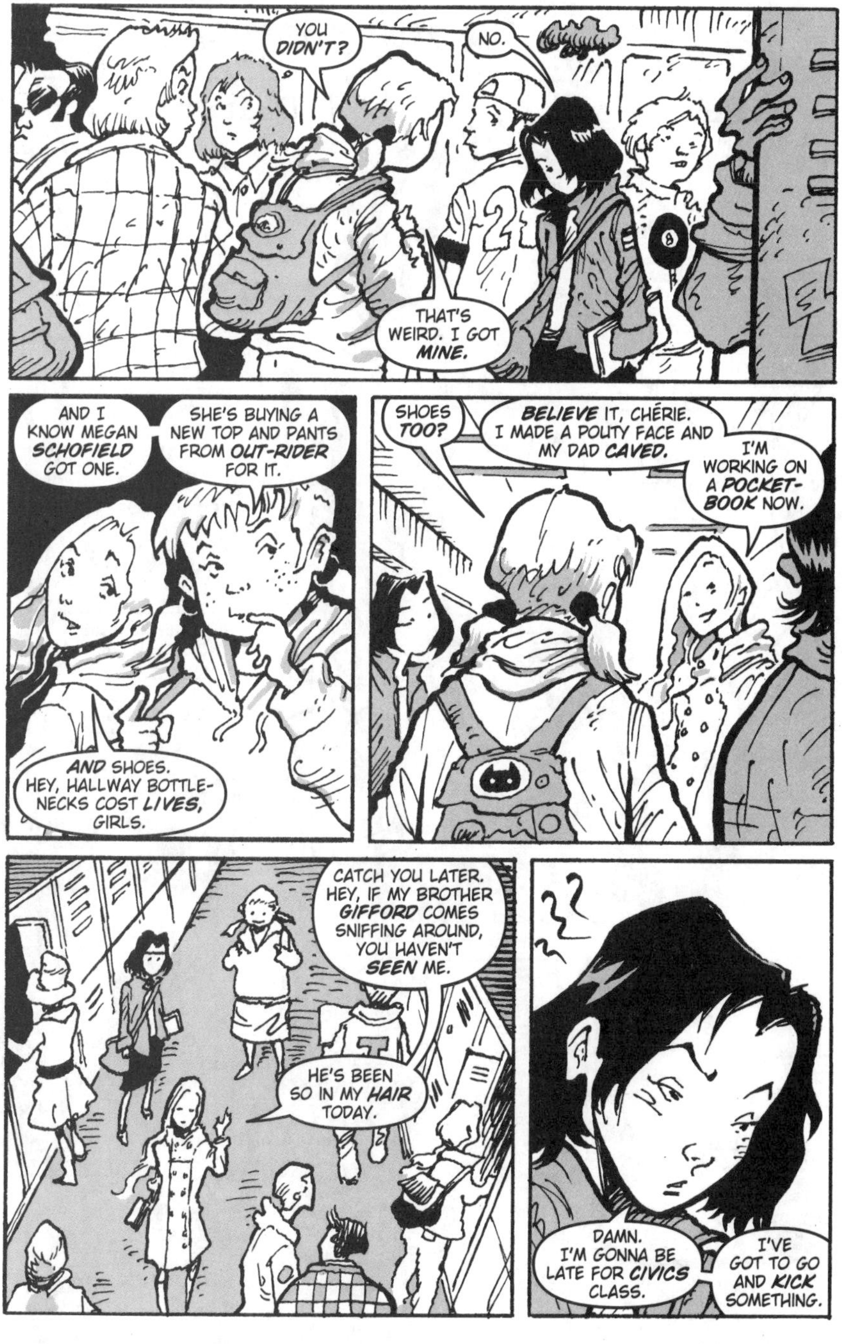
YOU DIDN'T?
NO.
THAT'S WEIRD. I GOT MINE.
AND I KNOW MEGAN SCHOFIELD GOT ONE.
SHE'S BUYING A NEW TOP AND PANTS FROM OUT-RIDER FOR IT.
AND SHOES. HEY, HALLWAY BOTTLE-NECKS COST LIVES, GIRLS.
SHOES TOO?
BELIEVE IT, CHÉRIE. I MADE A POUTY FACE AND MY DAD CAVED.
I'M WORKING ON A POCKET-BOOK NOW.
CATCH YOU LATER. HEY, IF MY BROTHER GIFFORD COMES SNIFFING AROUND, YOU HAVEN'T SEEN ME.
HE'S BEEN SO IN MY HAIR TODAY.
DAMN. I'M GONNA BE LATE FOR CIVICS CLASS.
I'VE GOT TO GO AND KICK SOMETHING.

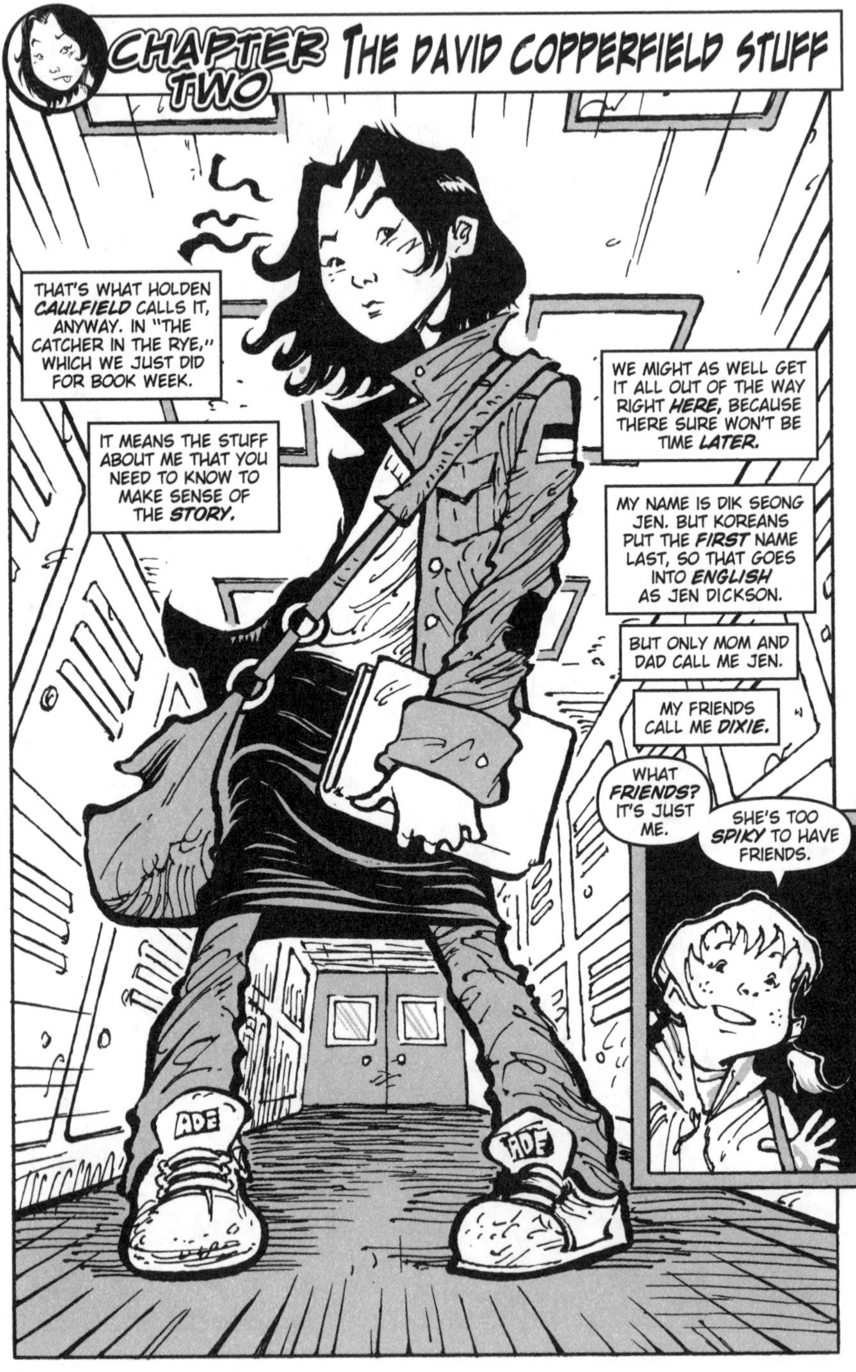
CHAPTER TWO
THE DAVID COPPERFIELD STUFF
THAT'S WHAT HOLDEN CAULFIELD CALLS IT, ANYWAY. IN "THE CATCHER IN THE RYE," WHICH WE JUST DID FOR BOOK WEEK.
IT MEANS THE STUFF ABOUT ME THAT YOU NEED TO KNOW TO MAKE SENSE OF THE STORY.
WE MIGHT AS WELL GET IT ALL OUT OF THE WAY RIGHT HERE, BECAUSE THERE SURE WON'T BE TIME LATER.
MY NAME IS DIK SEONG JEN. BUT KOREANS PUT THE FIRST NAME LAST, SO THAT GOES INTO ENGLISH AS JEN DICKSON.
BUT ONLY MOM AND DAD CALL ME JEN.
MY FRIENDS CALL ME DIXIE.
WHAT FRIENDS? IT'S JUST ME.
SHE'S TOO SPIKY TO HAVE FRIENDS.
ADE
ADE

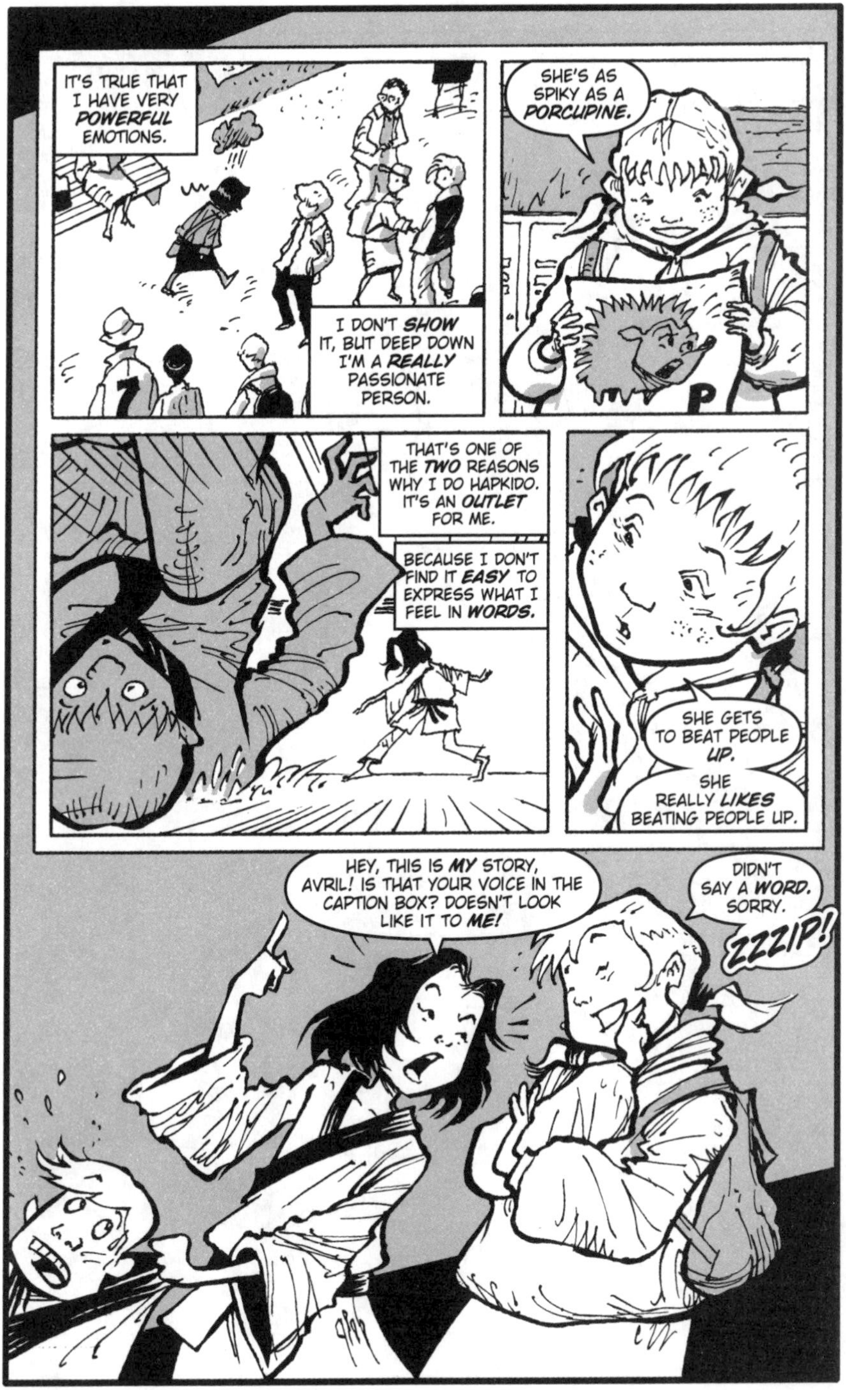

IT'S TRUE THAT I HAVE VERY POWERFUL EMOTIONS.
I DON'T SHOW IT, BUT DEEP DOWN I'M A REALLY PASSIONATE PERSON.
SHE'S AS SPIKY AS A PORCUPINE.
P
THAT'S ONE OF THE TWO REASONS WHY I DO HAPKIDO. IT'S AN OUTLET FOR ME.
BECAUSE I DON'T FIND IT EASY TO EXPRESS WHAT I FEEL IN WORDS.
SHE GETS TO BEAT PEOPLE UP.
SHE REALLY LIKES BEATING PEOPLE UP.
HEY, THIS IS MY STORY, AVRIL! IS THAT YOUR VOICE IN THE CAPTION BOX? DOESN'T LOOK LIKE IT TO ME!
DIDN'T SAY A WORD. SORRY.
ZZZIP!

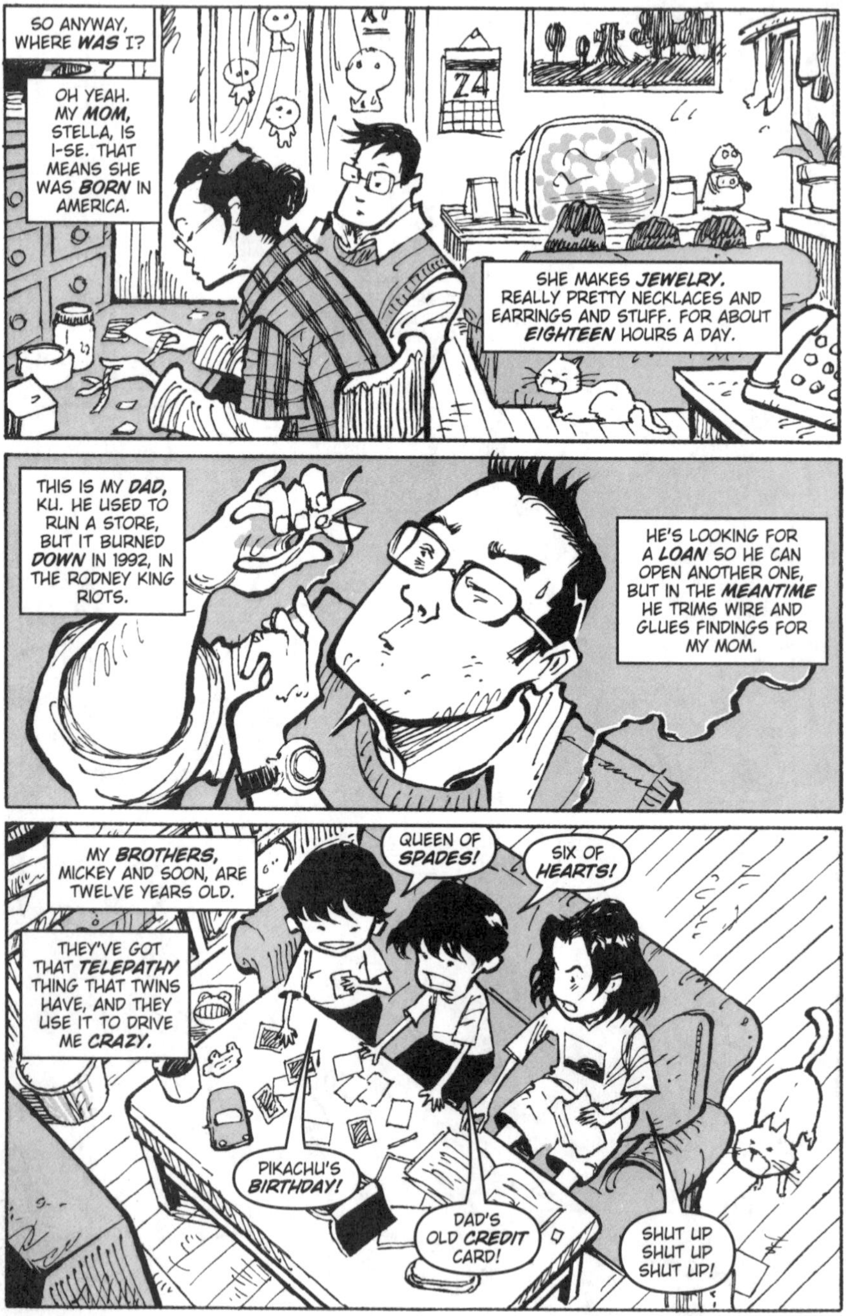
SO ANYWAY, WHERE WAS I?
OH YEAH. MY MOM, STELLA, IS I-SE. THAT MEANS SHE WAS BORN IN AMERICA.
SHE MAKES JEWELRY. REALLY PRETTY NECKLACES AND EARRINGS AND STUFF. FOR ABOUT EIGHTEEN HOURS A DAY.
THIS IS MY DAD, KU. HE USED TO RUN A STORE, BUT IT BURNED DOWN IN 1992, IN THE RODNEY KING RIOTS.
HE'S LOOKING FOR A LOAN SO HE CAN OPEN ANOTHER ONE, BUT IN THE MEANTIME HE TRIMS WIRE AND GLUES FINDINGS FOR MY MOM.
MY BROTHERS, MICKEY AND SOON, ARE TWELVE YEARS OLD.
THEY'VE GOT THAT TELEPATHY THING THAT TWINS HAVE, AND THEY USE IT TO DRIVE ME CRAZY.
QUEEN OF SPADES!
SIX OF HEARTS!
PIKACHU'S BIRTHDAY!
DAD'S OLD CREDIT CARD!
SHUT UP SHUT UP SHUT UP!

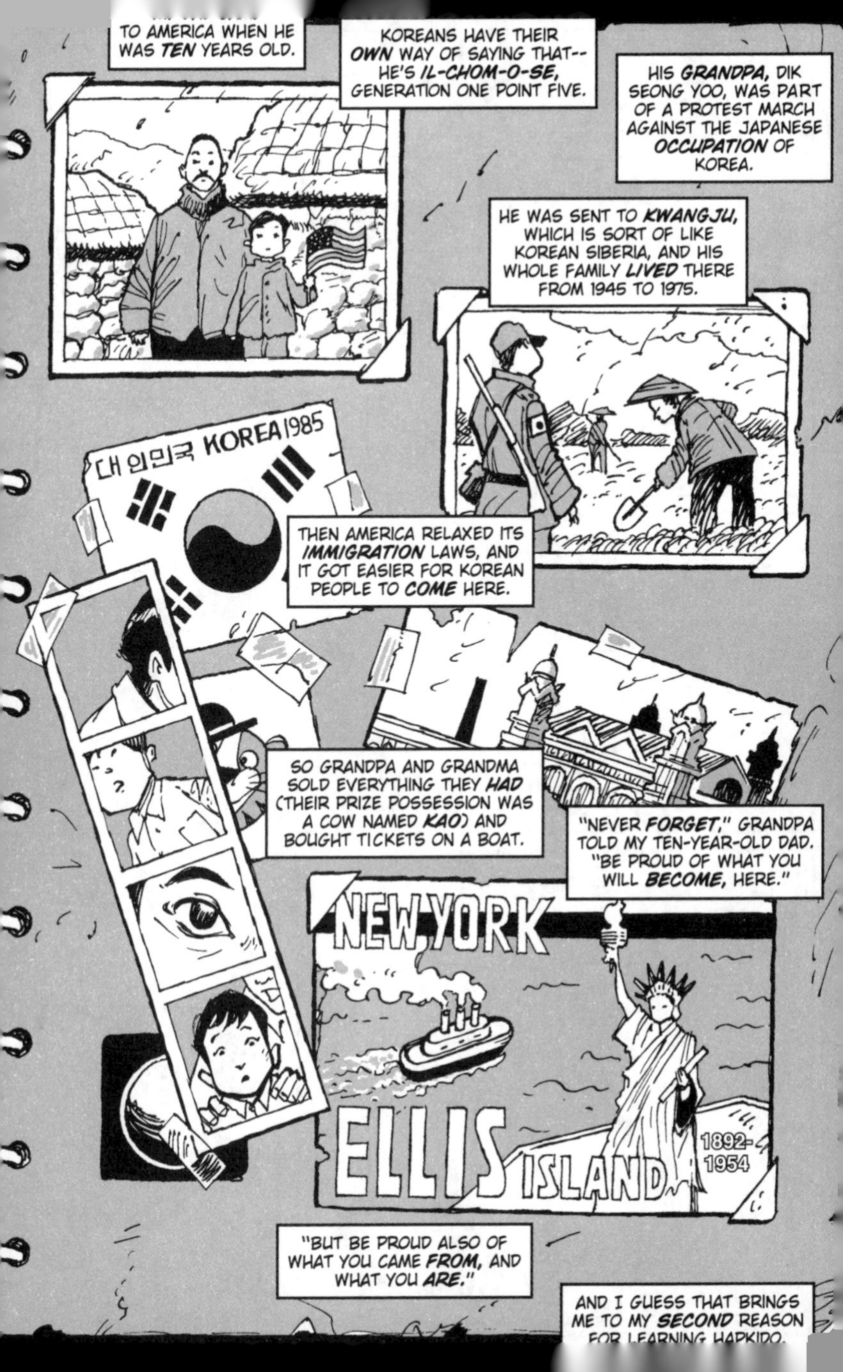

TO AMERICA WHEN HE WAS TEN YEARS OLD.
KOREANS HAVE THEIR OWN WAY OF SAYING THAT-- HE'S IL-CHOM-O-SE, GENERATION ONE POINT FIVE.
HIS GRANDPA, DIK SEONG YOO, WAS PART OF A PROTEST MARCH AGAINST THE JAPANESE OCCUPATION OF KOREA.
HE WAS SENT TO KWANGJU, WHICH IS SORT OF LIKE KOREAN SIBERIA, AND HIS WHOLE FAMILY LIVED THERE FROM 1945 TO 1975.
대한민국 KOREA 1985
THEN AMERICA RELAXED ITS IMMIGRATION LAWS, AND IT GOT EASIER FOR KOREAN PEOPLE TO COME HERE.
SO GRANDPA AND GRANDMA SOLD EVERYTHING THEY HAD (THEIR PRIZE POSSESSION WAS A COW NAMED KAO) AND BOUGHT TICKETS ON A BOAT.
"NEVER FORGET," GRANDPA TOLD MY TEN-YEAR-OLD DAD. "BE PROUD OF WHAT YOU WILL BECOME, HERE."
NEW YORK
ELLIS ISLAND
1892-1954
"BUT BE PROUD ALSO OF WHAT YOU CAME FROM, AND WHAT YOU ARE."
AND I GUESS THAT BRINGS ME TO MY SECOND REASON FOR LEARNING HAPKIDO.

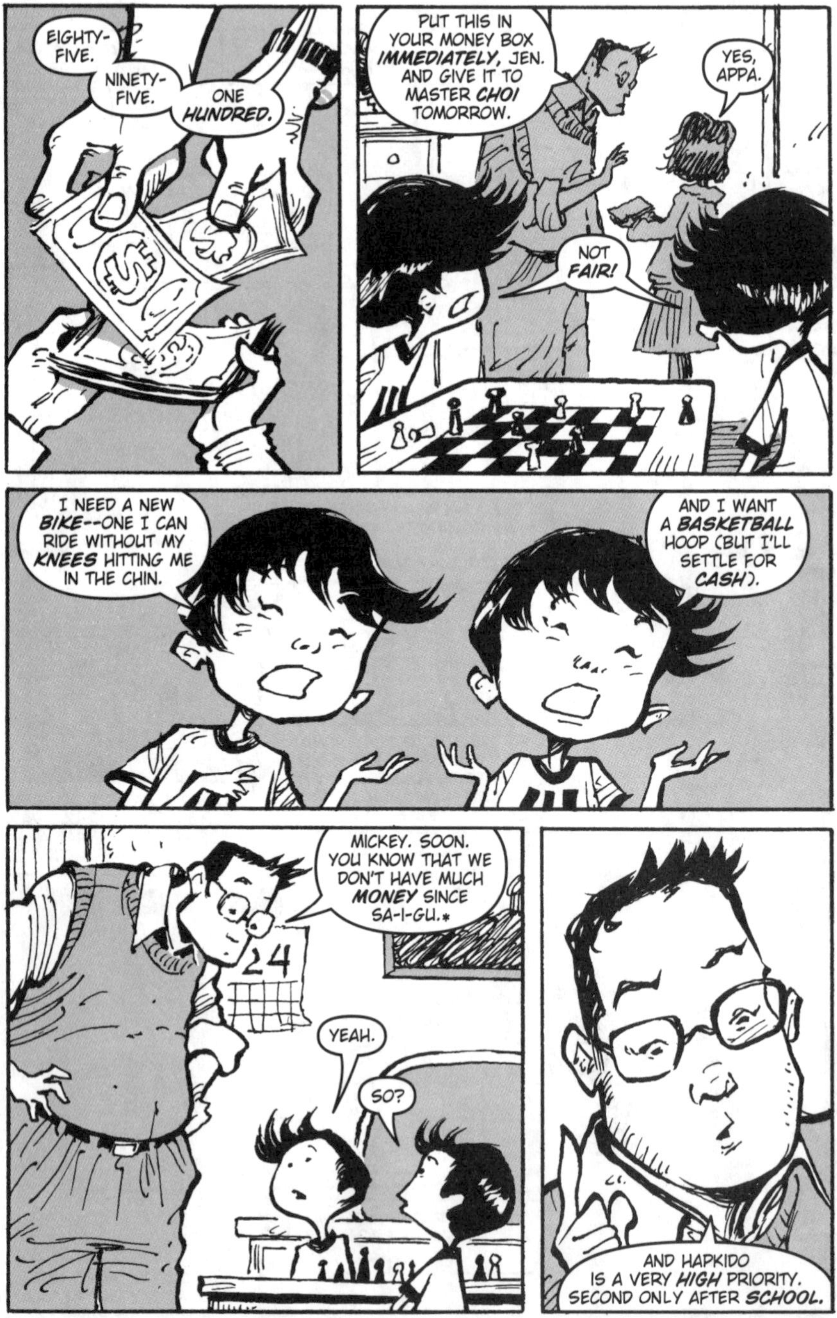
EIGHTY-FIVE.
NINETY-FIVE.
ONE HUNDRED.
PUT THIS IN YOUR MONEY BOX IMMEDIATELY, JEN. AND GIVE IT TO MASTER CHOI TOMORROW.
YES, APPA.
NOT FAIR!
I NEED A NEW BIKE--ONE I CAN RIDE WITHOUT MY KNEES HITTING ME IN THE CHIN.
AND I WANT A BASKETBALL HOOP (BUT I'LL SETTLE FOR CASH).
MICKEY. SOON. YOU KNOW THAT WE DON'T HAVE MUCH MONEY SINCE SA-I-GU.*
24
YEAH.
SO?
AND HAPKIDO IS A VERY HIGH PRIORITY. SECOND ONLY AFTER SCHOOL.

*WHAT KOREANS CALL THE RODNEY KING RIOTS--LITERALLY "APRIL 29TH."

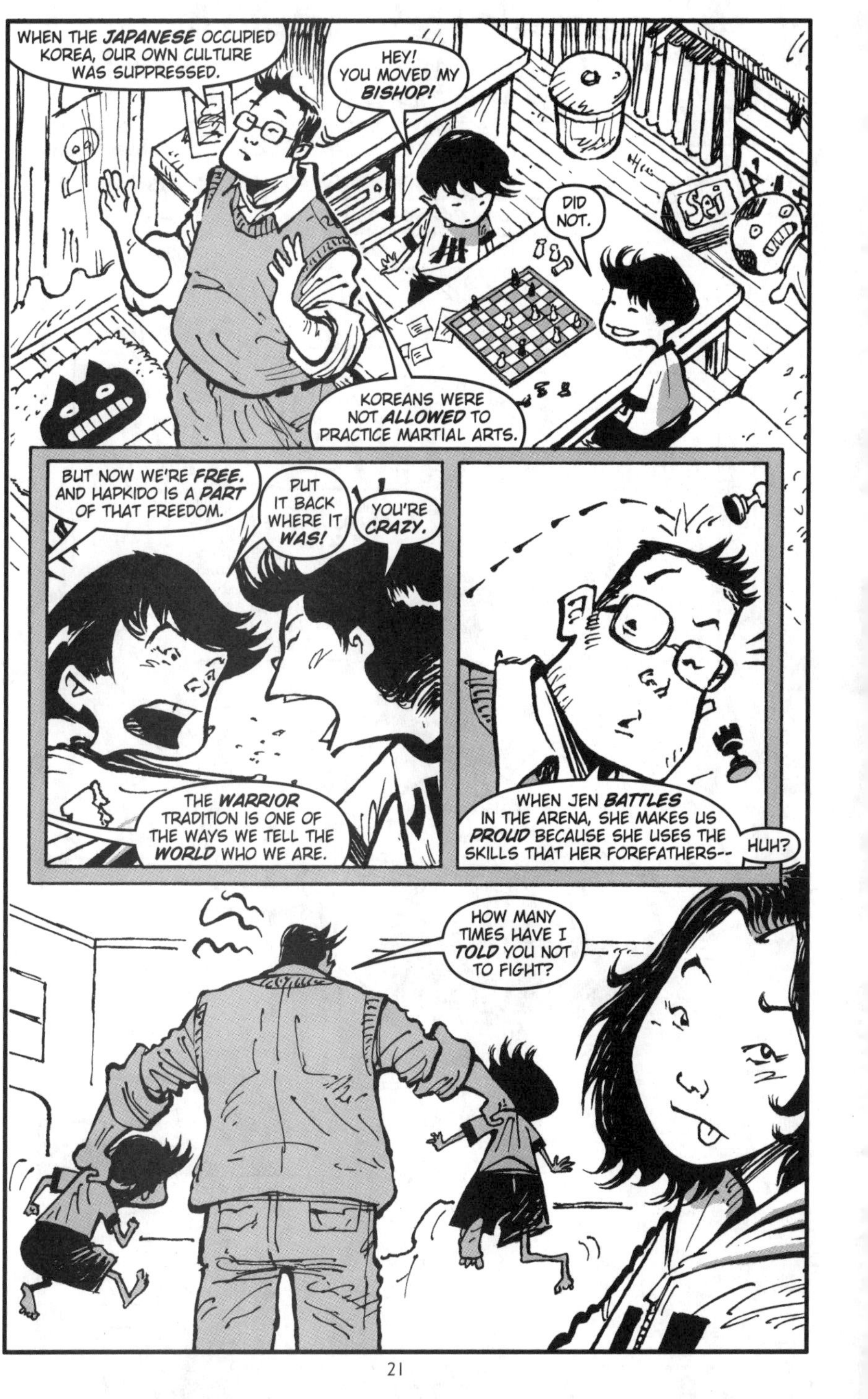
WHEN THE JAPANESE OCCUPIED KOREA, OUR OWN CULTURE WAS SUPPRESSED.
HEY! YOU MOVED MY BISHOP!
DID NOT.
KOREANS WERE NOT ALLOWED TO PRACTICE MARTIAL ARTS.
BUT NOW WE'RE FREE. AND HAPKIDO IS A PART OF THAT FREEDOM.
PUT IT BACK WHERE IT WAS!
YOU'RE CRAZY.
THE WARRIOR TRADITION IS ONE OF THE WAYS WE TELL THE WORLD WHO WE ARE.
WHEN JEN BATTLES IN THE ARENA, SHE MAKES US PROUD BECAUSE SHE USES THE SKILLS THAT HER FOREFATHERS--
HUH?
HOW MANY TIMES HAVE I TOLD YOU NOT TO FIGHT?

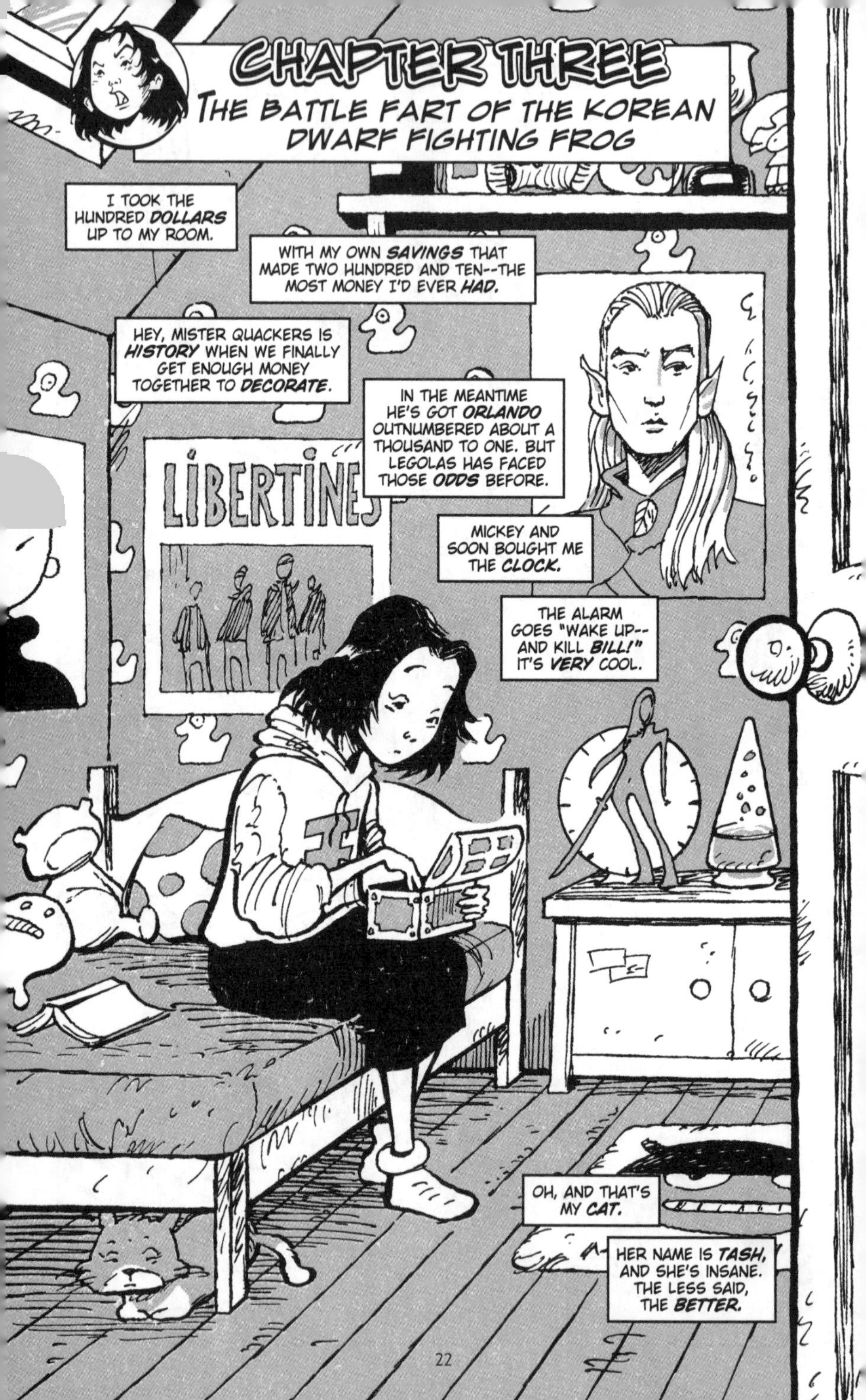
CHAPTER THREE
THE BATTLE FART OF THE KOREAN DWARF FIGHTING FROG
I TOOK THE HUNDRED DOLLARS UP TO MY ROOM.
WITH MY OWN SAVINGS THAT MADE TWO HUNDRED AND TEN--THE MOST MONEY I'D EVER HAD.
HEY, MISTER QUACKERS IS HISTORY WHEN WE FINALLY GET ENOUGH MONEY TOGETHER TO DECORATE.
IN THE MEANTIME HE'S GOT ORLANDO OUTNUMBERED ABOUT A THOUSAND TO ONE. BUT LEGOLAS HAS FACED THOSE ODDS BEFORE.
LIBERTINES
MICKEY AND SOON BOUGHT ME THE CLOCK.
THE ALARM GOES "WAKE UP--AND KILL BILL!" IT'S VERY COOL.
OH, AND THAT'S MY CAT.
HER NAME IS TASH, AND SHE'S INSANE. THE LESS SAID, THE BETTER.

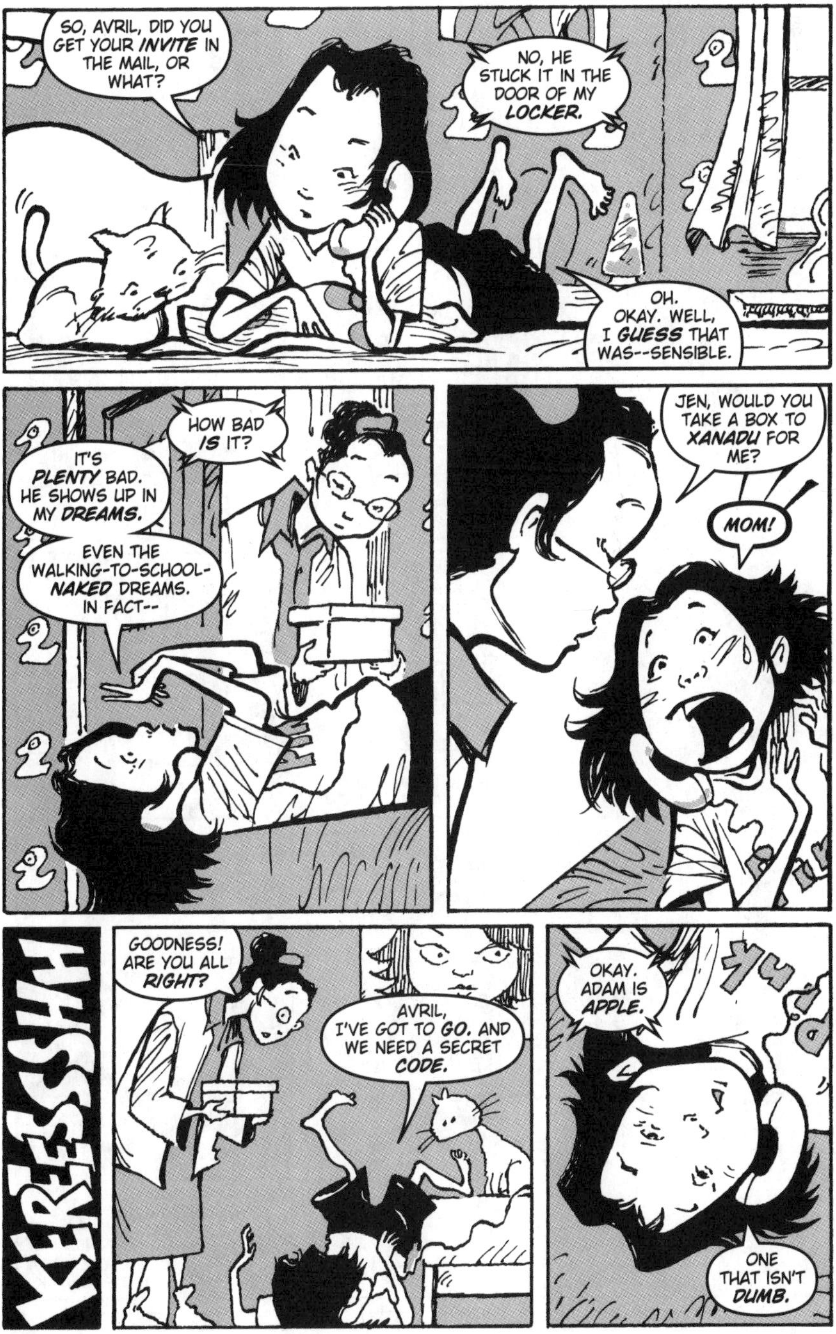
SO, AVRIL, DID YOU GET YOUR INVITE IN THE MAIL, OR WHAT?
NO, HE STUCK IT IN THE DOOR OF MY LOCKER.
OH. OKAY. WELL, I GUESS THAT WAS--SENSIBLE.
HOW BAD IS IT?
IT'S PLENTY BAD. HE SHOWS UP IN MY DREAMS.
EVEN THE WALKING-TO-SCHOOL-NAKED DREAMS. IN FACT--
JEN, WOULD YOU TAKE A BOX TO XANADU FOR ME?
MOM!
KEREESSHH
GOODNESS! ARE YOU ALL RIGHT?
AVRIL, I'VE GOT TO GO. AND WE NEED A SECRET CODE.
OKAY. ADAM IS APPLE.
ONE THAT ISN'T DUMB.

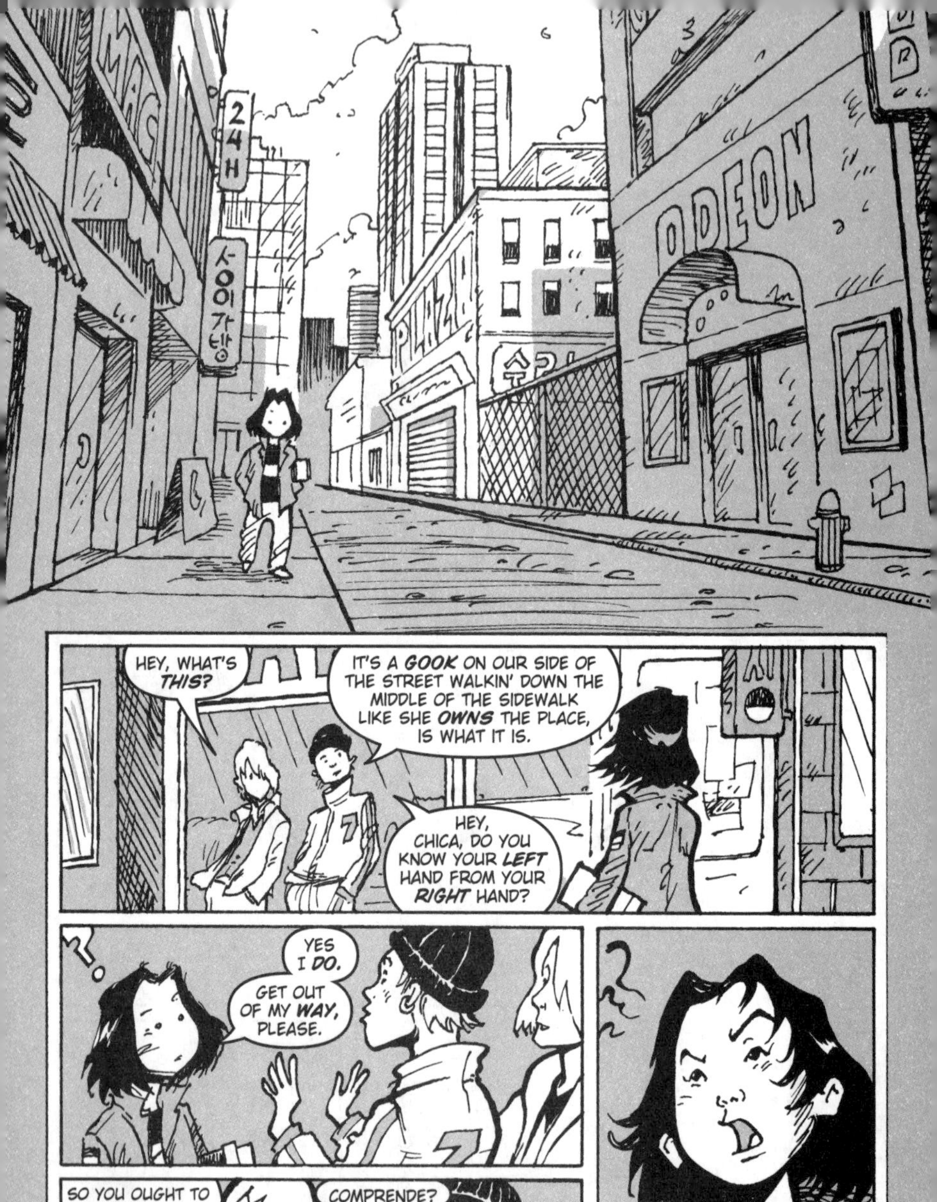
24H
ODEON
HEY, WHAT'S THIS?
IT'S A GOOK ON OUR SIDE OF THE STREET WALKIN' DOWN THE MIDDLE OF THE SIDEWALK LIKE SHE OWNS THE PLACE, IS WHAT IT IS.
HEY, CHICA, DO YOU KNOW YOUR LEFT HAND FROM YOUR RIGHT HAND?
YES I DO.
GET OUT OF MY WAY, PLEASE.
SO YOU OUGHT TO BE ABLE TO TELL THE GOOK SIDE OF THE STREET FROM OUR SIDE...
COMPRENDE?
YEAH. YOU BELONG OVER THERE.
I'M GOING TO A STORE THAT'S ON THIS SIDE OF THE STREET.
AND YOU DON'T OWN THE SIDEWALK.

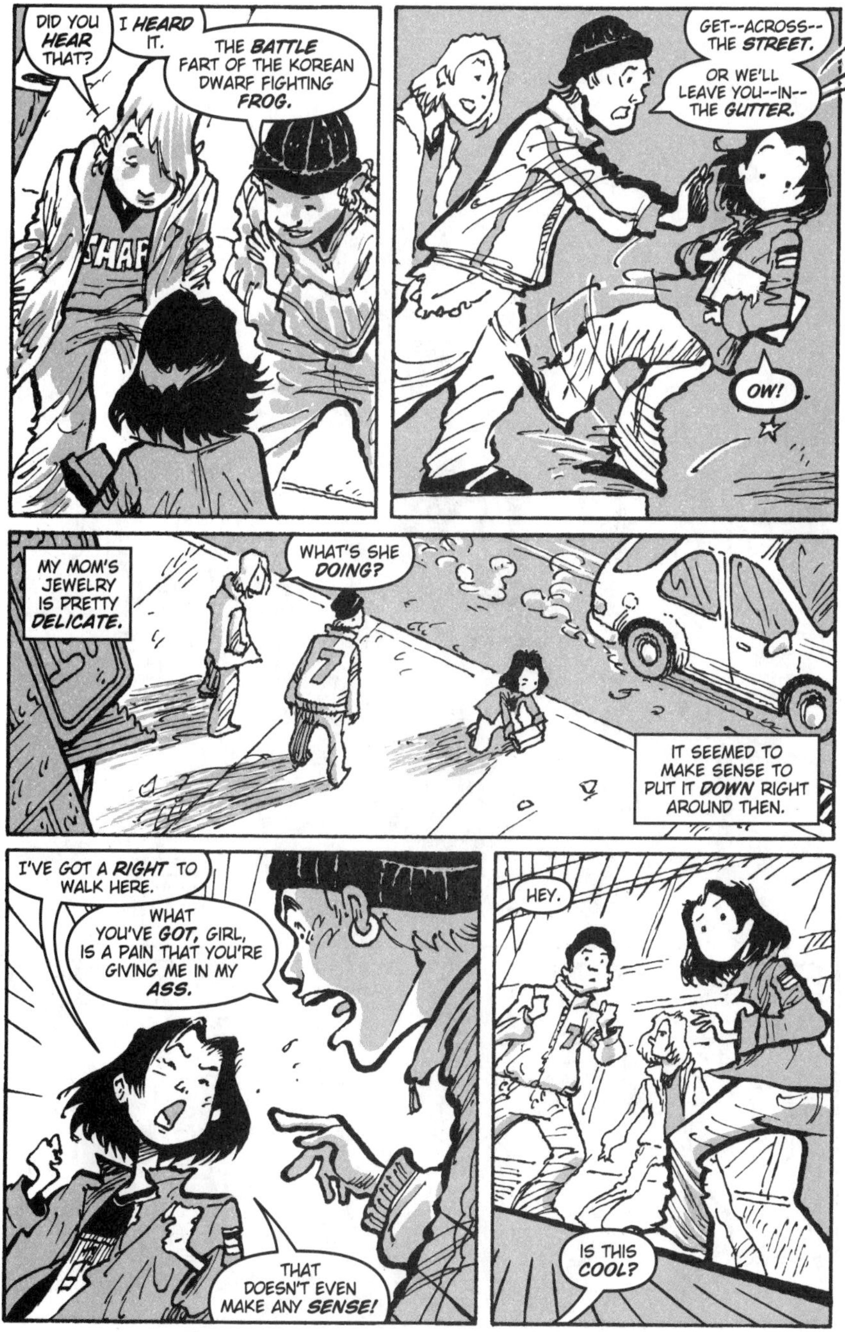
DID YOU HEAR THAT?
I HEARD IT.
THE BATTLE FART OF THE KOREAN DWARF FIGHTING FROG.
GET--ACROSS--THE STREET.
OR WE'LL LEAVE YOU--IN--THE GUTTER.
OW!
MY MOM'S JEWELRY IS PRETTY DELICATE.
WHAT'S SHE DOING?
IT SEEMED TO MAKE SENSE TO PUT IT DOWN RIGHT AROUND THEN.
I'VE GOT A RIGHT TO WALK HERE.
WHAT YOU'VE GOT, GIRL, IS A PAIN THAT YOU'RE GIVING ME IN MY ASS.
THAT DOESN'T EVEN MAKE ANY SENSE!
HEY.
IS THIS COOL?

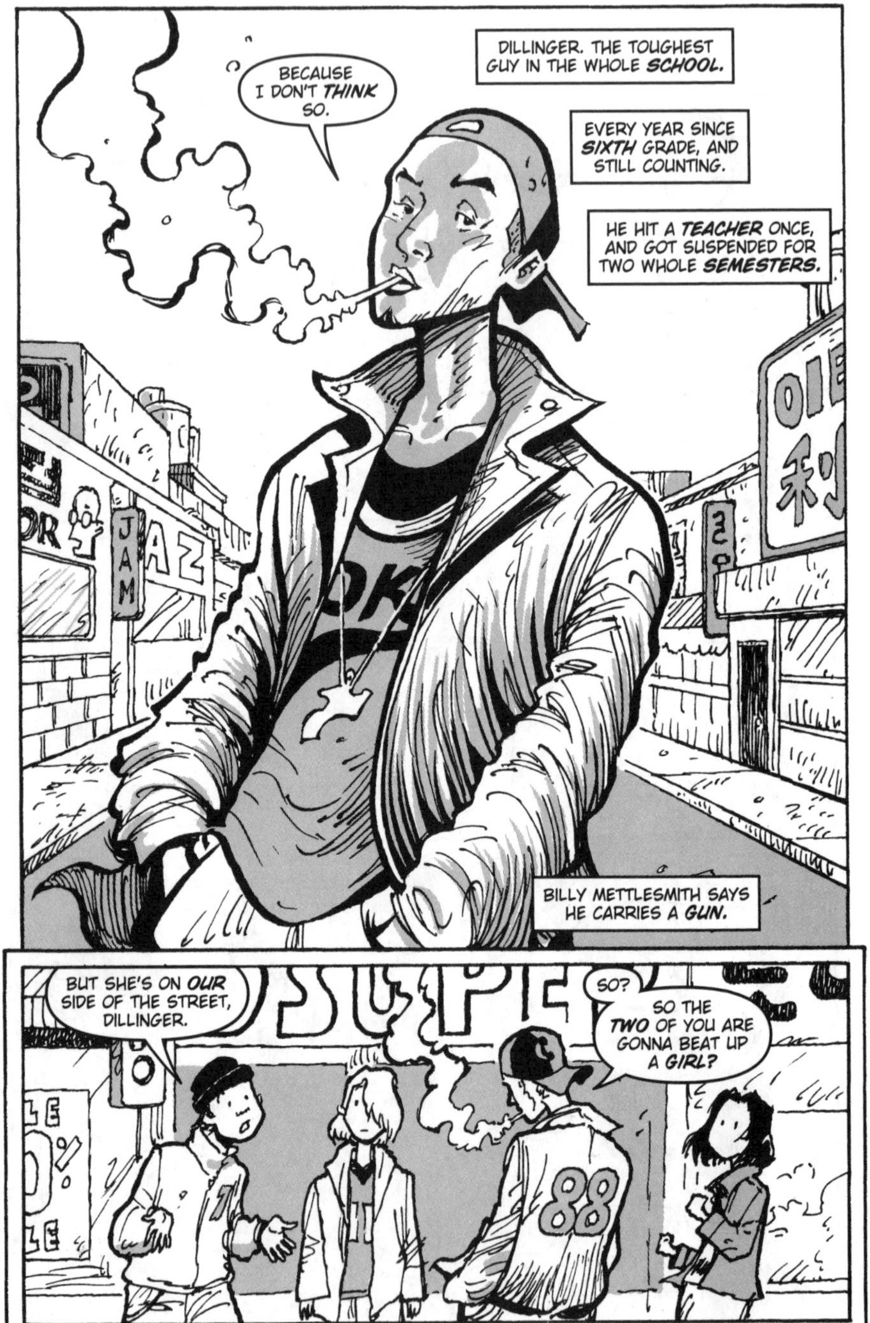
BECAUSE I DON'T THINK SO.
DILLINGER. THE TOUGHEST GUY IN THE WHOLE SCHOOL.
EVERY YEAR SINCE SIXTH GRADE, AND STILL COUNTING.
HE HIT A TEACHER ONCE, AND GOT SUSPENDED FOR TWO WHOLE SEMESTERS.
BILLY METTLESMITH SAYS HE CARRIES A GUN.
BUT SHE'S ON OUR SIDE OF THE STREET, DILLINGER.
SO?
SO THE TWO OF YOU ARE GONNA BEAT UP A GIRL?

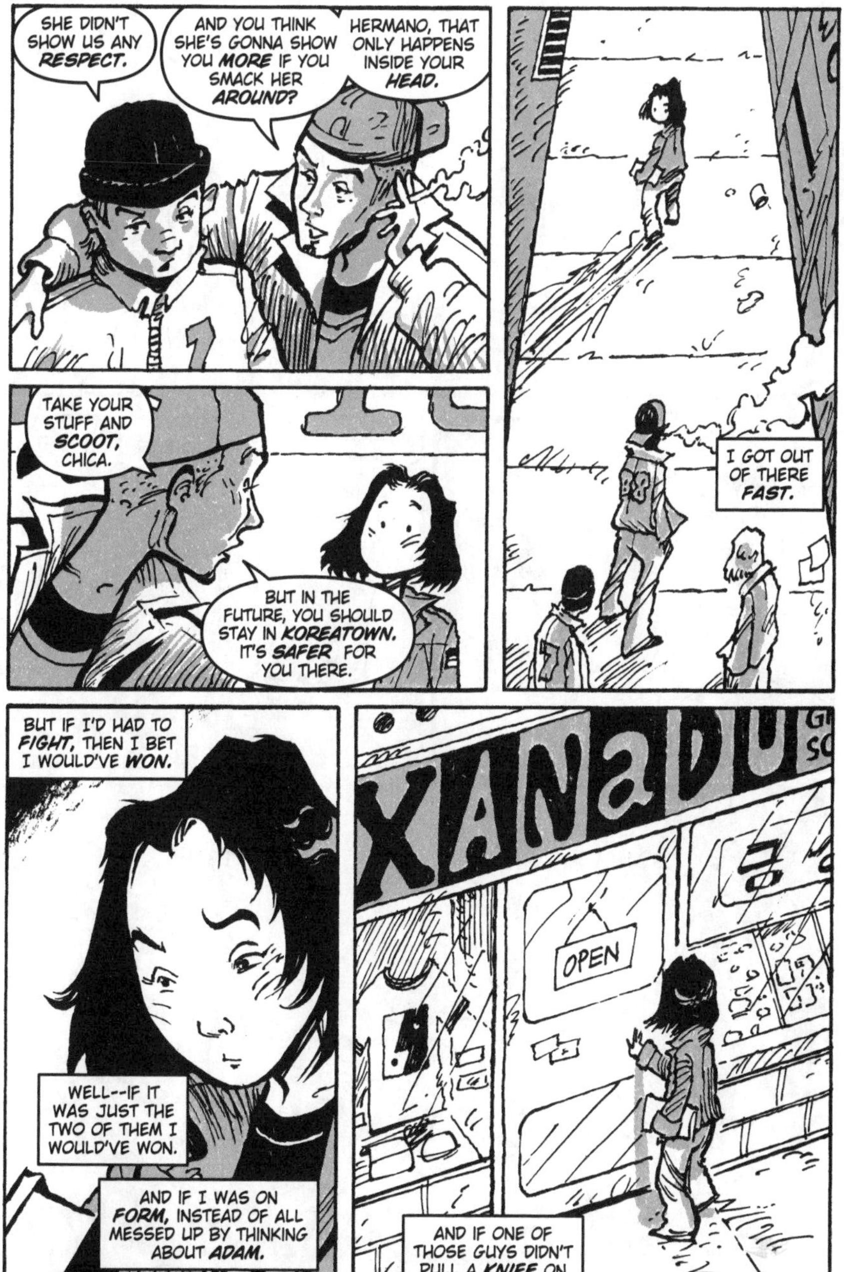
SHE DIDN'T SHOW US ANY RESPECT.
AND YOU THINK SHE'S GONNA SHOW YOU MORE IF YOU SMACK HER AROUND?
HERMANO, THAT ONLY HAPPENS INSIDE YOUR HEAD.
I GOT OUT OF THERE FAST.
TAKE YOUR STUFF AND SCOOT, CHICA.
BUT IN THE FUTURE, YOU SHOULD STAY IN KOREATOWN. IT'S SAFER FOR YOU THERE.
BUT IF I'D HAD TO FIGHT, THEN I BET I WOULD'VE WON.
WELL--IF IT WAS JUST THE TWO OF THEM I WOULD'VE WON.
AND IF I WAS ON FORM, INSTEAD OF ALL MESSED UP BY THINKING ABOUT ADAM.
XANaDU
OPEN
AND IF ONE OF THOSE GUYS DIDN'T PULL A KNIFE ON ME OR SOMETHING.

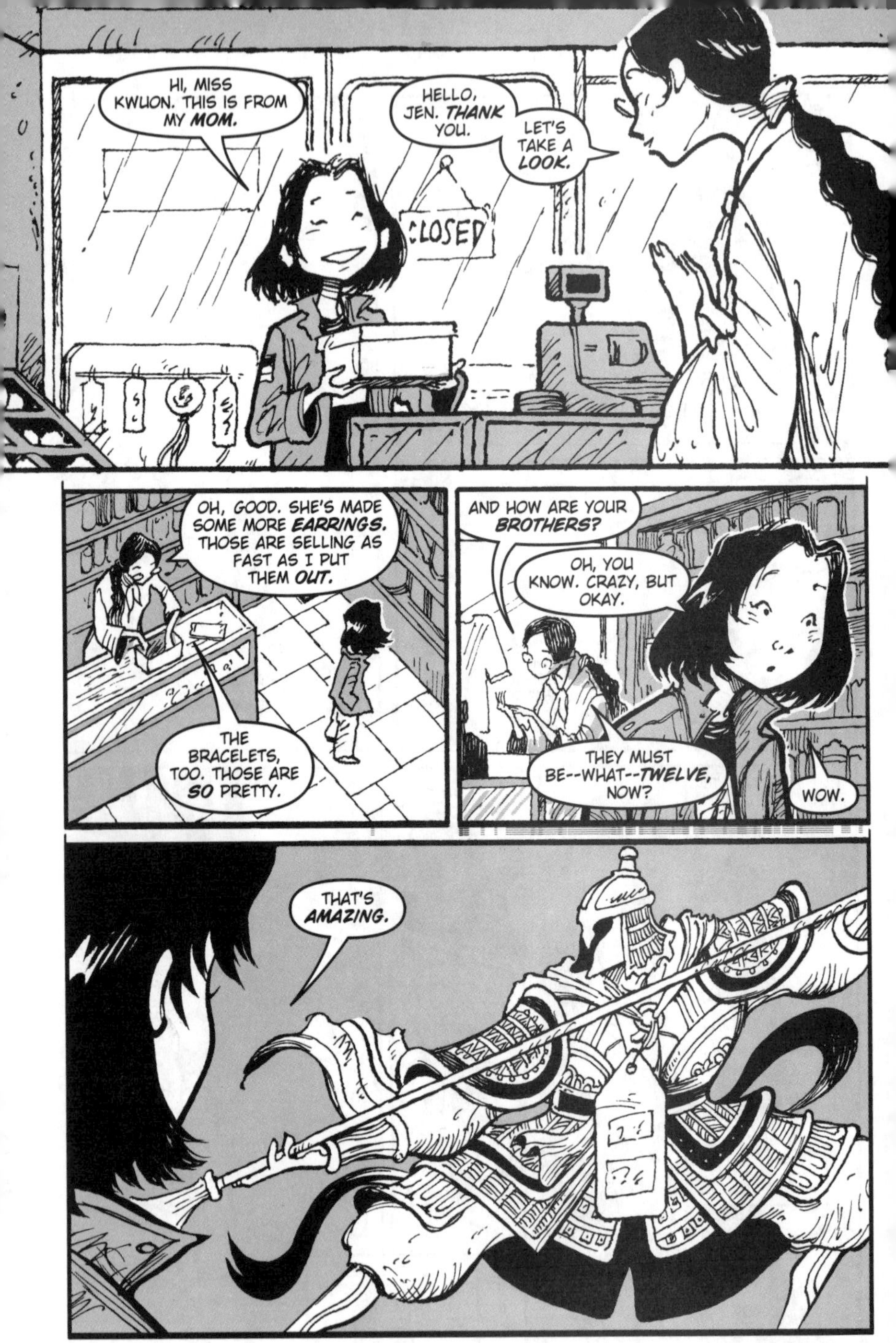
HI, MISS KWUON. THIS IS FROM MY MOM.
HELLO, JEN. THANK YOU.
LET'S TAKE A LOOK.
CLOSED
OH, GOOD. SHE'S MADE SOME MORE EARRINGS. THOSE ARE SELLING AS FAST AS I PUT THEM OUT.
THE BRACELETS, TOO. THOSE ARE SO PRETTY.
AND HOW ARE YOUR BROTHERS?
OH, YOU KNOW. CRAZY, BUT OKAY.
THEY MUST BE--WHAT--TWELVE, NOW?
WOW.
THAT'S AMAZING.

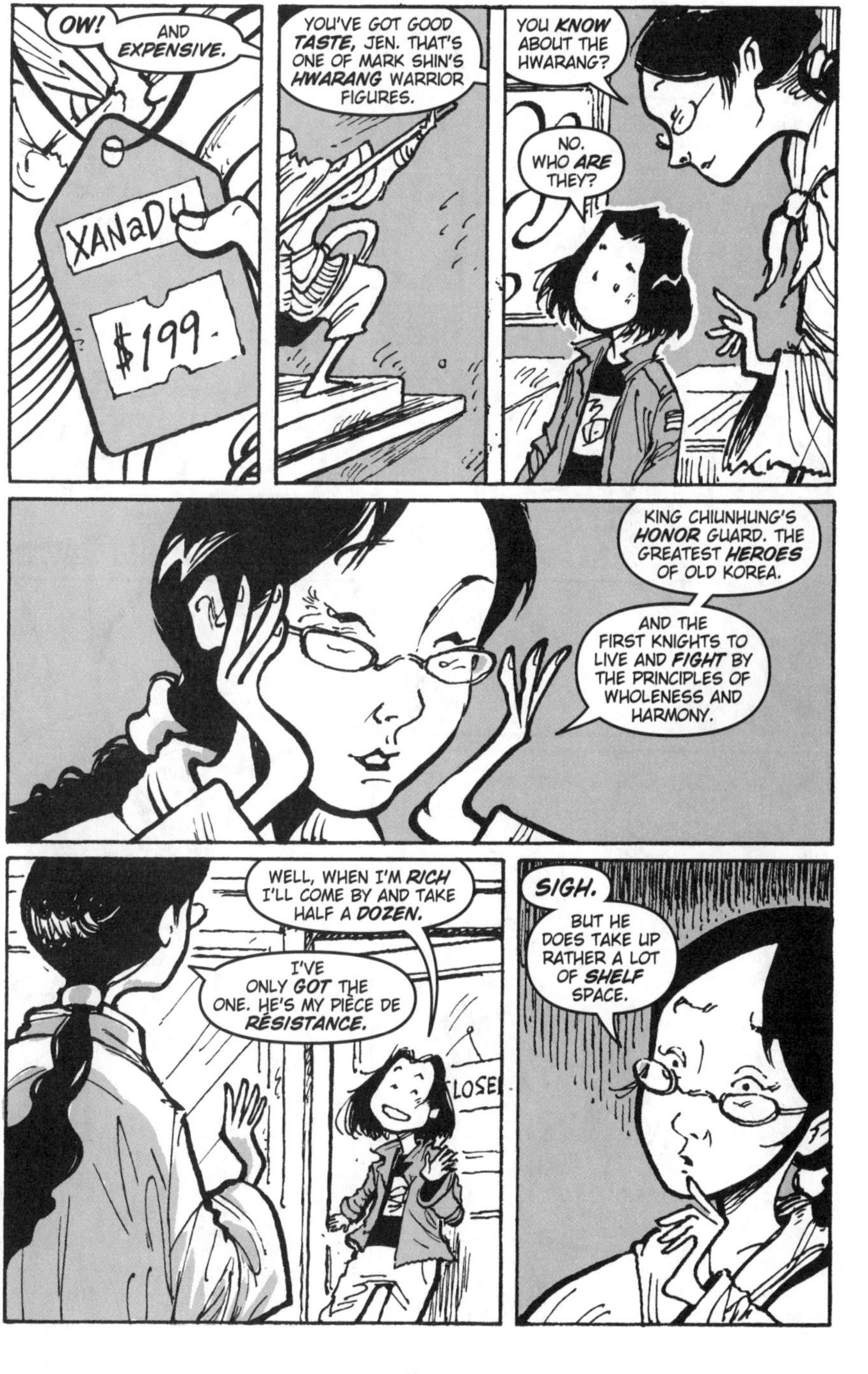
OW!
AND EXPENSIVE.
XANaDU
$199.
YOU'VE GOT GOOD TASTE, JEN. THAT'S ONE OF MARK SHIN'S HWARANG WARRIOR FIGURES.
YOU KNOW ABOUT THE HWARANG?
NO. WHO ARE THEY?
KING CHIUNHUNG'S HONOR GUARD. THE GREATEST HEROES OF OLD KOREA.
AND THE FIRST KNIGHTS TO LIVE AND FIGHT BY THE PRINCIPLES OF WHOLENESS AND HARMONY.
WELL, WHEN I'M RICH I'LL COME BY AND TAKE HALF A DOZEN.
I'VE ONLY GOT THE ONE. HE'S MY PIÈCE DE RÉSISTANCE.
SIGH.
BUT HE DOES TAKE UP RATHER A LOT OF SHELF SPACE.

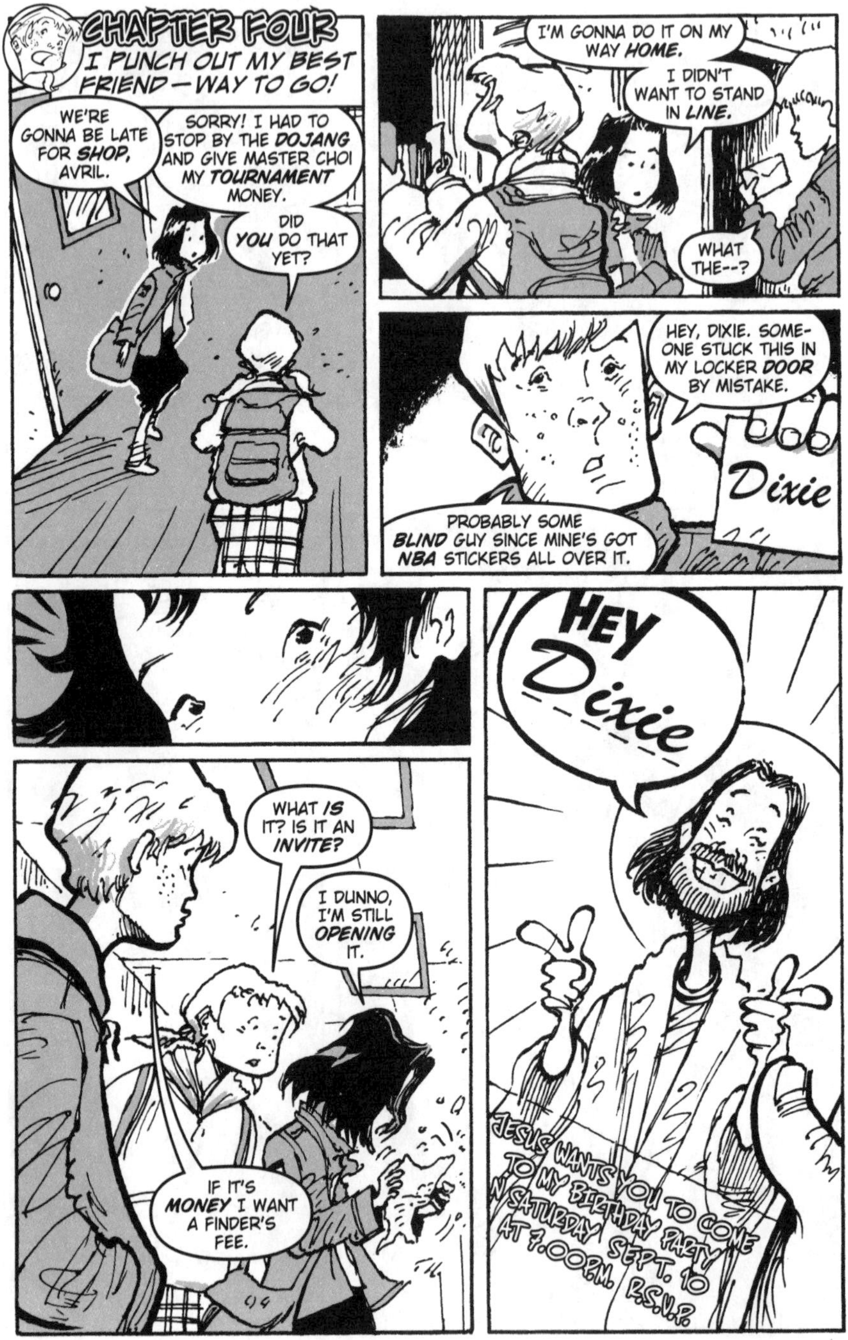
CHAPTER FOUR
I PUNCH OUT MY BEST FRIEND—WAY TO GO!
WE'RE GONNA BE LATE FOR SHOP, AVRIL.
SORRY! I HAD TO STOP BY THE DOJANG AND GIVE MASTER CHOI MY TOURNAMENT MONEY.
DID YOU DO THAT YET?
I'M GONNA DO IT ON MY WAY HOME.
I DIDN'T WANT TO STAND IN LINE.
WHAT THE--?
HEY, DIXIE. SOMEONE STUCK THIS IN MY LOCKER DOOR BY MISTAKE.
Dixie
PROBABLY SOME BLIND GUY SINCE MINE'S GOT NBA STICKERS ALL OVER IT.
WHAT IS IT? IS IT AN INVITE?
I DUNNO, I'M STILL OPENING IT.
IF IT'S MONEY I WANT A FINDER'S FEE.
HEY Dixie
JESUS WANTS YOU TO COME TO MY BIRTHDAY PARTY
N SATURDAY SEPT. 10
AT 7:00P.M. R.S.V.P.

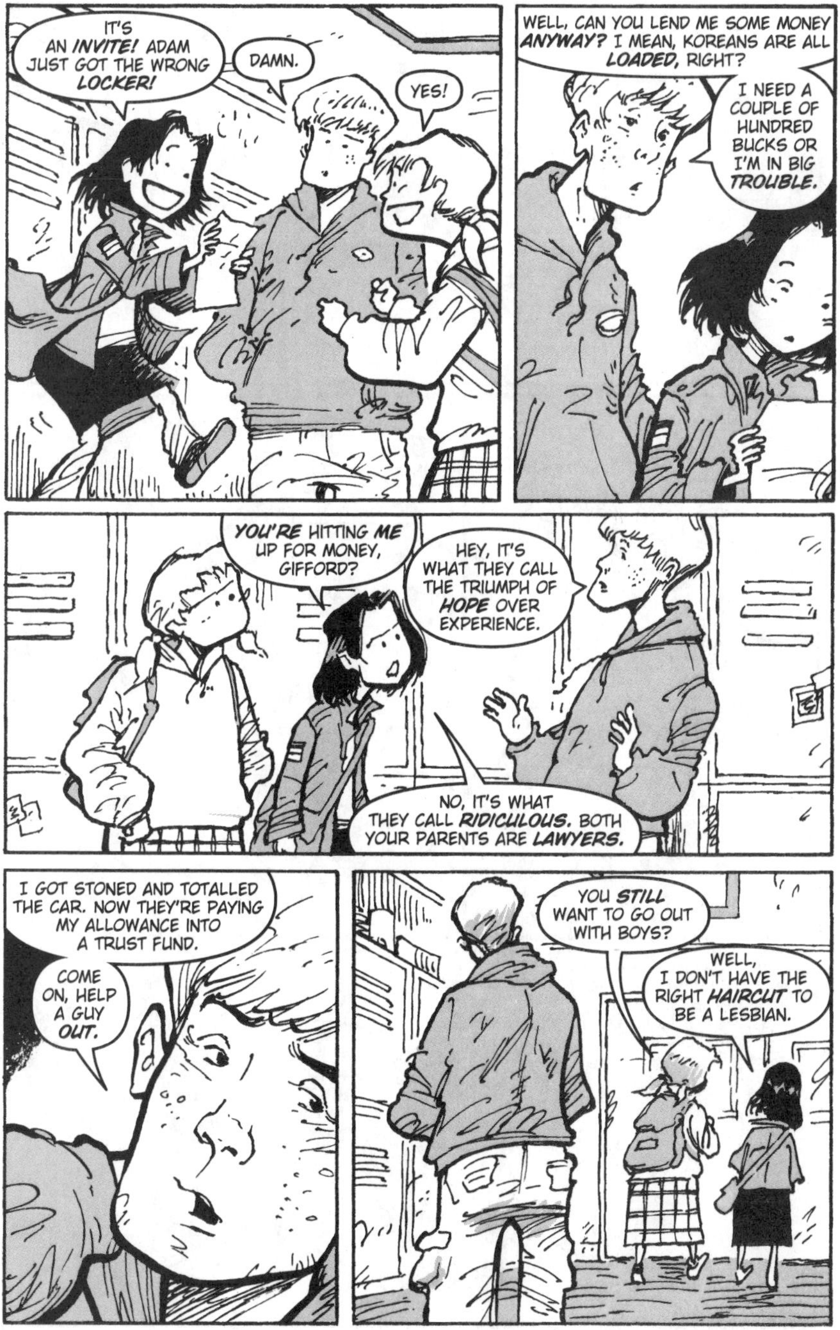
IT'S AN INVITE! ADAM JUST GOT THE WRONG LOCKER!
DAMN.
YES!
WELL, CAN YOU LEND ME SOME MONEY ANYWAY? I MEAN, KOREANS ARE ALL LOADED, RIGHT?
I NEED A COUPLE OF HUNDRED BUCKS OR I'M IN BIG TROUBLE.
YOU'RE HITTING ME UP FOR MONEY, GIFFORD?
HEY, IT'S WHAT THEY CALL THE TRIUMPH OF HOPE OVER EXPERIENCE.
NO, IT'S WHAT THEY CALL RIDICULOUS. BOTH YOUR PARENTS ARE LAWYERS.
I GOT STONED AND TOTALLED THE CAR. NOW THEY'RE PAYING MY ALLOWANCE INTO A TRUST FUND.
COME ON, HELP A GUY OUT.
YOU STILL WANT TO GO OUT WITH BOYS?
WELL, I DON'T HAVE THE RIGHT HAIRCUT TO BE A LESBIAN.

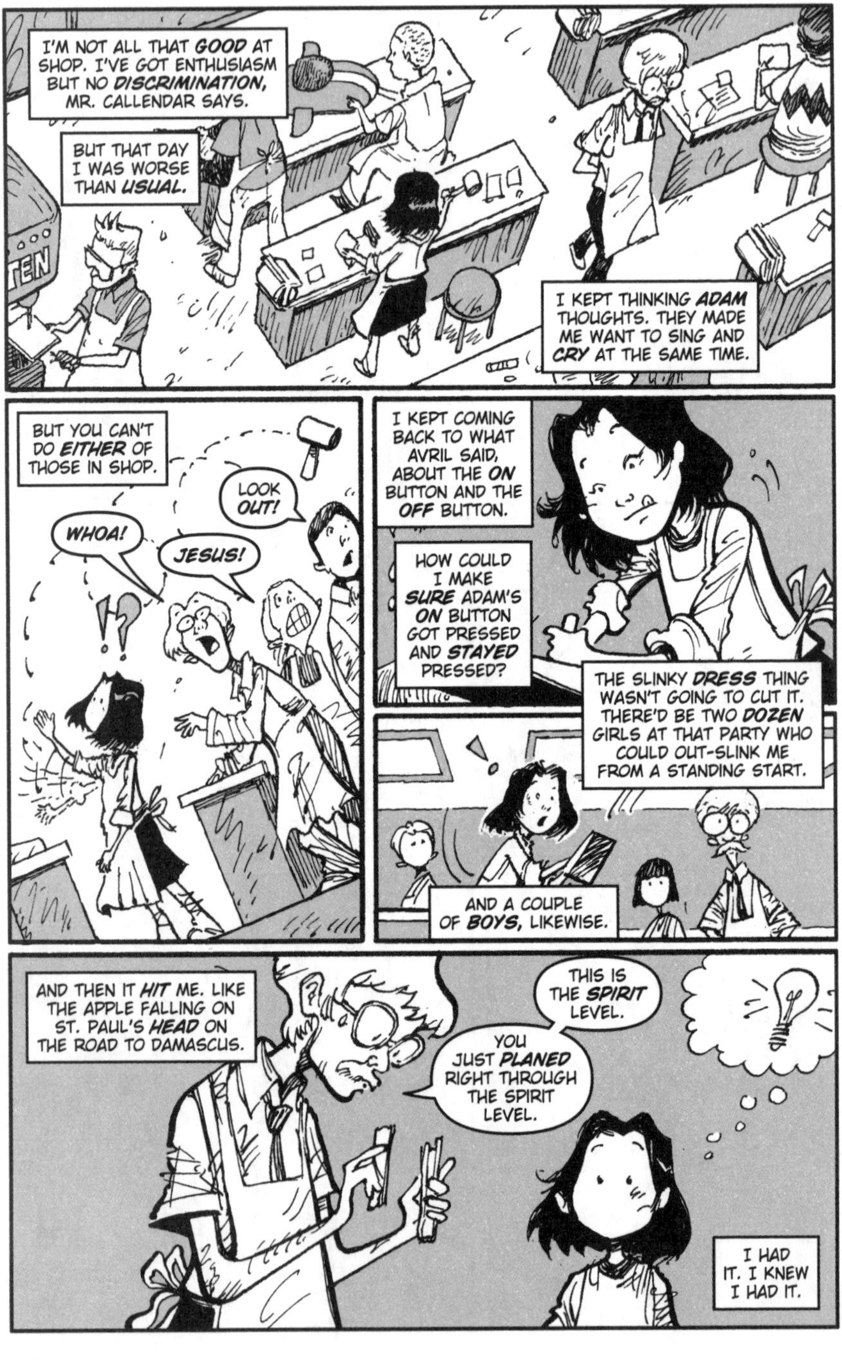
I'M NOT ALL THAT GOOD AT SHOP. I'VE GOT ENTHUSIASM BUT NO DISCRIMINATION, MR. CALLENDAR SAYS.
BUT THAT DAY I WAS WORSE THAN USUAL.
I KEPT THINKING ADAM THOUGHTS. THEY MADE ME WANT TO SING AND CRY AT THE SAME TIME.
BUT YOU CAN'T DO EITHER OF THOSE IN SHOP.
LOOK OUT!
WHOA!
JESUS!
I KEPT COMING BACK TO WHAT AVRIL SAID, ABOUT THE ON BUTTON AND THE OFF BUTTON.
HOW COULD I MAKE SURE ADAM'S ON BUTTON GOT PRESSED AND STAYED PRESSED?
THE SLINKY DRESS THING WASN'T GOING TO CUT IT. THERE'D BE TWO DOZEN GIRLS AT THAT PARTY WHO COULD OUT-SLINK ME FROM A STANDING START.
AND A COUPLE OF BOYS, LIKEWISE.
AND THEN IT HIT ME. LIKE THE APPLE FALLING ON ST. PAUL'S HEAD ON THE ROAD TO DAMASCUS.
THIS IS THE SPIRIT LEVEL.
YOU JUST PLANED RIGHT THROUGH THE SPIRIT LEVEL.
I HAD IT. I KNEW I HAD IT.

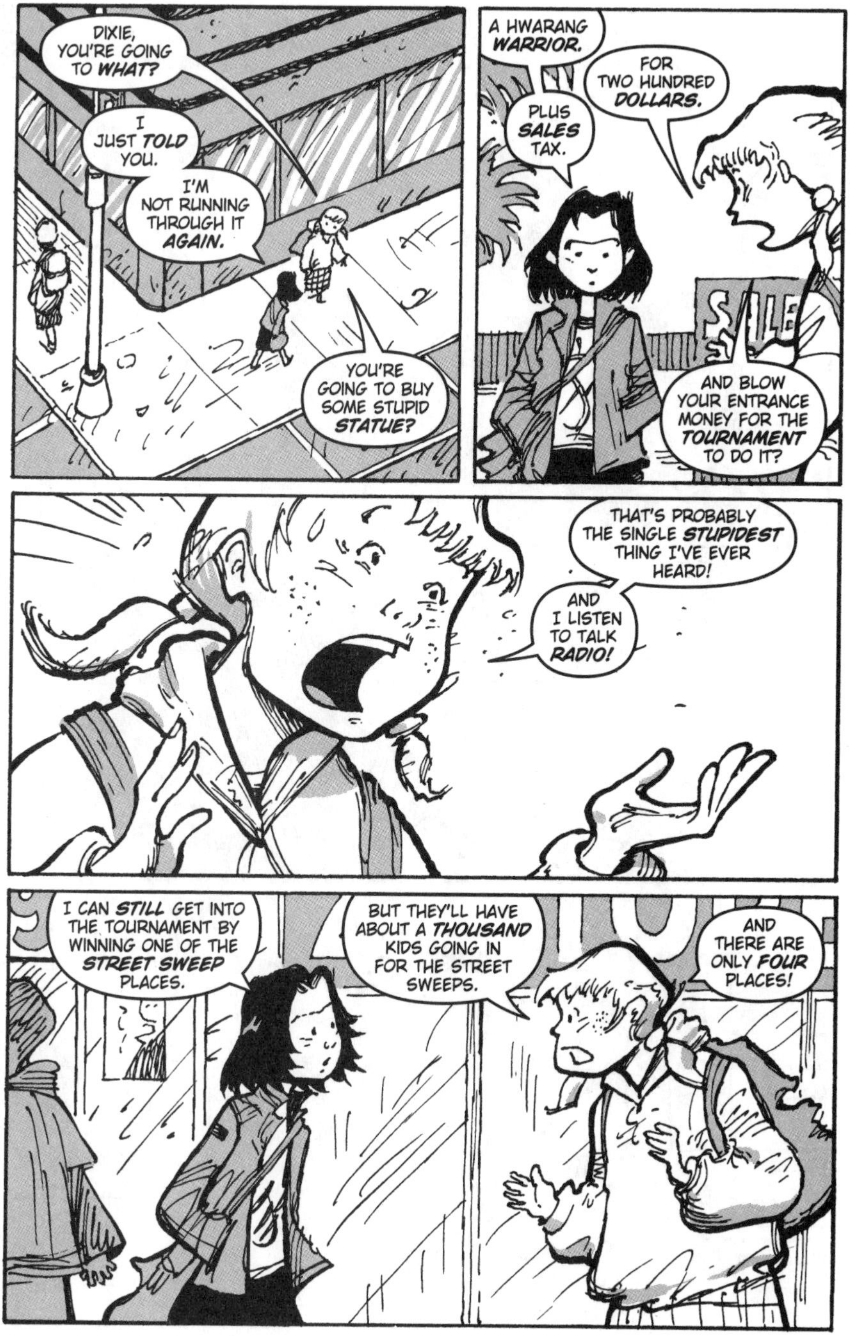
DIXIE, YOU'RE GOING TO WHAT?
I JUST TOLD YOU.
I'M NOT RUNNING THROUGH IT AGAIN.
YOU'RE GOING TO BUY SOME STUPID STATUE?
A HWARANG WARRIOR.
FOR TWO HUNDRED DOLLARS.
PLUS SALES TAX.
AND BLOW YOUR ENTRANCE MONEY FOR THE TOURNAMENT TO DO IT?
THAT'S PROBABLY THE SINGLE STUPIDEST THING I'VE EVER HEARD!
AND I LISTEN TO TALK RADIO!
I CAN STILL GET INTO THE TOURNAMENT BY WINNING ONE OF THE STREET SWEEP PLACES.
BUT THEY'LL HAVE ABOUT A THOUSAND KIDS GOING IN FOR THE STREET SWEEPS.
AND THERE ARE ONLY FOUR PLACES!

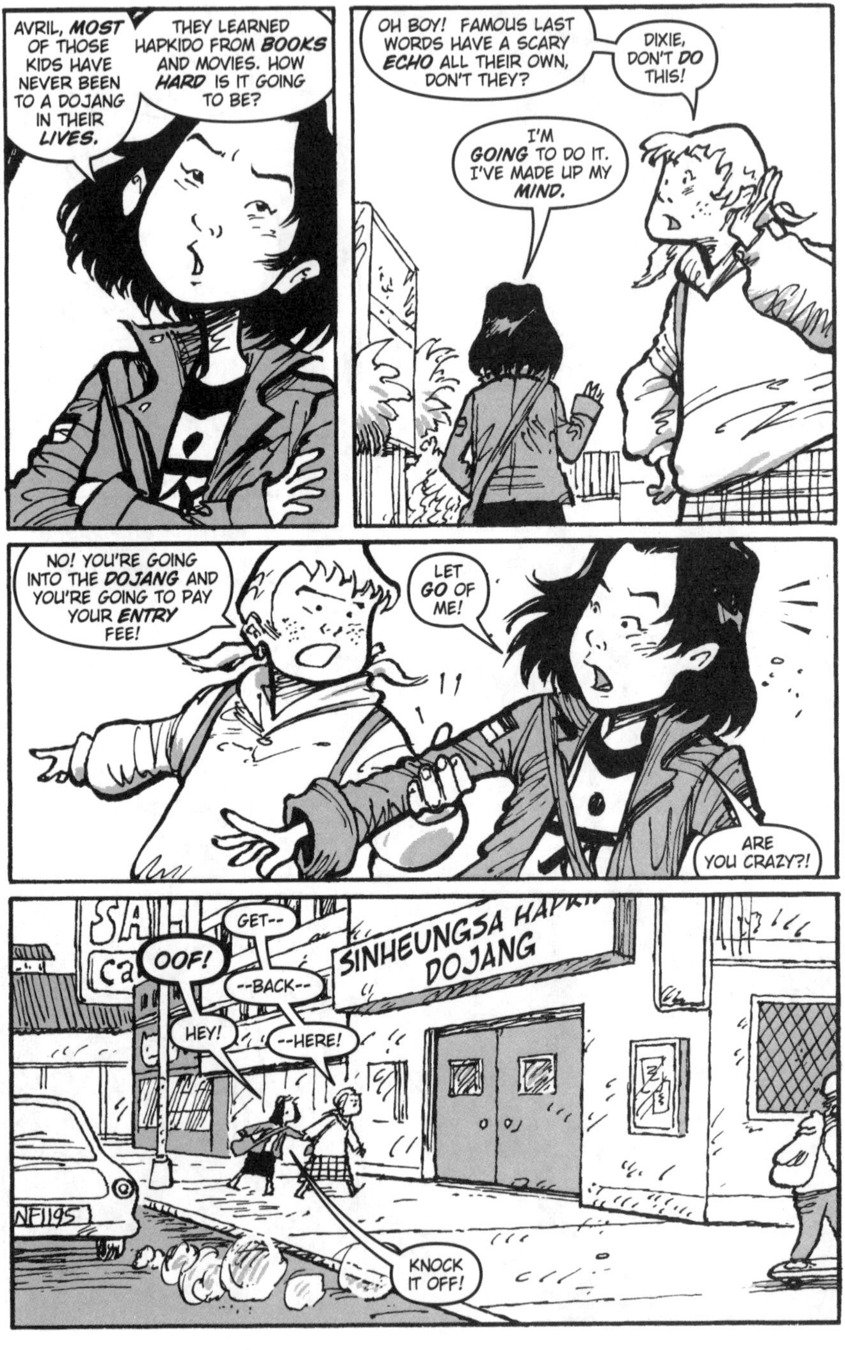
AVRIL, MOST OF THOSE KIDS HAVE NEVER BEEN TO A DOJANG IN THEIR LIVES.
THEY LEARNED HAPKIDO FROM BOOKS AND MOVIES. HOW HARD IS IT GOING TO BE?
OH BOY! FAMOUS LAST WORDS HAVE A SCARY ECHO ALL THEIR OWN, DON'T THEY?
DIXIE, DON'T DO THIS!
I'M GOING TO DO IT. I'VE MADE UP MY MIND.
NO! YOU'RE GOING INTO THE DOJANG AND YOU'RE GOING TO PAY YOUR ENTRY FEE!
LET GO OF ME!
ARE YOU CRAZY?!
SINHEUNGSA HAPKI
DOJANG
GET--
OOF!
--BACK--
HEY!
--HERE!
KNOCK IT OFF!

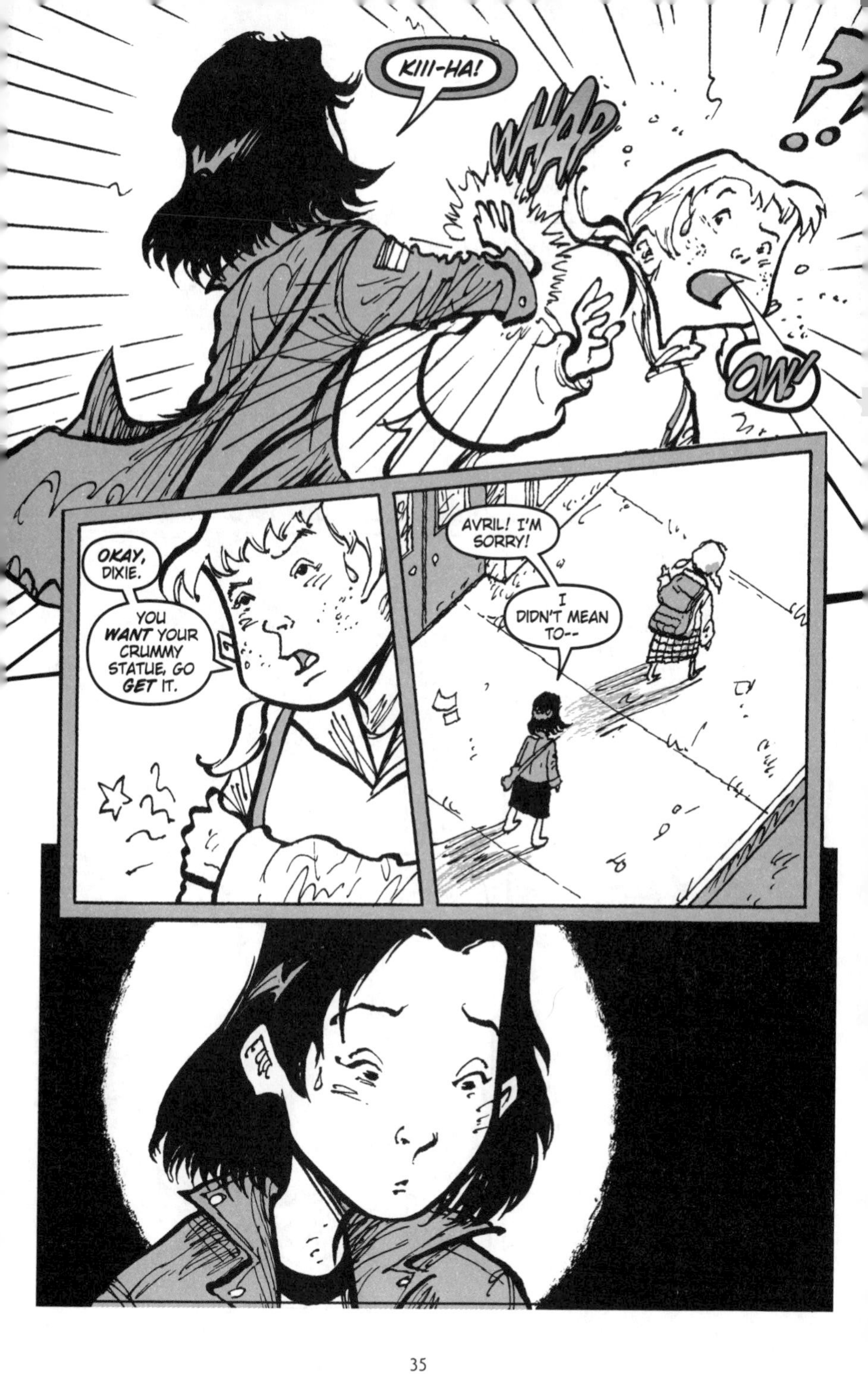
KIII-HA!
WHAP
?!
OW!
OKAY, DIXIE.
YOU WANT YOUR CRUMMY STATUE, GO GET IT.
AVRIL! I'M SORRY!
I DIDN'T MEAN TO--

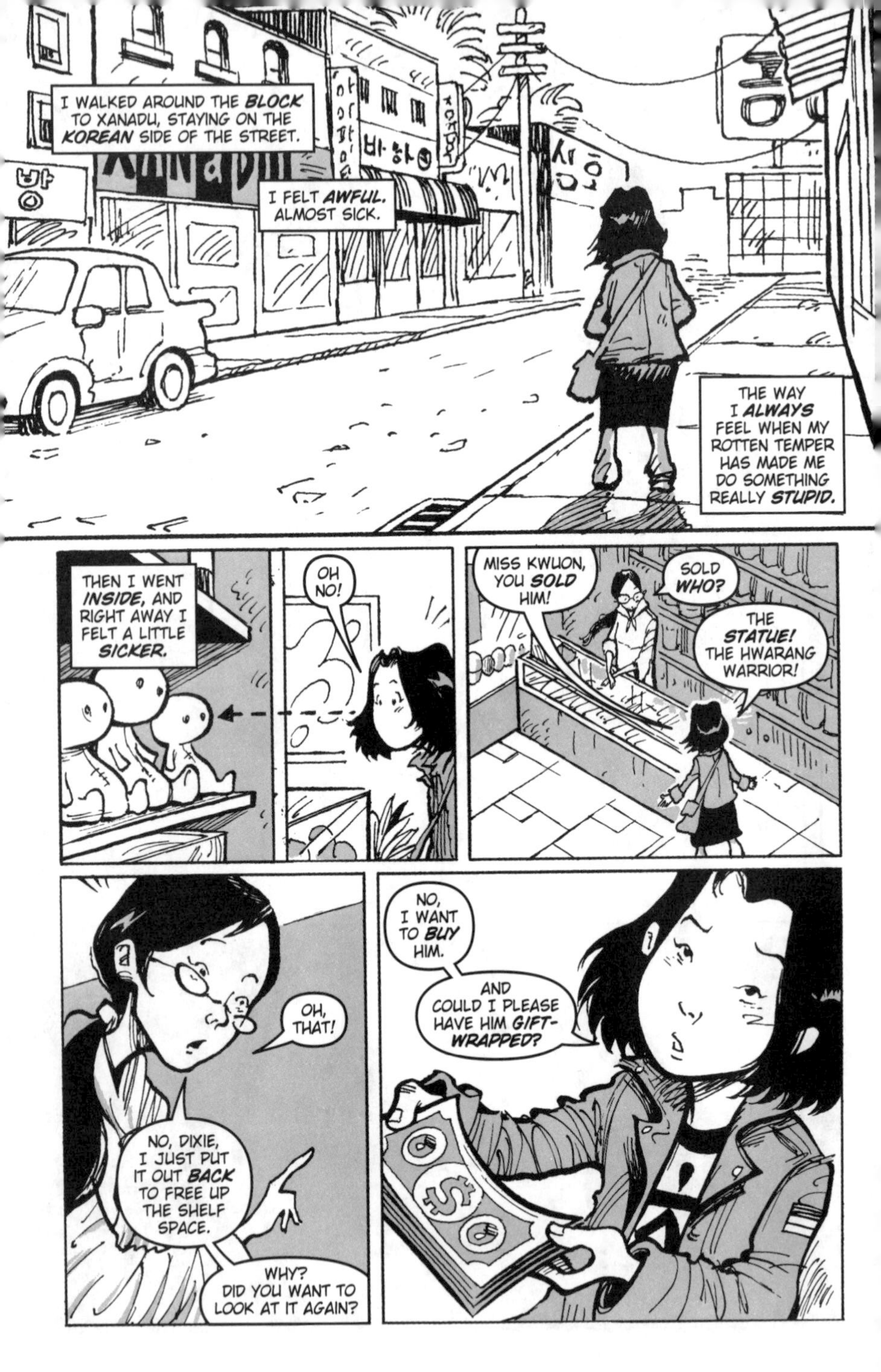
I WALKED AROUND THE BLOCK TO XANADU, STAYING ON THE KOREAN SIDE OF THE STREET.
I FELT AWFUL. ALMOST SICK.
THE WAY I ALWAYS FEEL WHEN MY ROTTEN TEMPER HAS MADE ME DO SOMETHING REALLY STUPID.
THEN I WENT INSIDE, AND RIGHT AWAY I FELT A LITTLE SICKER.
OH NO!
MISS KWUON, YOU SOLD HIM!
SOLD WHO?
THE STATUE! THE HWARANG WARRIOR!
OH, THAT!
NO, DIXIE, I JUST PUT IT OUT BACK TO FREE UP THE SHELF SPACE.
WHY? DID YOU WANT TO LOOK AT IT AGAIN?
NO, I WANT TO BUY HIM.
AND COULD I PLEASE HAVE HIM GIFT-WRAPPED?

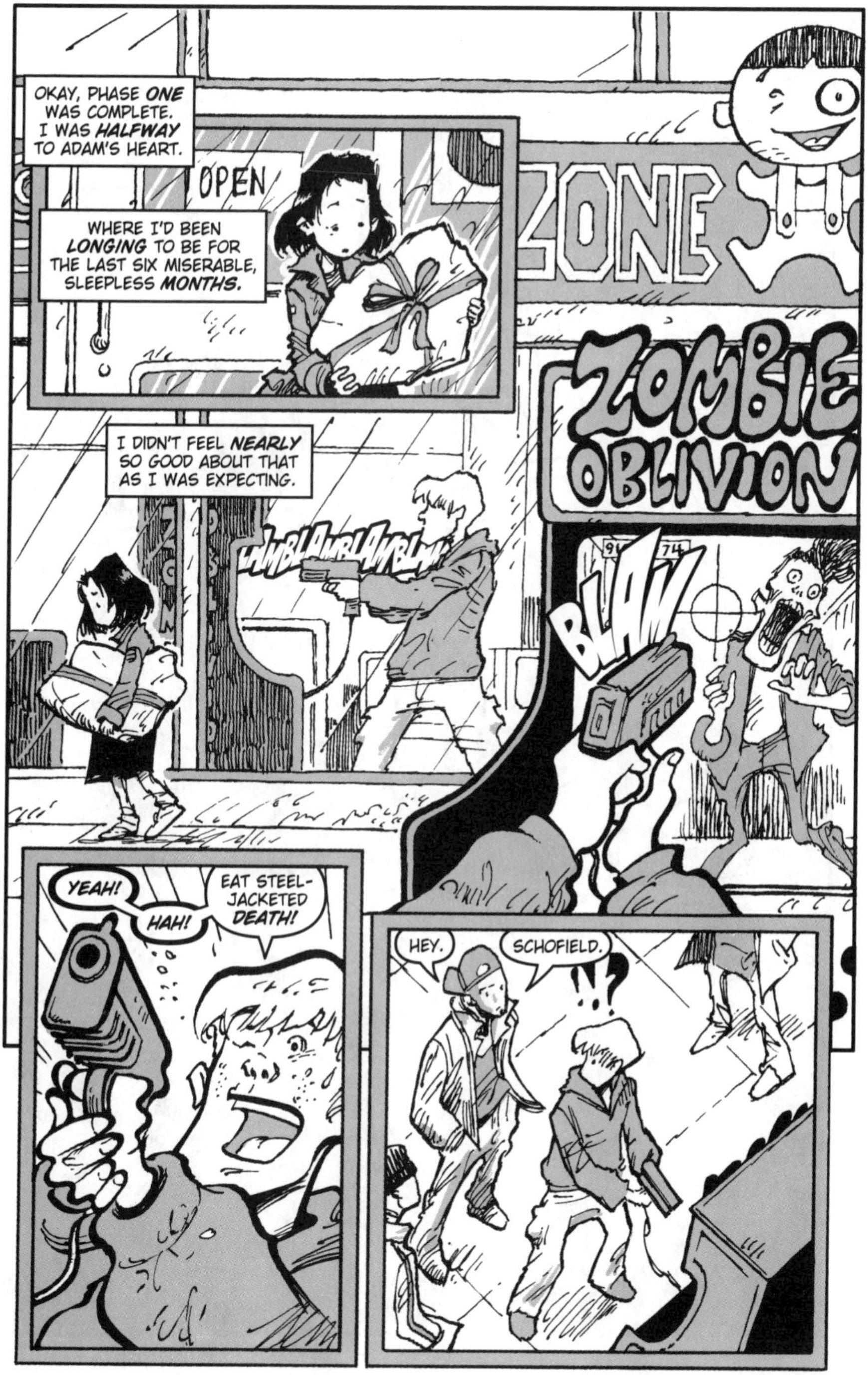

OKAY, PHASE ONE WAS COMPLETE. I WAS HALFWAY TO ADAM'S HEART.
OPEN
ZONE
WHERE I'D BEEN LONGING TO BE FOR THE LAST SIX MISERABLE, SLEEPLESS MONTHS.
ZOMBIE OBLIVION
I DIDN'T FEEL NEARLY SO GOOD ABOUT THAT AS I WAS EXPECTING.
BLAMBLAMBLAMBLAM
BLAM
YEAH!
HAH!
EAT STEEL-JACKETED DEATH!
HEY.
SCHOFIELD.
!?

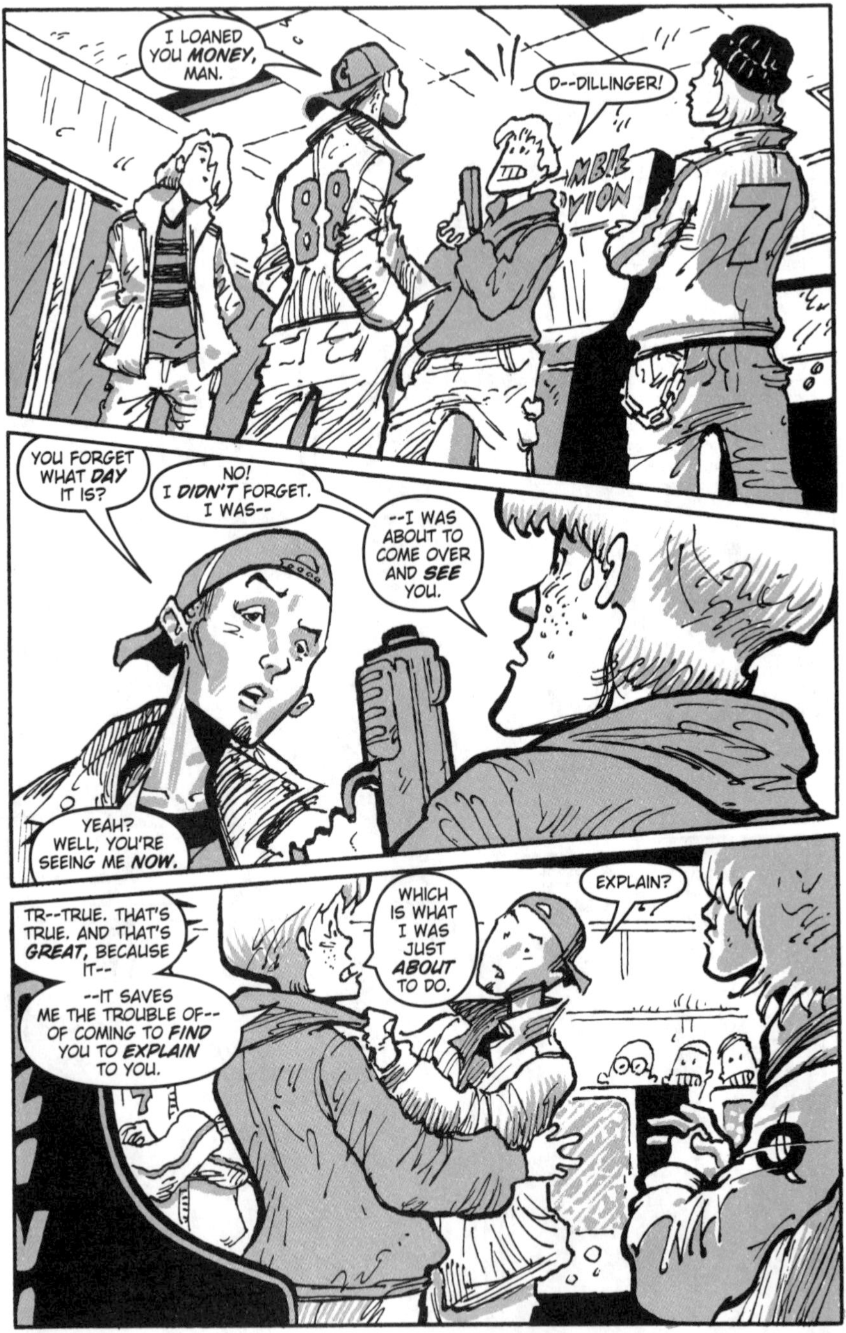
I LOANED YOU MONEY, MAN.
D--DILLINGER!
MBLE
VION
YOU FORGET WHAT DAY IT IS?
NO! I DIDN'T FORGET. I WAS--
--I WAS ABOUT TO COME OVER AND SEE YOU.
YEAH? WELL, YOU'RE SEEING ME NOW.
TR--TRUE. THAT'S TRUE. AND THAT'S GREAT, BECAUSE IT--
--IT SAVES ME THE TROUBLE OF-- OF COMING TO FIND YOU TO EXPLAIN TO YOU.
WHICH IS WHAT I WAS JUST ABOUT TO DO.
EXPLAIN?

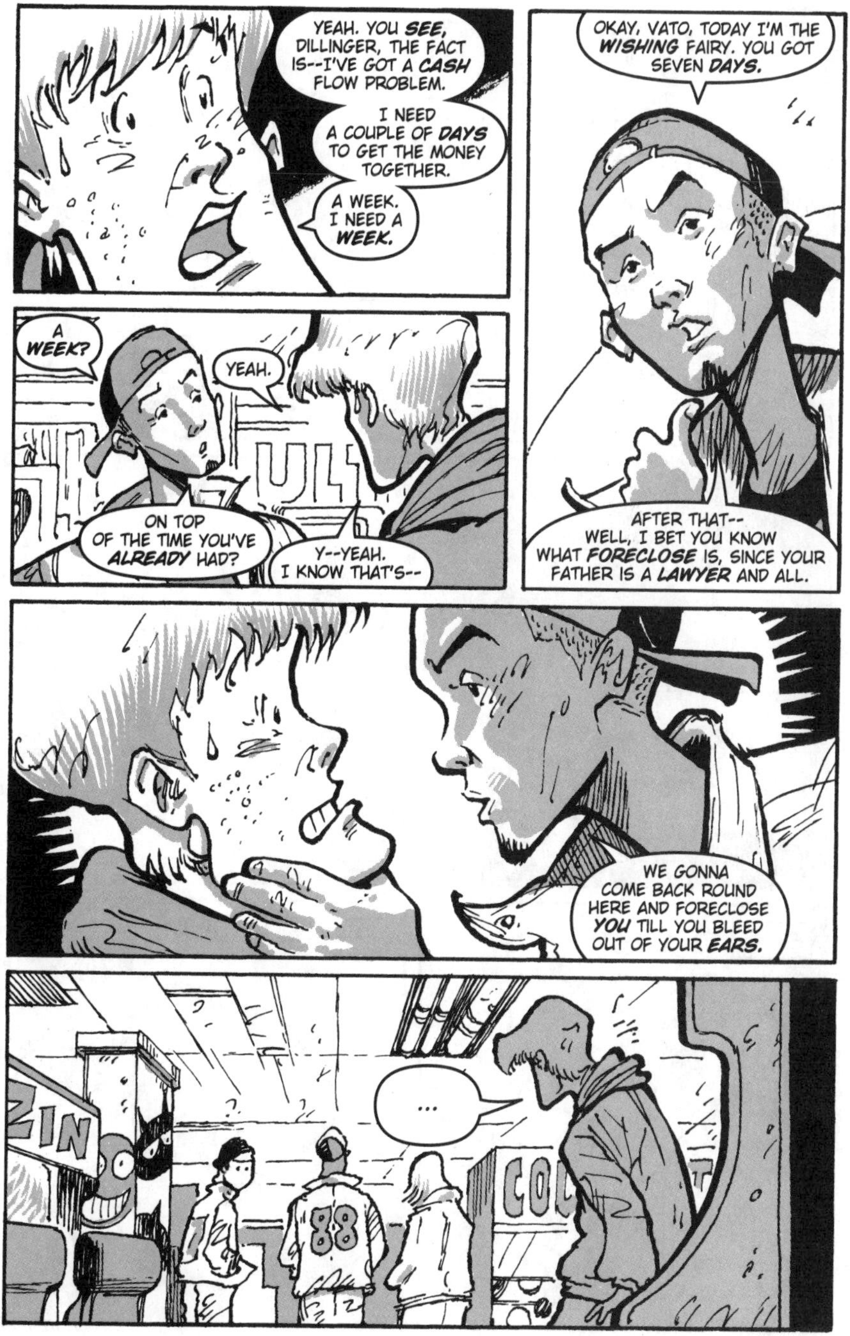
YEAH. YOU SEE, DILLINGER, THE FACT IS--I'VE GOT A CASH FLOW PROBLEM.
I NEED A COUPLE OF DAYS TO GET THE MONEY TOGETHER.
A WEEK. I NEED A WEEK.
A WEEK?
YEAH.
ON TOP OF THE TIME YOU'VE ALREADY HAD?
Y--YEAH. I KNOW THAT'S--
OKAY, VATO, TODAY I'M THE WISHING FAIRY. YOU GOT SEVEN DAYS.
AFTER THAT-- WELL, I BET YOU KNOW WHAT FORECLOSE IS, SINCE YOUR FATHER IS A LAWYER AND ALL.
WE GONNA COME BACK ROUND HERE AND FORECLOSE YOU TILL YOU BLEED OUT OF YOUR EARS.
...
ZIN
88
COU

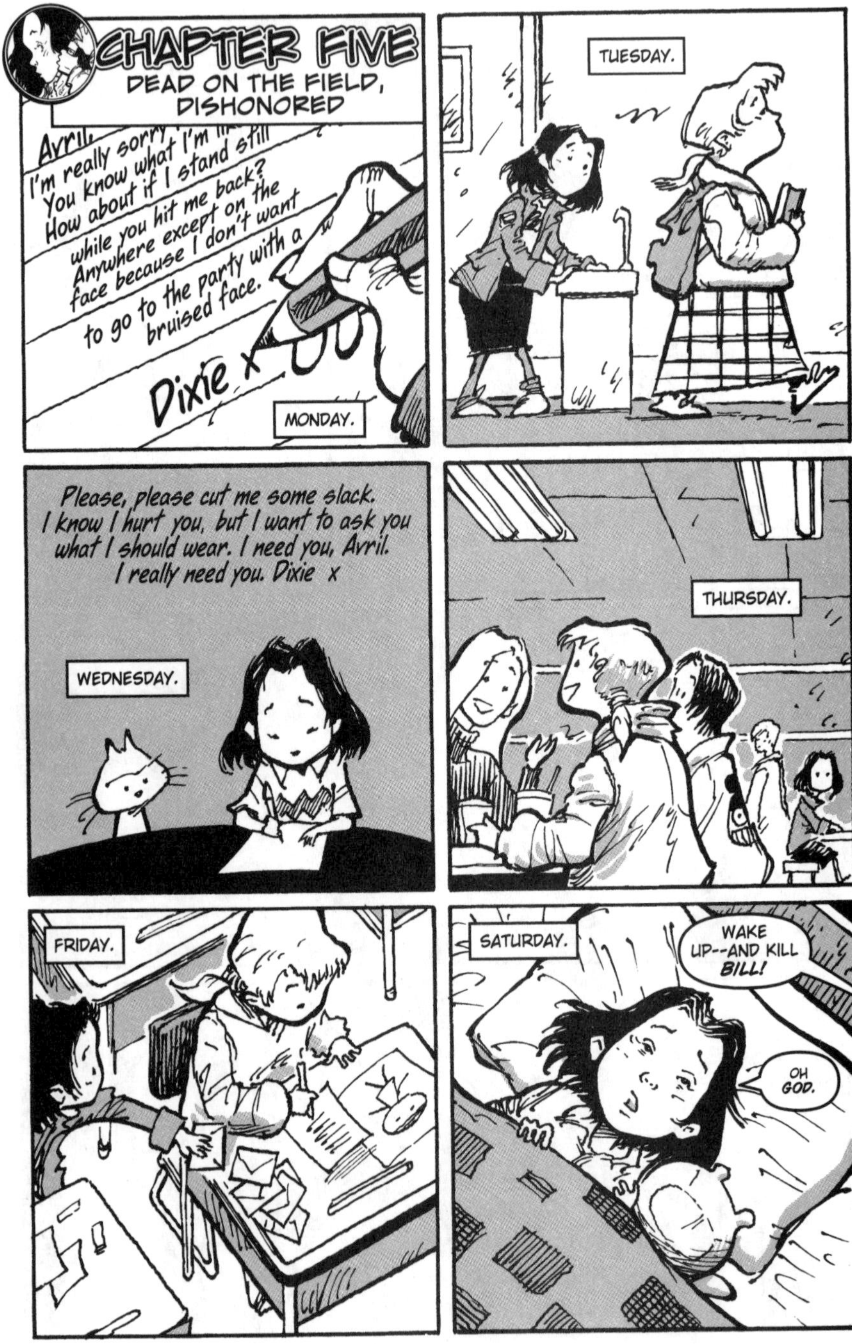
CHAPTER FIVE
DEAD ON THE FIELD, DISHONORED
Avril
I'm really sorry
You know what I'm
How about if I stand still
while you hit me back?
Anywhere except on the
face because I don't want
to go to the party with a
bruised face.
Dixie x
MONDAY.
TUESDAY.
Please, please cut me some slack.
I know I hurt you, but I want to ask you
what I should wear. I need you, Avril.
I really need you. Dixie x
WEDNESDAY.
THURSDAY.
FRIDAY.
SATURDAY.
WAKE UP--AND KILL BILL!
OH GOD.

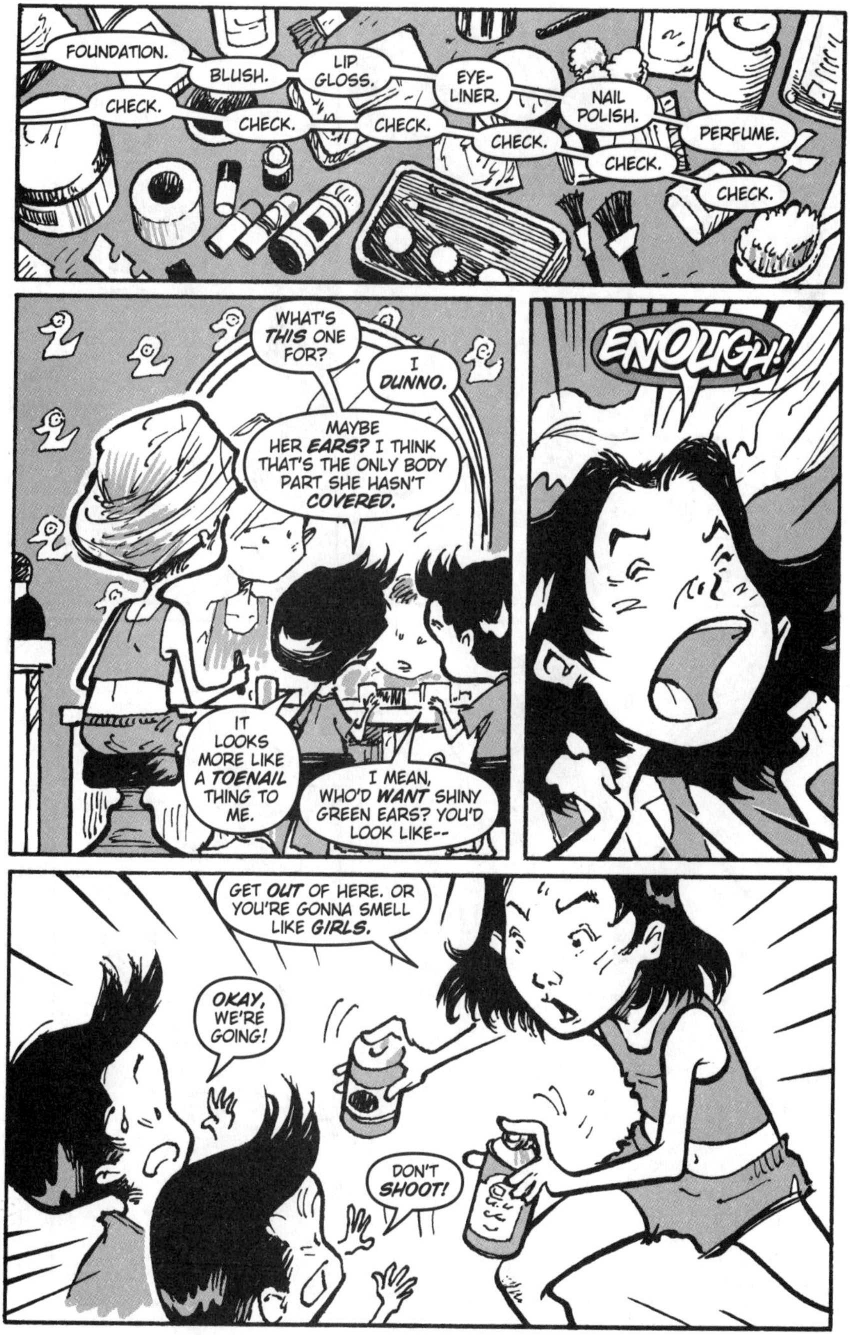
FOUNDATION.
CHECK.
BLUSH.
CHECK.
LIP GLOSS.
CHECK.
EYE-LINER.
CHECK.
NAIL POLISH.
CHECK.
PERFUME.
CHECK.
WHAT'S *THIS* ONE FOR?
I *DUNNO.*
MAYBE HER *EARS?* I THINK THAT'S THE ONLY BODY PART SHE HASN'T *COVERED.*
IT LOOKS MORE LIKE A *TOENAIL* THING TO ME.
I MEAN, WHO'D *WANT* SHINY GREEN EARS? YOU'D LOOK LIKE--
ENOUGH!
GET *OUT* OF HERE. OR YOU'RE GONNA SMELL LIKE *GIRLS.*
OKAY, WE'RE GOING!
DON'T *SHOOT!*

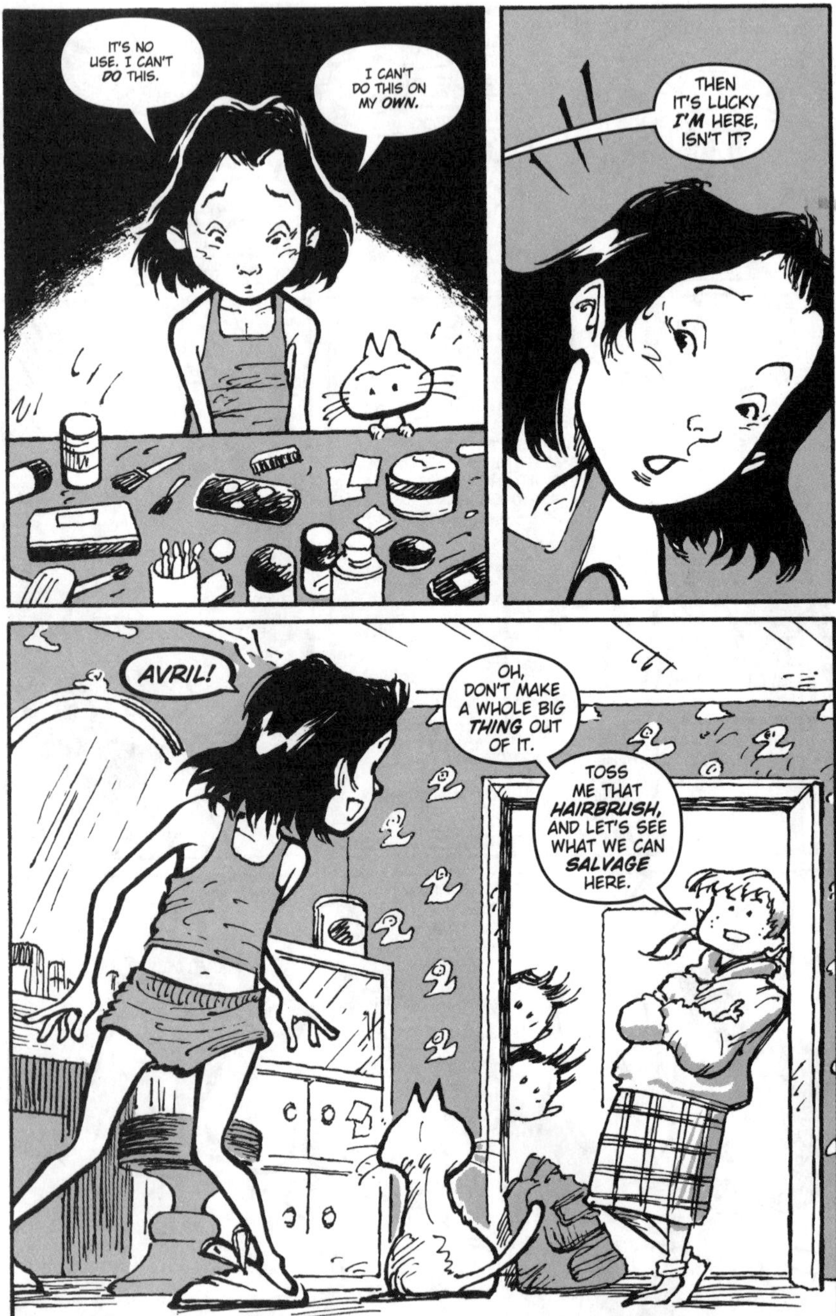
IT'S NO USE. I CAN'T *DO* THIS.
I CAN'T DO THIS ON MY *OWN.*
THEN IT'S LUCKY *I'M* HERE, ISN'T IT?
AVRIL!
OH, DON'T MAKE A WHOLE BIG *THING* OUT OF IT.
TOSS ME THAT *HAIRBRUSH,* AND LET'S SEE WHAT WE CAN *SALVAGE* HERE.

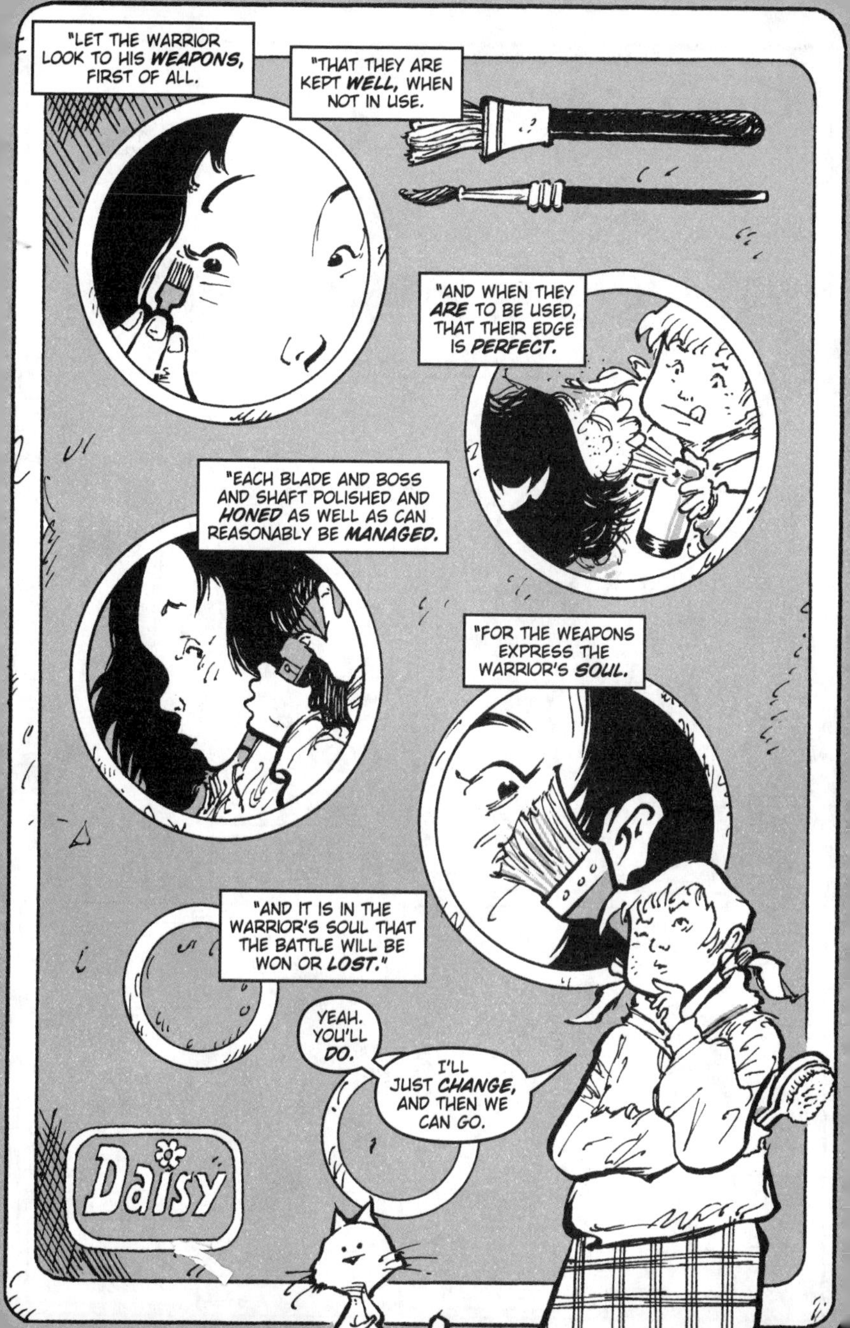
"LET THE WARRIOR LOOK TO HIS WEAPONS, FIRST OF ALL.
"THAT THEY ARE KEPT WELL, WHEN NOT IN USE.
"AND WHEN THEY ARE TO BE USED, THAT THEIR EDGE IS PERFECT.
"EACH BLADE AND BOSS AND SHAFT POLISHED AND HONED AS WELL AS CAN REASONABLY BE MANAGED.
"FOR THE WEAPONS EXPRESS THE WARRIOR'S SOUL.
"AND IT IS IN THE WARRIOR'S SOUL THAT THE BATTLE WILL BE WON OR LOST."
YEAH. YOU'LL DO.
I'LL JUST CHANGE, AND THEN WE CAN GO.
Daisy

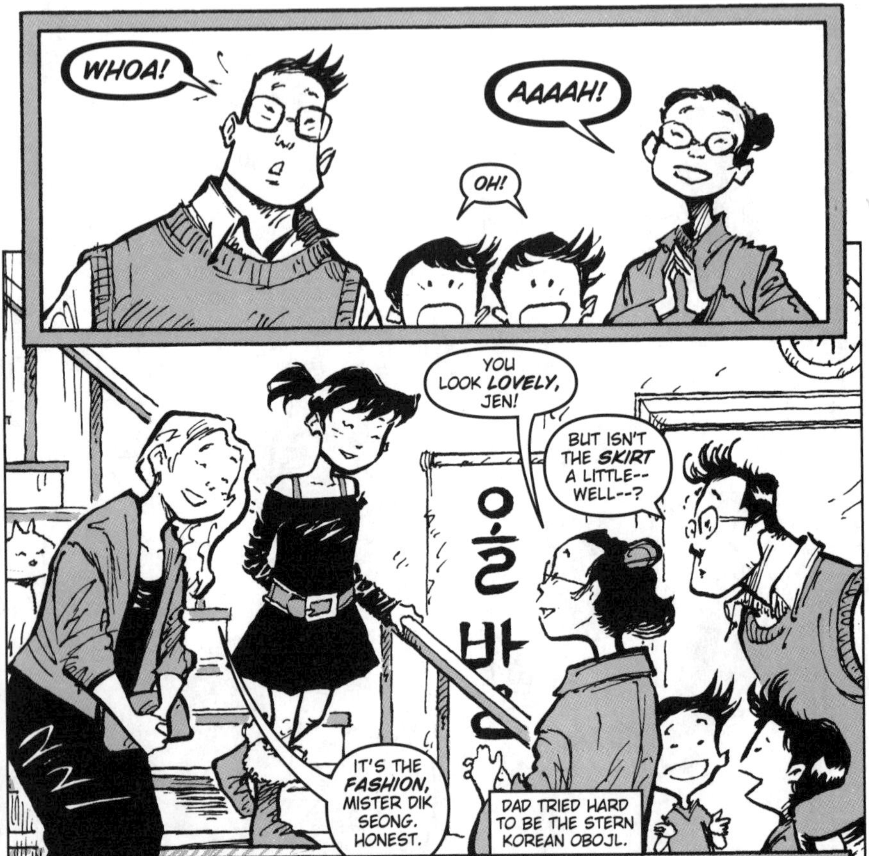
WHOA!
AAAAH!
OH!
YOU LOOK LOVELY, JEN!
BUT ISN'T THE SKIRT A LITTLE-- WELL--?
IT'S THE FASHION, MISTER DIK SEONG. HONEST.
DAD TRIED HARD TO BE THE STERN KOREAN OBOJI.
WELL, YOU BE BACK BY ELEVEN O'CLOCK, THAT'S ALL.
I WILL, DAD.
AND-- HAVE A GREAT TIME.
BUT AS USUAL, HE DIDN'T QUITE MANAGE IT.
MEGAN SCHOFIELD HAD OFFERED US A LIFT IN HER BIG BROTHER HARRISON'S JEEP.
SO I GAVE MICKEY AND SOON ONE LAST WAVE, AND WE RODE OFF--

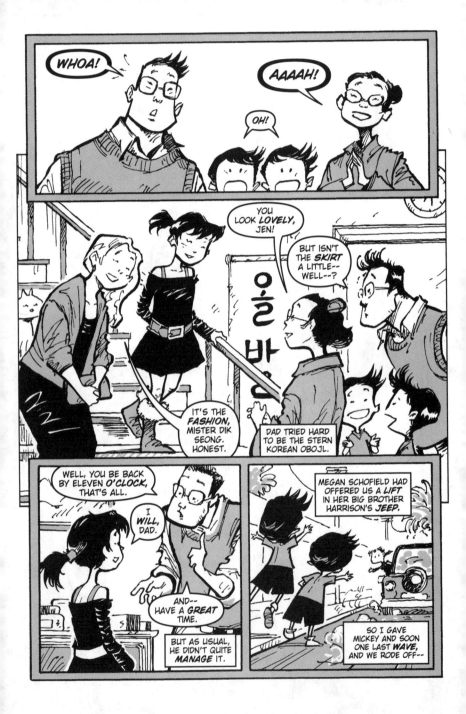

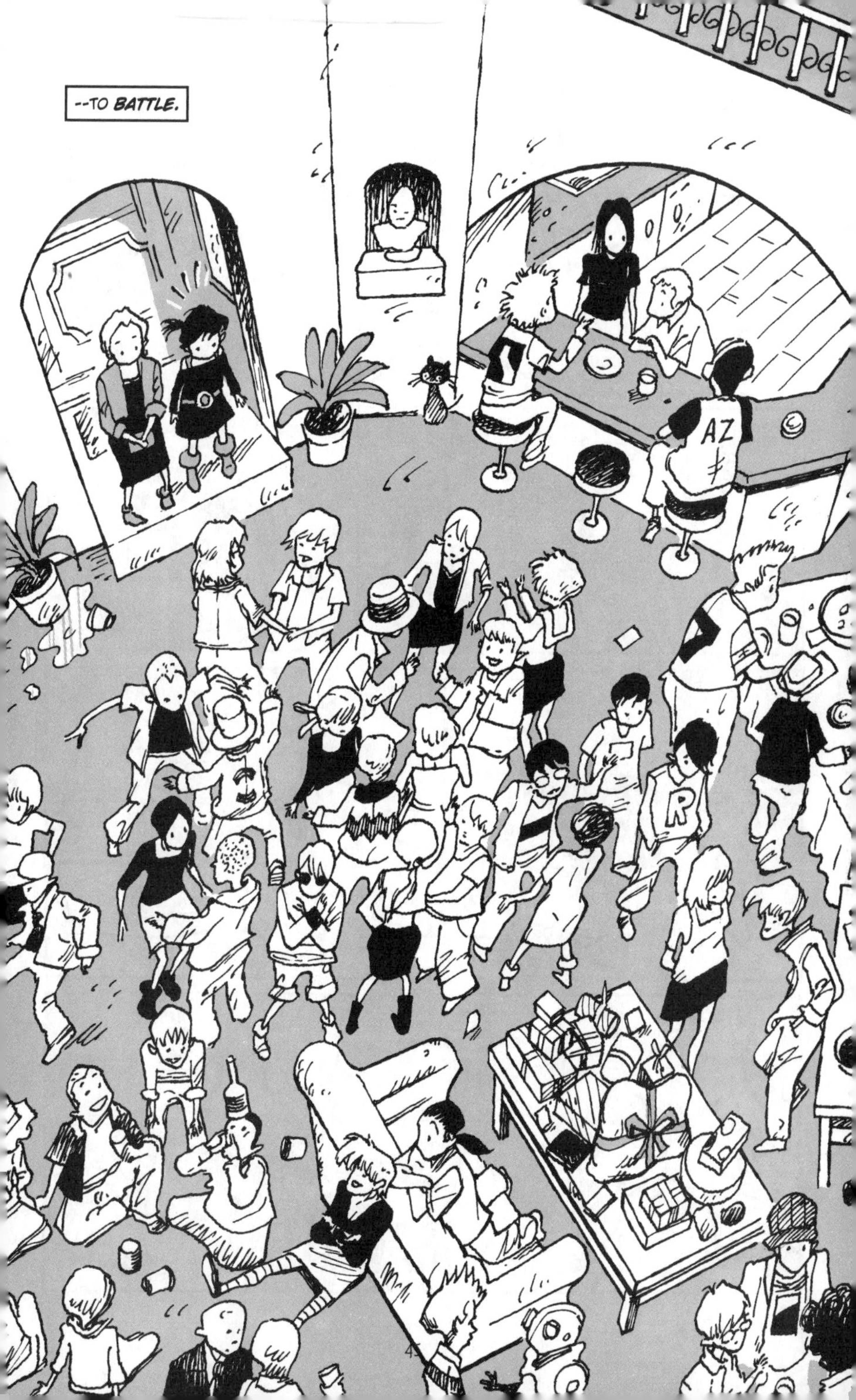
--TO BATTLE.

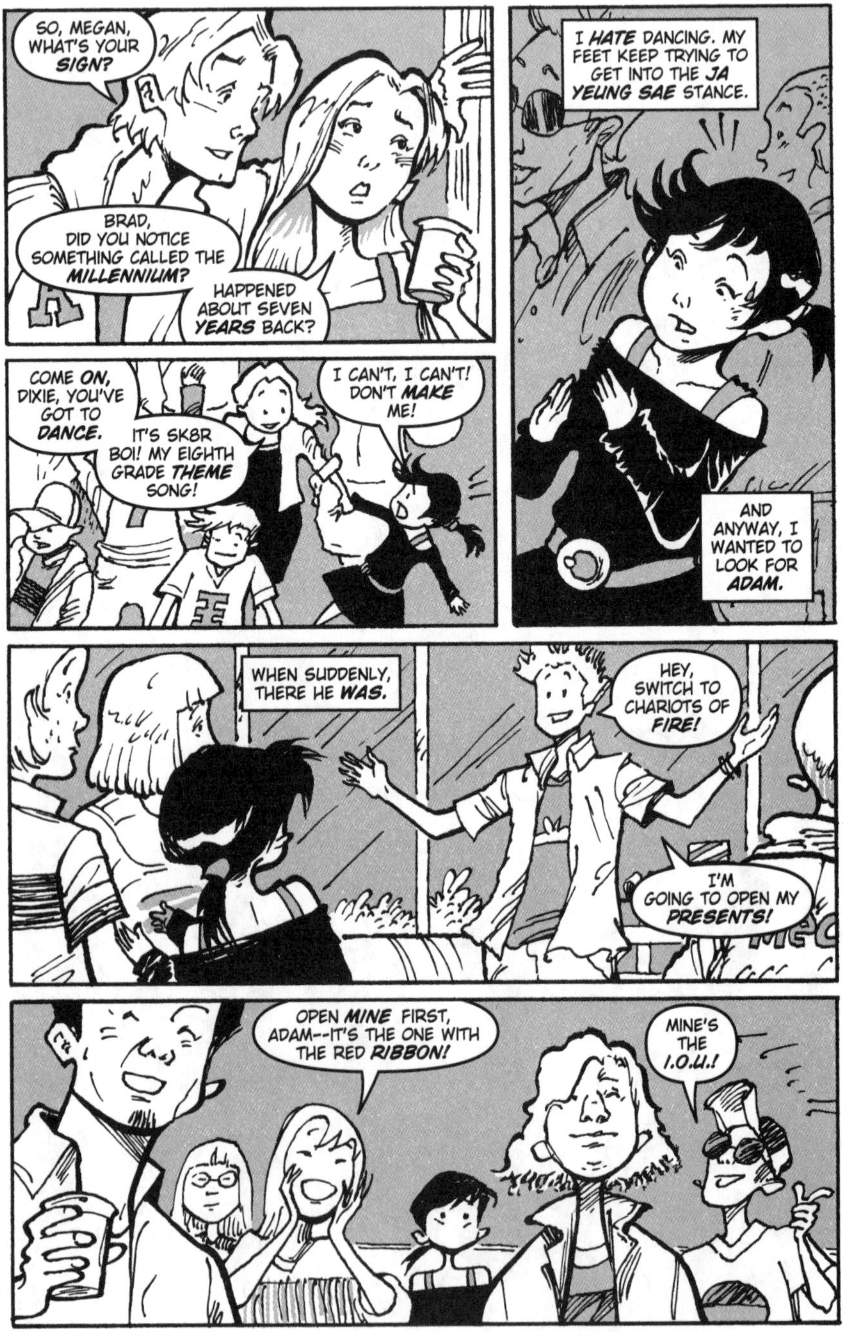
SO, MEGAN, WHAT'S YOUR SIGN?
BRAD, DID YOU NOTICE SOMETHING CALLED THE MILLENNIUM?
HAPPENED ABOUT SEVEN YEARS BACK?
I HATE DANCING. MY FEET KEEP TRYING TO GET INTO THE JA YEUNG SAE STANCE.
COME ON, DIXIE, YOU'VE GOT TO DANCE.
IT'S SK8R BOI! MY EIGHTH GRADE THEME SONG!
I CAN'T, I CAN'T! DON'T MAKE ME!
AND ANYWAY, I WANTED TO LOOK FOR ADAM.
WHEN SUDDENLY, THERE HE WAS.
HEY, SWITCH TO CHARIOTS OF FIRE!
I'M GOING TO OPEN MY PRESENTS!
OPEN MINE FIRST, ADAM--IT'S THE ONE WITH THE RED RIBBON!
MINE'S THE I.O.U.!

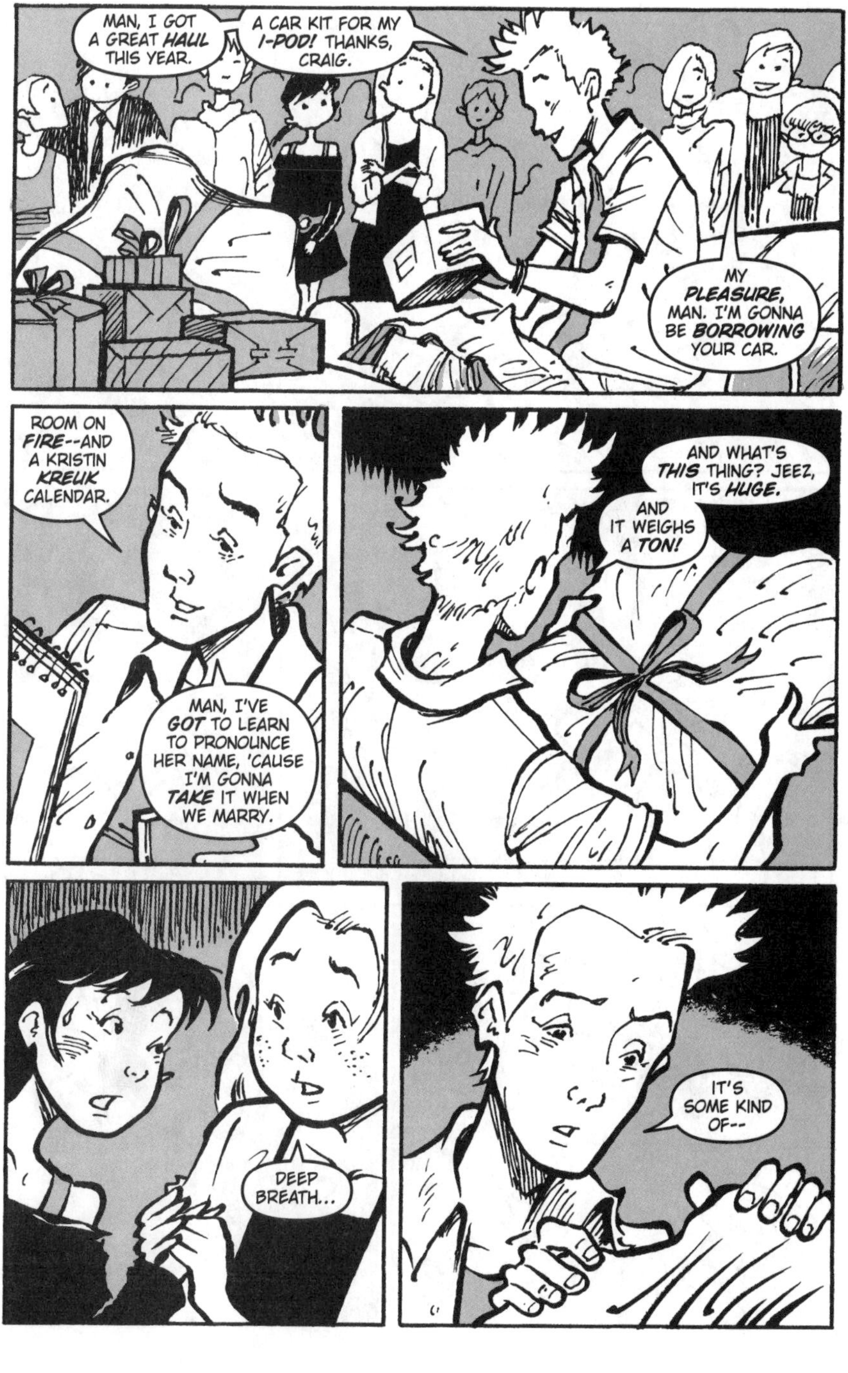
MAN, I GOT A GREAT HAUL THIS YEAR.
A CAR KIT FOR MY I-POD! THANKS, CRAIG.
MY PLEASURE, MAN. I'M GONNA BE BORROWING YOUR CAR.
ROOM ON FIRE--AND A KRISTIN KREUK CALENDAR.
MAN, I'VE GOT TO LEARN TO PRONOUNCE HER NAME, 'CAUSE I'M GONNA TAKE IT WHEN WE MARRY.
AND WHAT'S THIS THING? JEEZ, IT'S HUGE.
AND IT WEIGHS A TON!
DEEP BREATH...
IT'S SOME KIND OF--

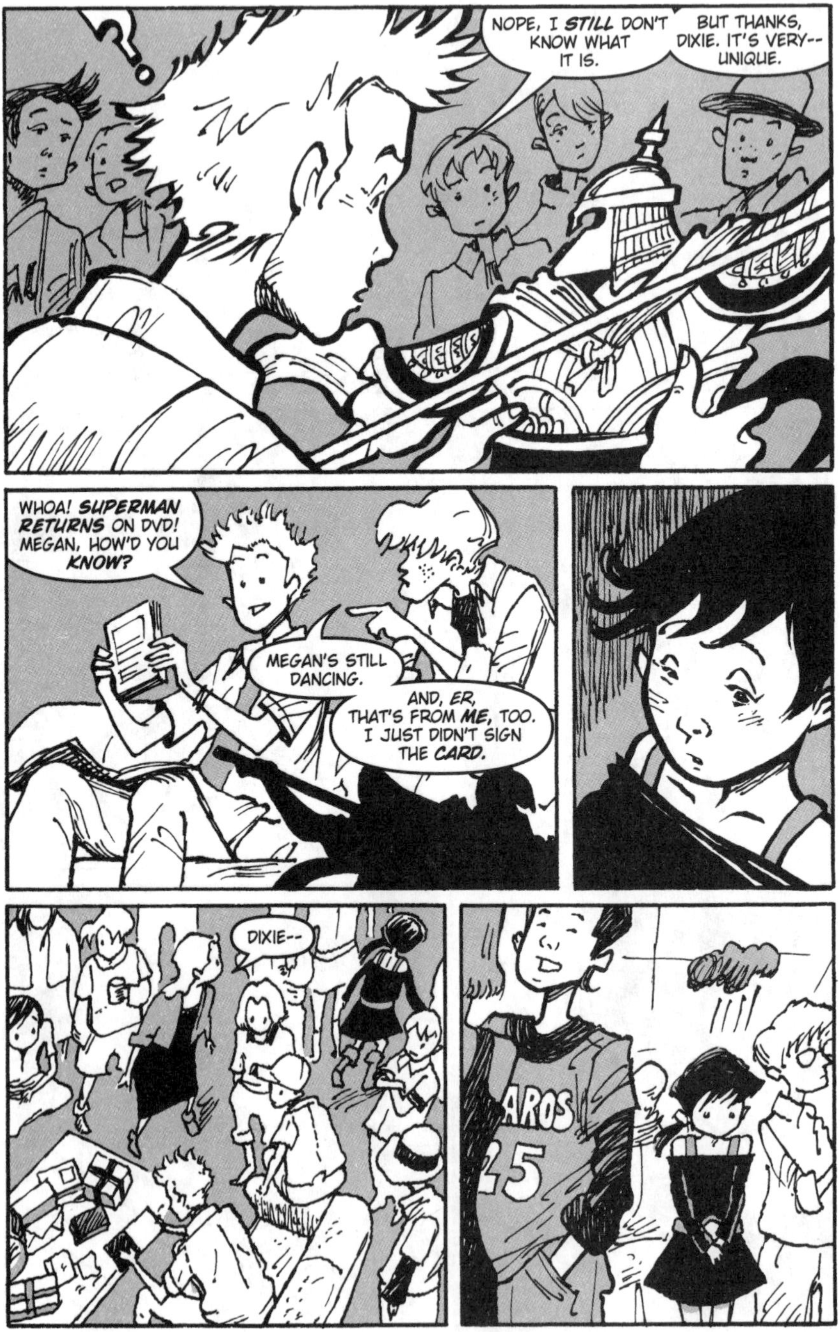
NOPE, I STILL DON'T KNOW WHAT IT IS.
BUT THANKS, DIXIE. IT'S VERY--UNIQUE.
WHOA! SUPERMAN RETURNS ON DVD! MEGAN, HOW'D YOU KNOW?
MEGAN'S STILL DANCING.
AND, ER, THAT'S FROM ME, TOO. I JUST DIDN'T SIGN THE CARD.
DIXIE--
AROS
25

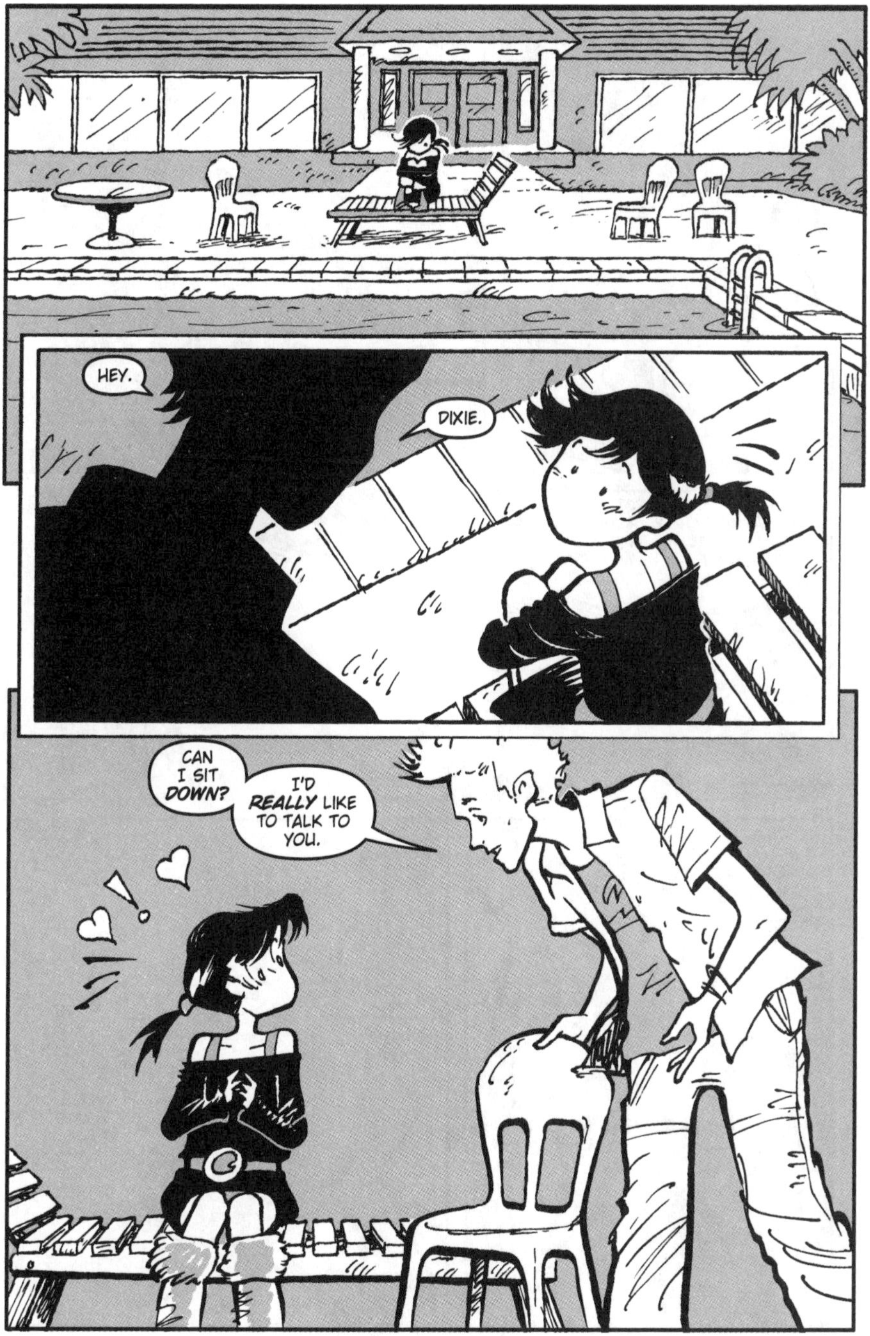
HEY.
DIXIE.
CAN I SIT DOWN?
I'D REALLY LIKE TO TALK TO YOU.
!

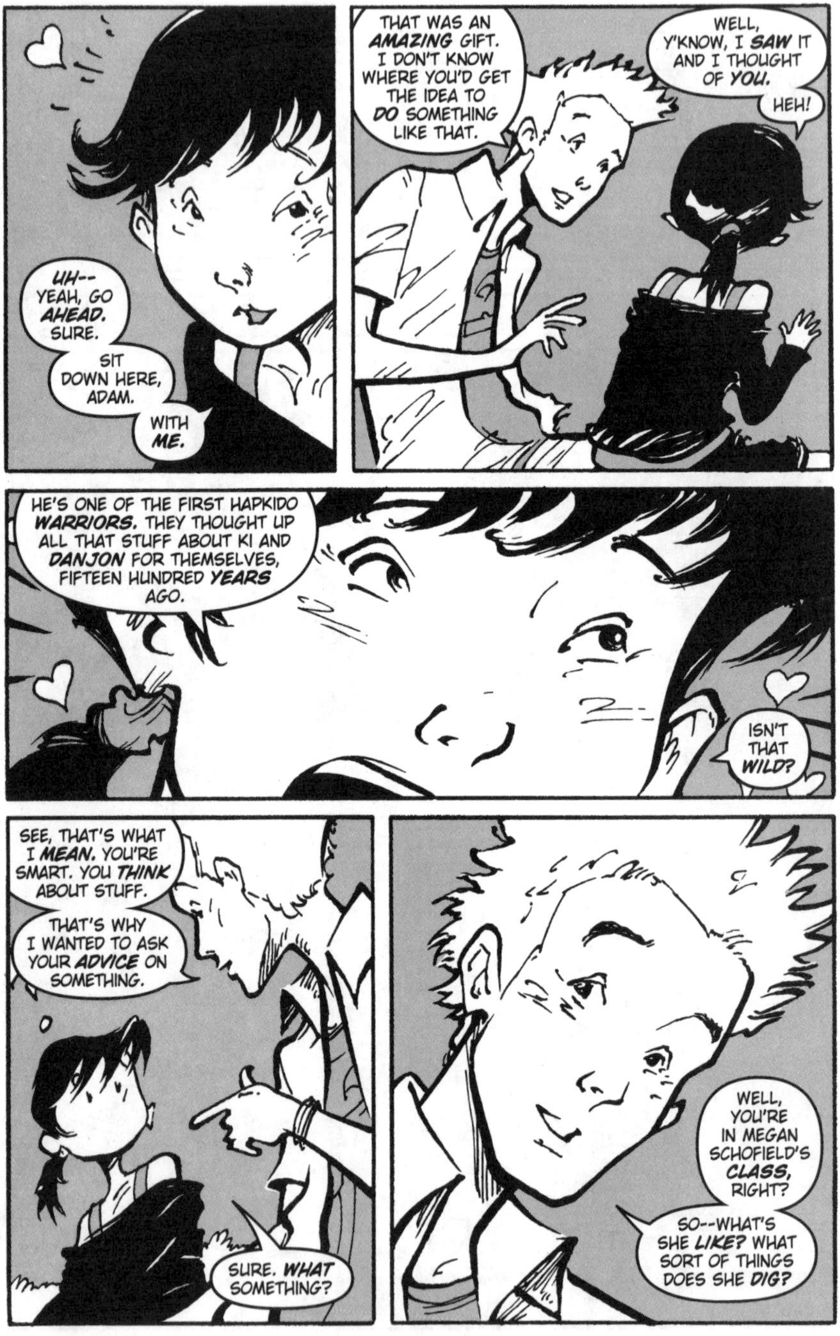
UH-- YEAH, GO AHEAD. SURE.
SIT DOWN HERE, ADAM.
WITH ME.
THAT WAS AN AMAZING GIFT. I DON'T KNOW WHERE YOU'D GET THE IDEA TO DO SOMETHING LIKE THAT.
WELL, Y'KNOW, I SAW IT AND I THOUGHT OF YOU.
HEH!
HE'S ONE OF THE FIRST HAPKIDO WARRIORS. THEY THOUGHT UP ALL THAT STUFF ABOUT KI AND DANJON FOR THEMSELVES, FIFTEEN HUNDRED YEARS AGO.
ISN'T THAT WILD?
SEE, THAT'S WHAT I MEAN. YOU'RE SMART. YOU THINK ABOUT STUFF.
THAT'S WHY I WANTED TO ASK YOUR ADVICE ON SOMETHING.
SURE. WHAT SOMETHING?
WELL, YOU'RE IN MEGAN SCHOFIELD'S CLASS, RIGHT?
SO--WHAT'S SHE LIKE? WHAT SORT OF THINGS DOES SHE DIG?

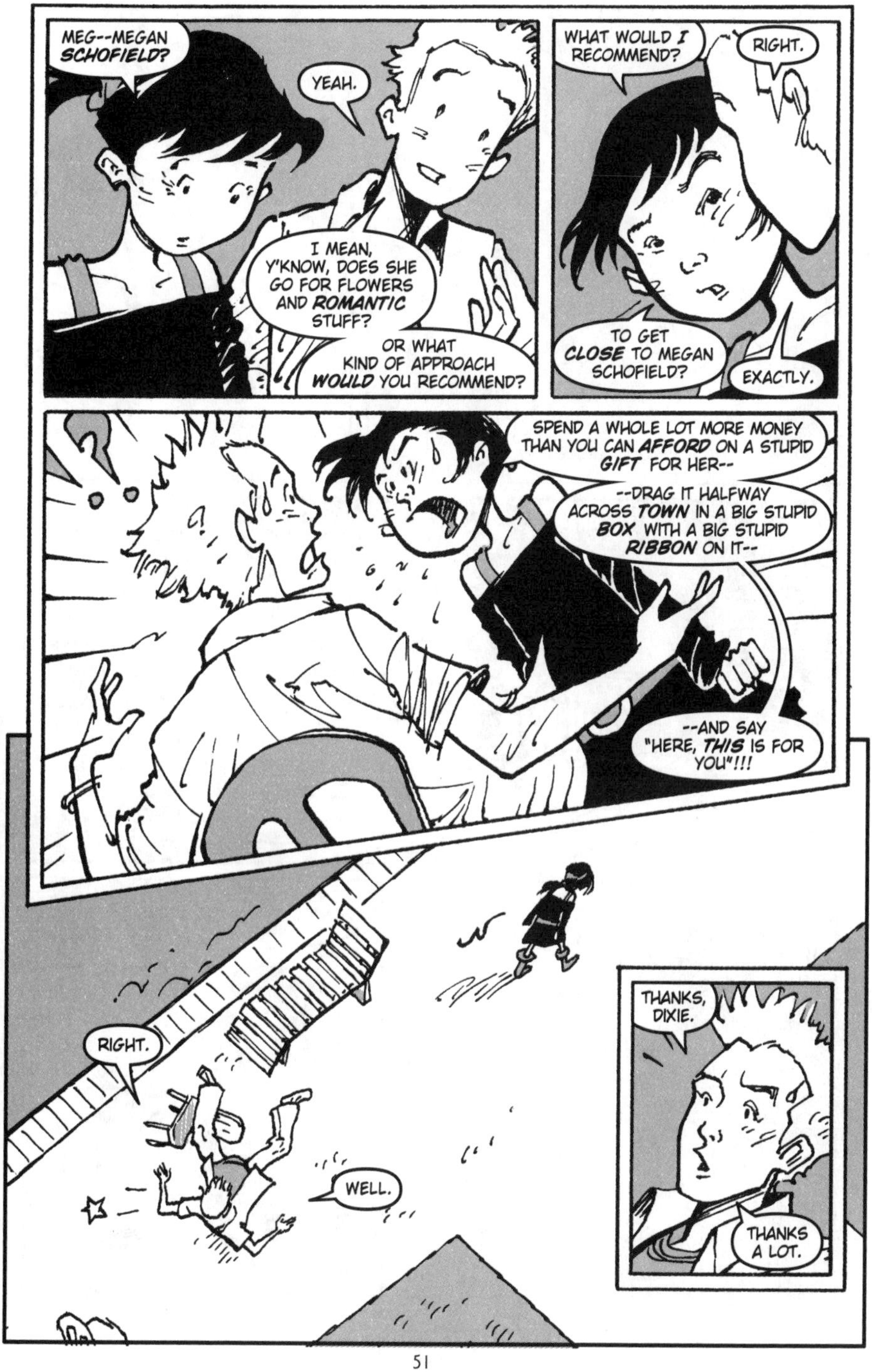

MEG--MEGAN SCHOFIELD?
YEAH.
I MEAN, Y'KNOW, DOES SHE GO FOR FLOWERS AND ROMANTIC STUFF?
OR WHAT KIND OF APPROACH WOULD YOU RECOMMEND?
WHAT WOULD I RECOMMEND?
RIGHT.
TO GET CLOSE TO MEGAN SCHOFIELD?
EXACTLY.
SPEND A WHOLE LOT MORE MONEY THAN YOU CAN AFFORD ON A STUPID GIFT FOR HER--
--DRAG IT HALFWAY ACROSS TOWN IN A BIG STUPID BOX WITH A BIG STUPID RIBBON ON IT--
--AND SAY "HERE, THIS IS FOR YOU"!!!
RIGHT.
WELL.
THANKS, DIXIE.
THANKS A LOT.

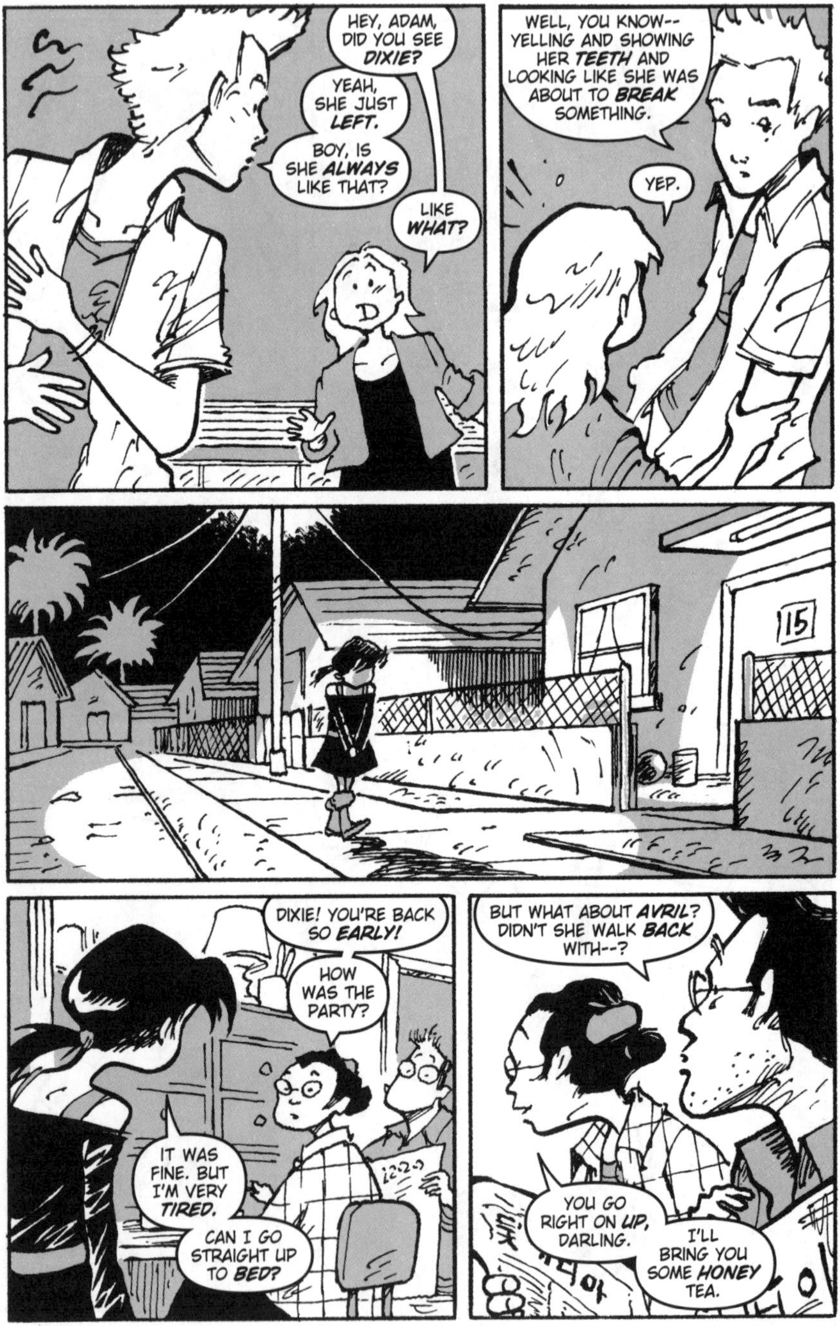
HEY, ADAM, DID YOU SEE DIXIE?
YEAH, SHE JUST LEFT.
BOY, IS SHE ALWAYS LIKE THAT?
LIKE WHAT?
WELL, YOU KNOW-- YELLING AND SHOWING HER TEETH AND LOOKING LIKE SHE WAS ABOUT TO BREAK SOMETHING.
YEP.
15
DIXIE! YOU'RE BACK SO EARLY!
HOW WAS THE PARTY?
IT WAS FINE. BUT I'M VERY TIRED.
CAN I GO STRAIGHT UP TO BED?
BUT WHAT ABOUT AVRIL? DIDN'T SHE WALK BACK WITH--?
YOU GO RIGHT ON UP, DARLING.
I'LL BRING YOU SOME HONEY TEA.

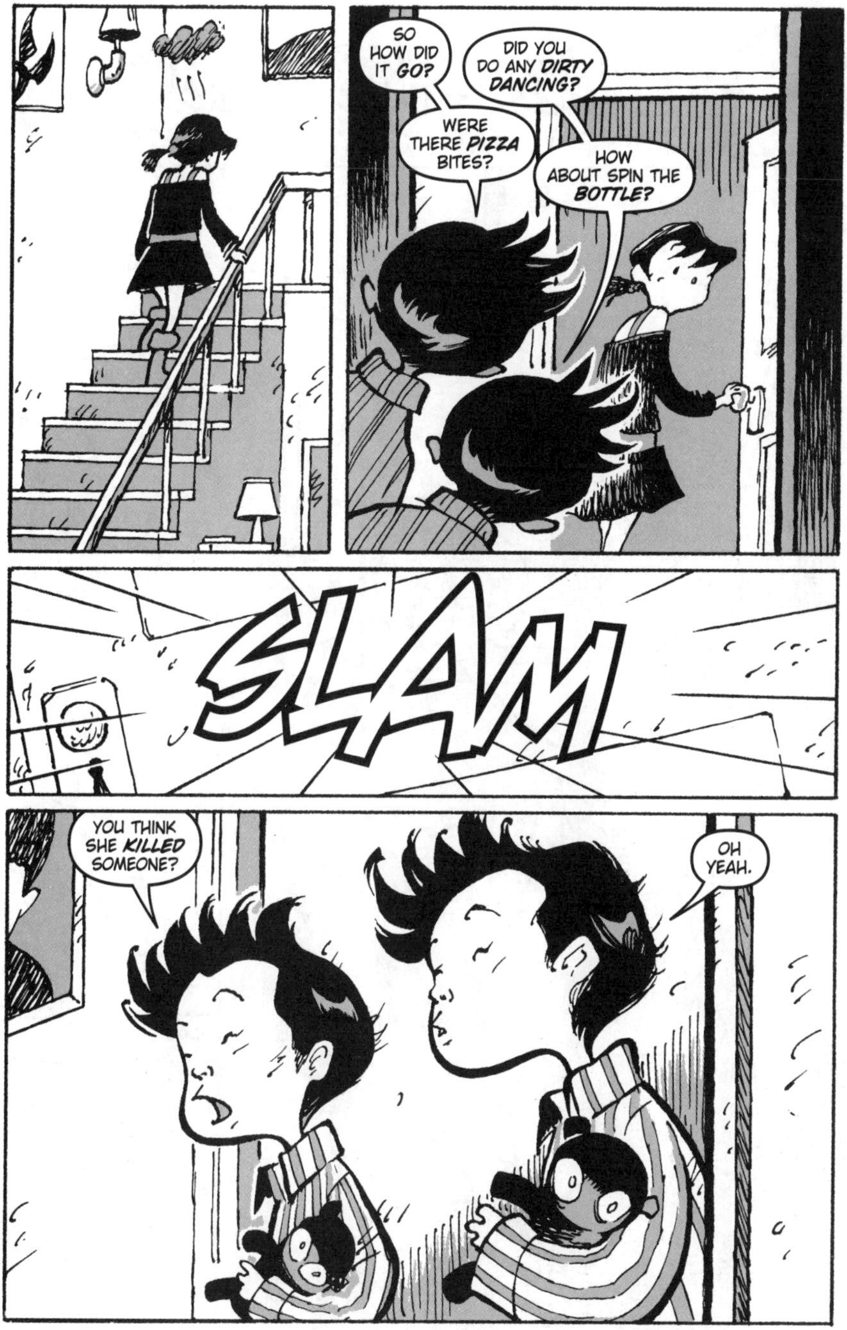
SO HOW DID IT GO?
DID YOU DO ANY DIRTY DANCING?
WERE THERE PIZZA BITES?
HOW ABOUT SPIN THE BOTTLE?
SLAM
YOU THINK SHE KILLED SOMEONE?
OH YEAH.

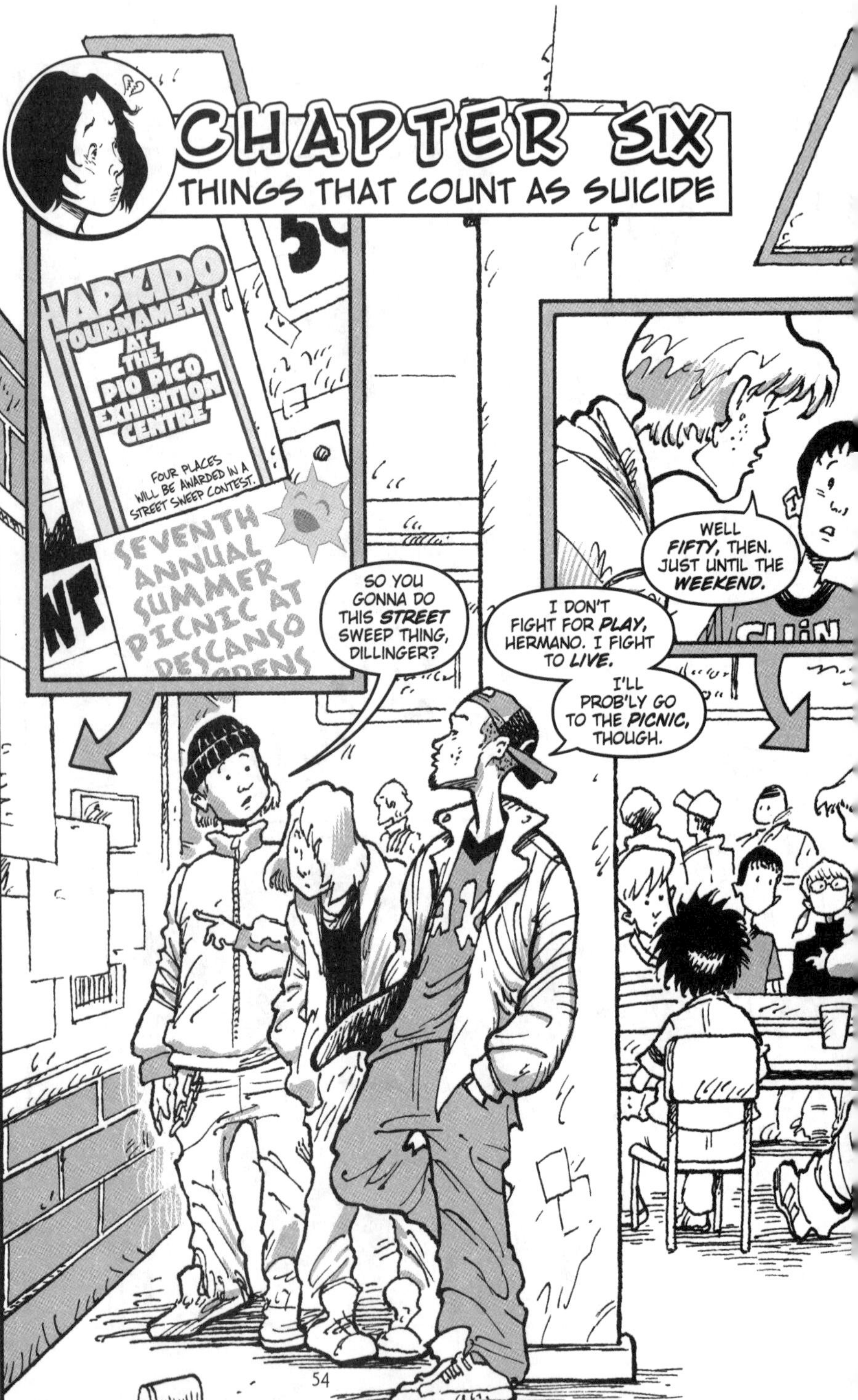
CHAPTER SIX
THINGS THAT COUNT AS SUICIDE
HAPKIDO TOURNAMENT AT THE PIO PICO EXHIBITION CENTRE
FOUR PLACES WILL BE AWARDED IN A STREET SWEEP CONTEST.
SEVENTH ANNUAL SUMMER PICNIC AT DESCANSO
WELL FIFTY, THEN. JUST UNTIL THE WEEKEND.
SO YOU GONNA DO THIS STREET SWEEP THING, DILLINGER?
I DON'T FIGHT FOR PLAY, HERMANO. I FIGHT TO LIVE.
I'LL PROB'LY GO TO THE PICNIC, THOUGH.

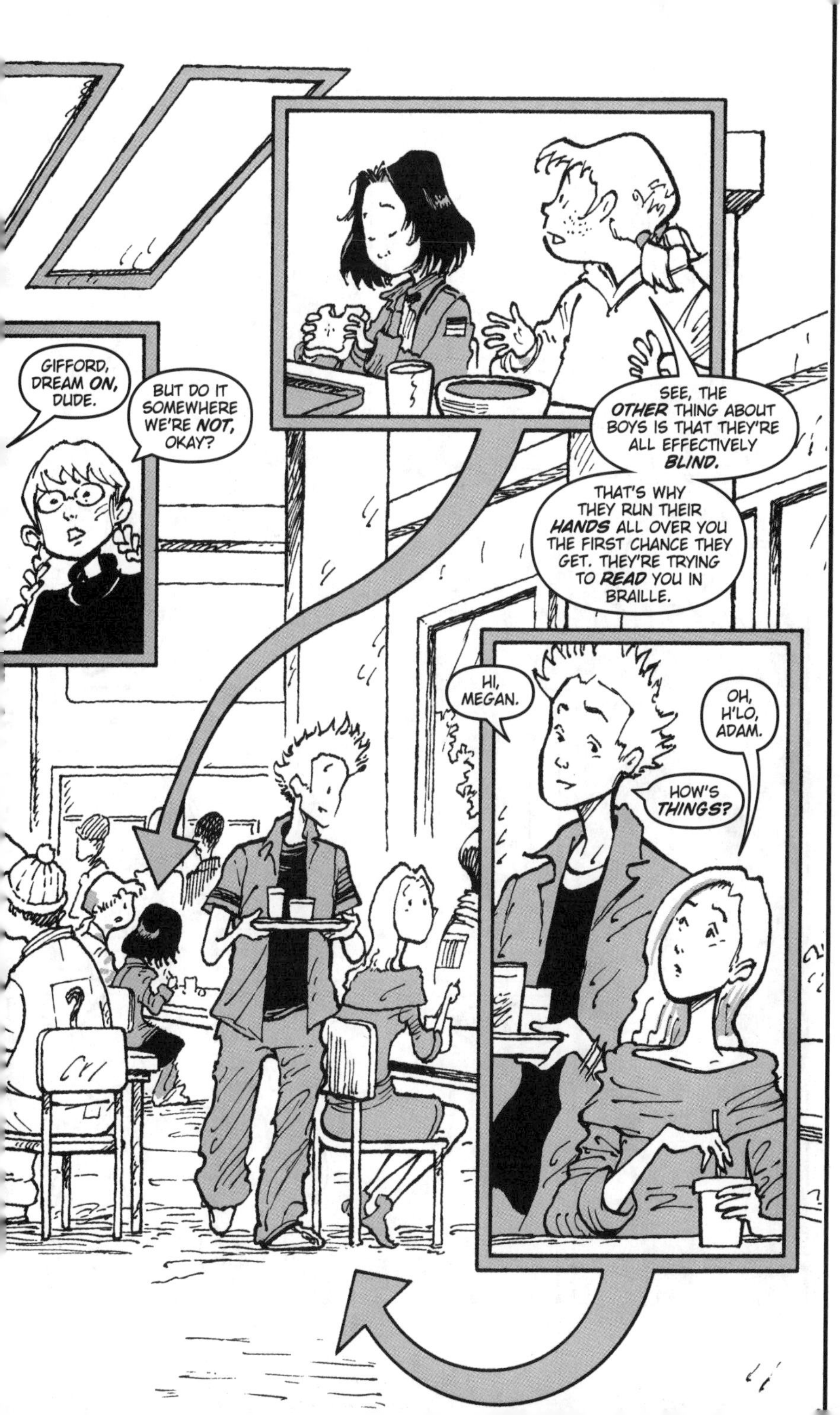
GIFFORD, DREAM *ON,* DUDE.
BUT DO IT SOMEWHERE WE'RE *NOT,* OKAY?
SEE, THE *OTHER* THING ABOUT BOYS IS THAT THEY'RE ALL EFFECTIVELY *BLIND.*
THAT'S WHY THEY RUN THEIR *HANDS* ALL OVER YOU THE FIRST CHANCE THEY GET. THEY'RE TRYING TO *READ* YOU IN BRAILLE.
HI, MEGAN.
OH, H'LO, ADAM.
HOW'S *THINGS?*

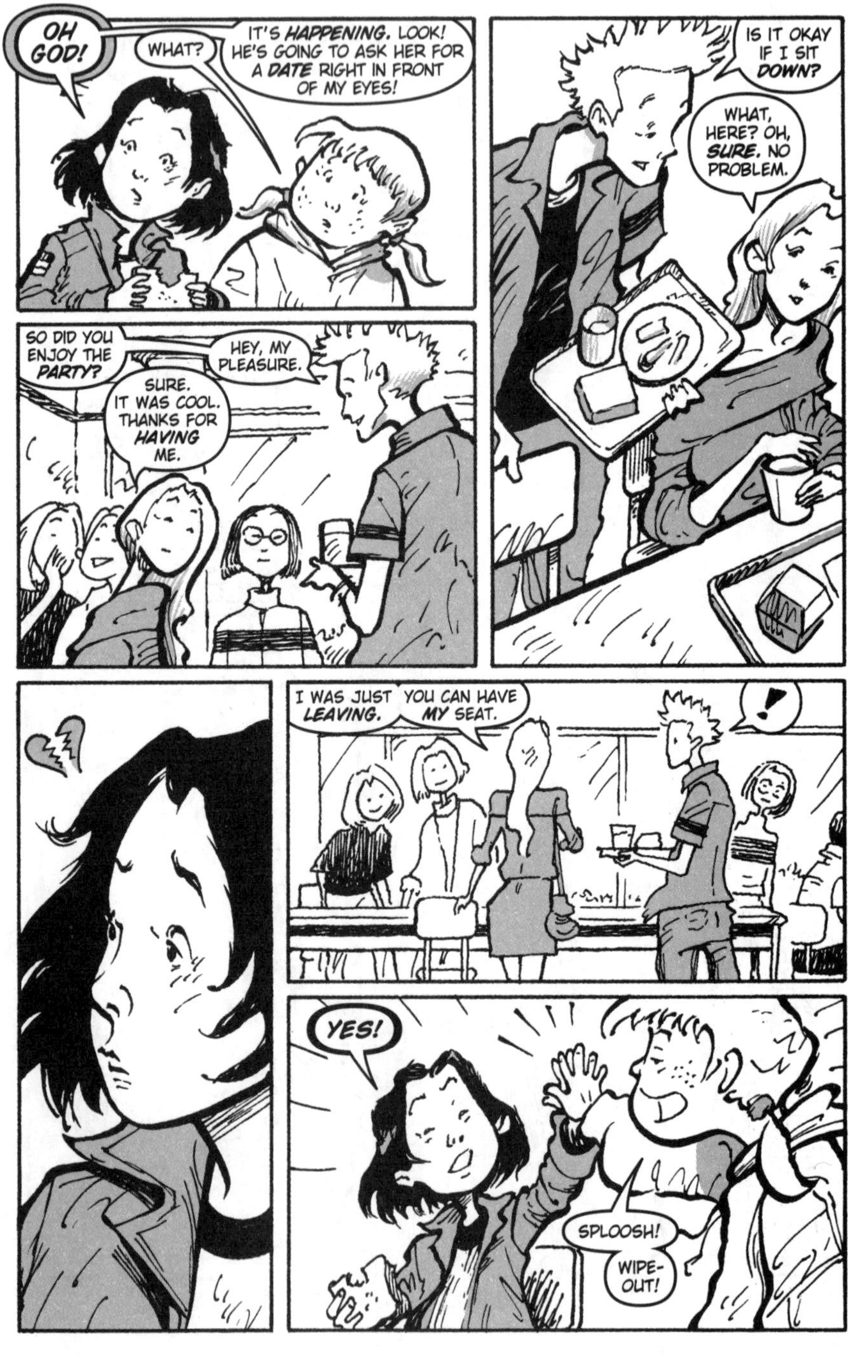
OH GOD!
WHAT?
IT'S HAPPENING. LOOK! HE'S GOING TO ASK HER FOR A DATE RIGHT IN FRONT OF MY EYES!
IS IT OKAY IF I SIT DOWN?
WHAT, HERE? OH, SURE. NO PROBLEM.
SO DID YOU ENJOY THE PARTY?
SURE. IT WAS COOL. THANKS FOR HAVING ME.
HEY, MY PLEASURE.
I WAS JUST LEAVING.
YOU CAN HAVE MY SEAT.
!
YES!
SPLOOSH!
WIPE-OUT!

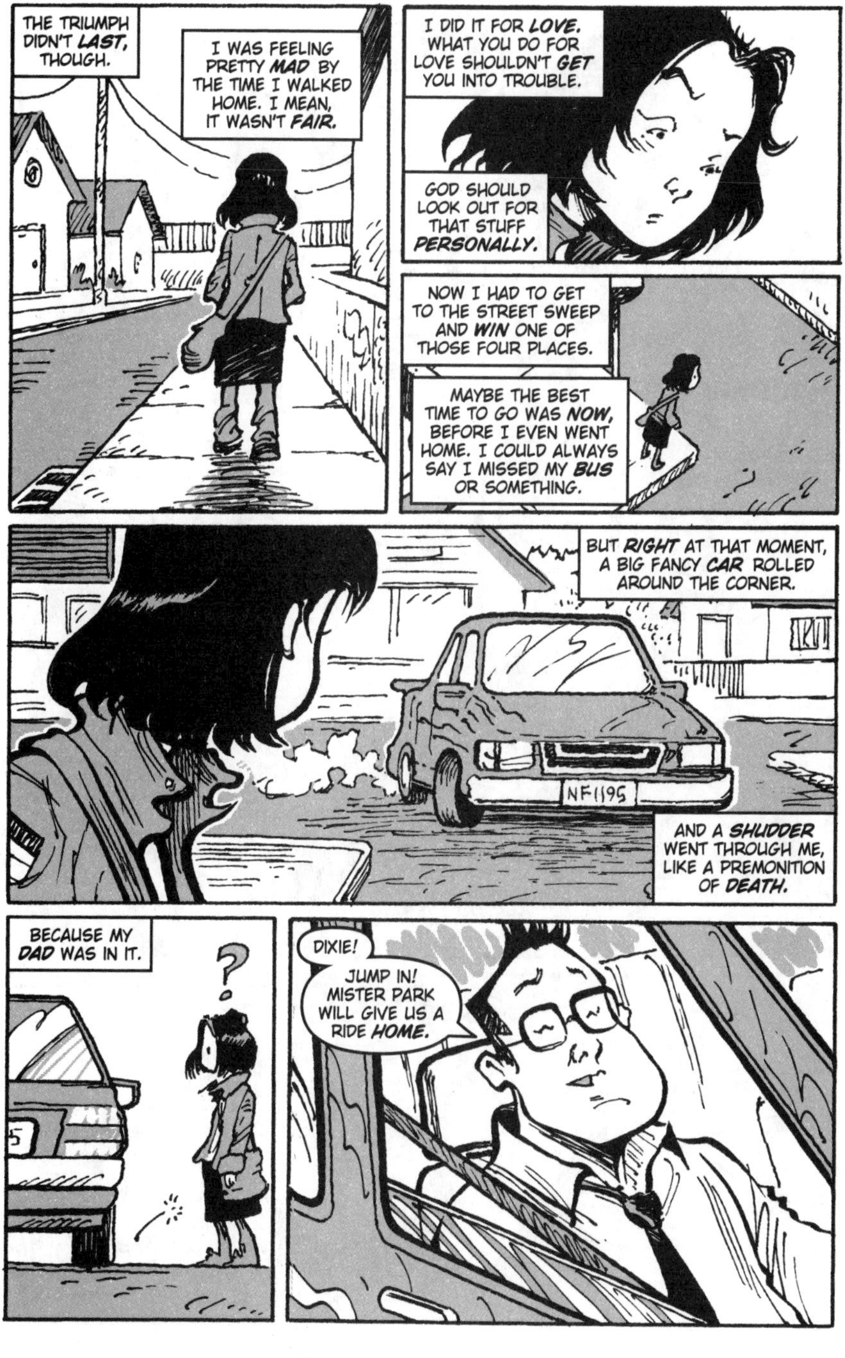
THE TRIUMPH DIDN'T LAST, THOUGH.
I WAS FEELING PRETTY MAD BY THE TIME I WALKED HOME. I MEAN, IT WASN'T FAIR.
I DID IT FOR LOVE. WHAT YOU DO FOR LOVE SHOULDN'T GET YOU INTO TROUBLE.
GOD SHOULD LOOK OUT FOR THAT STUFF PERSONALLY.
NOW I HAD TO GET TO THE STREET SWEEP AND WIN ONE OF THOSE FOUR PLACES.
MAYBE THE BEST TIME TO GO WAS NOW, BEFORE I EVEN WENT HOME. I COULD ALWAYS SAY I MISSED MY BUS OR SOMETHING.
BUT RIGHT AT THAT MOMENT, A BIG FANCY CAR ROLLED AROUND THE CORNER.
NF1195
AND A SHUDDER WENT THROUGH ME, LIKE A PREMONITION OF DEATH.
BECAUSE MY DAD WAS IN IT.
?
DIXIE!
JUMP IN! MISTER PARK WILL GIVE US A RIDE HOME.

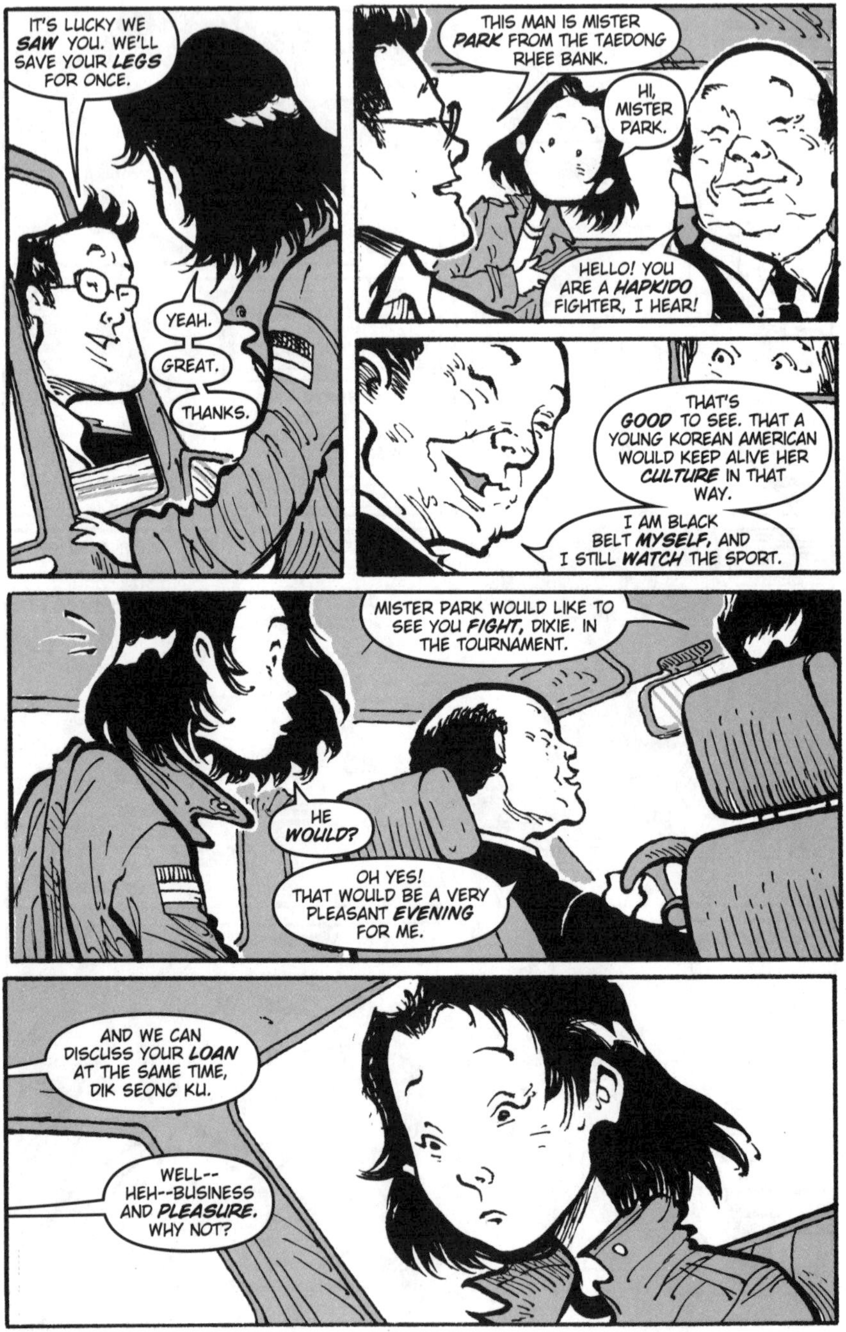
IT'S LUCKY WE SAW YOU. WE'LL SAVE YOUR LEGS FOR ONCE.
YEAH.
GREAT.
THANKS.
THIS MAN IS MISTER PARK FROM THE TAEDONG RHEE BANK.
HI, MISTER PARK.
HELLO! YOU ARE A HAPKIDO FIGHTER, I HEAR!
THAT'S GOOD TO SEE. THAT A YOUNG KOREAN AMERICAN WOULD KEEP ALIVE HER CULTURE IN THAT WAY.
I AM BLACK BELT MYSELF, AND I STILL WATCH THE SPORT.
MISTER PARK WOULD LIKE TO SEE YOU FIGHT, DIXIE. IN THE TOURNAMENT.
HE WOULD?
OH YES! THAT WOULD BE A VERY PLEASANT EVENING FOR ME.
AND WE CAN DISCUSS YOUR LOAN AT THE SAME TIME, DIK SEONG KU.
WELL-- HEH--BUSINESS AND PLEASURE. WHY NOT?

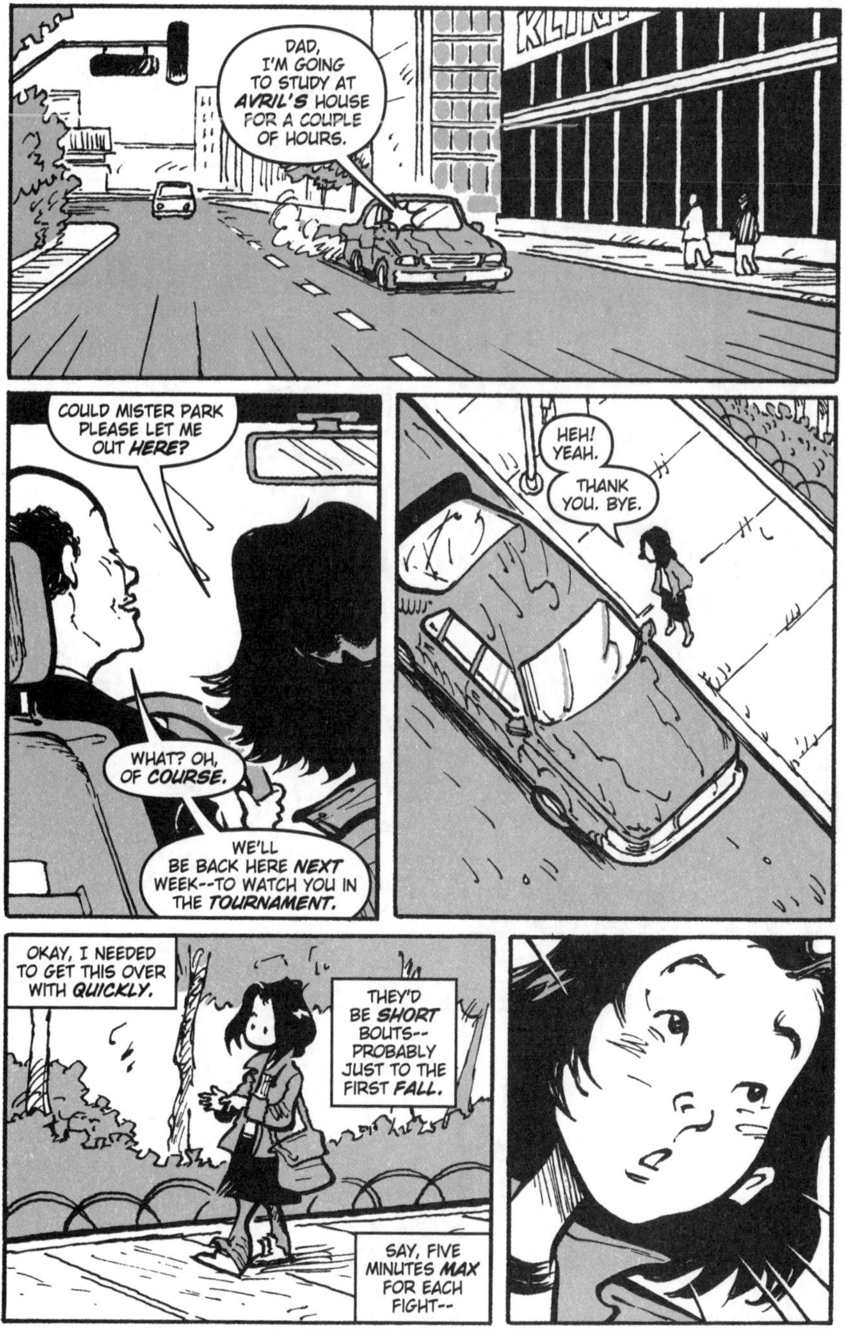
DAD, I'M GOING TO STUDY AT AVRIL'S HOUSE FOR A COUPLE OF HOURS.
COULD MISTER PARK PLEASE LET ME OUT HERE?
WHAT? OH, OF COURSE.
WE'LL BE BACK HERE NEXT WEEK--TO WATCH YOU IN THE TOURNAMENT.
HEH! YEAH.
THANK YOU. BYE.
OKAY, I NEEDED TO GET THIS OVER WITH QUICKLY.
THEY'D BE SHORT BOUTS--PROBABLY JUST TO THE FIRST FALL.
SAY, FIVE MINUTES MAX FOR EACH FIGHT--

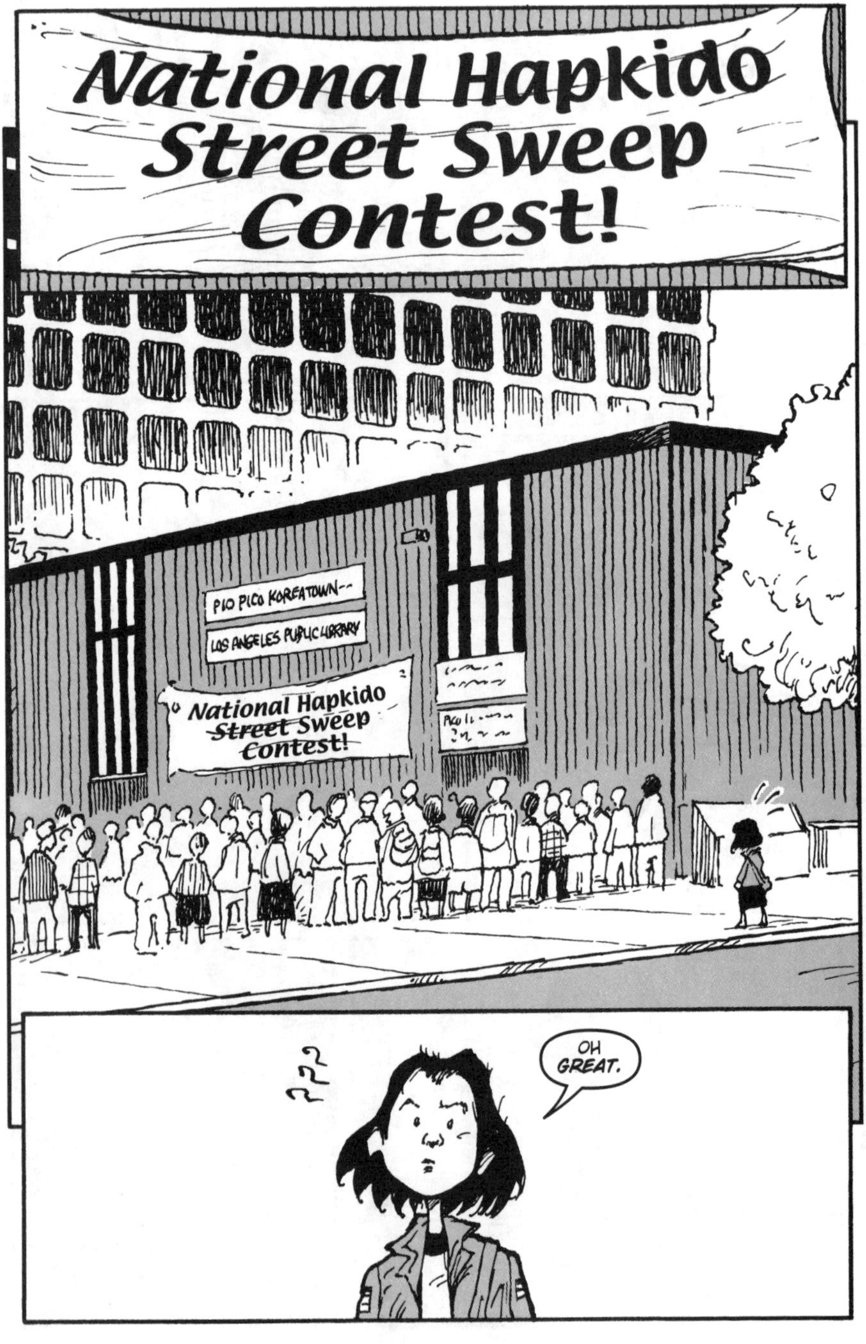
National Hapkido Street Sweep Contest!
PIO PICO KOREATOWN
LOS ANGELES PUBLIC LIBRARY
National Hapkido Street Sweep Contest!
OH GREAT.

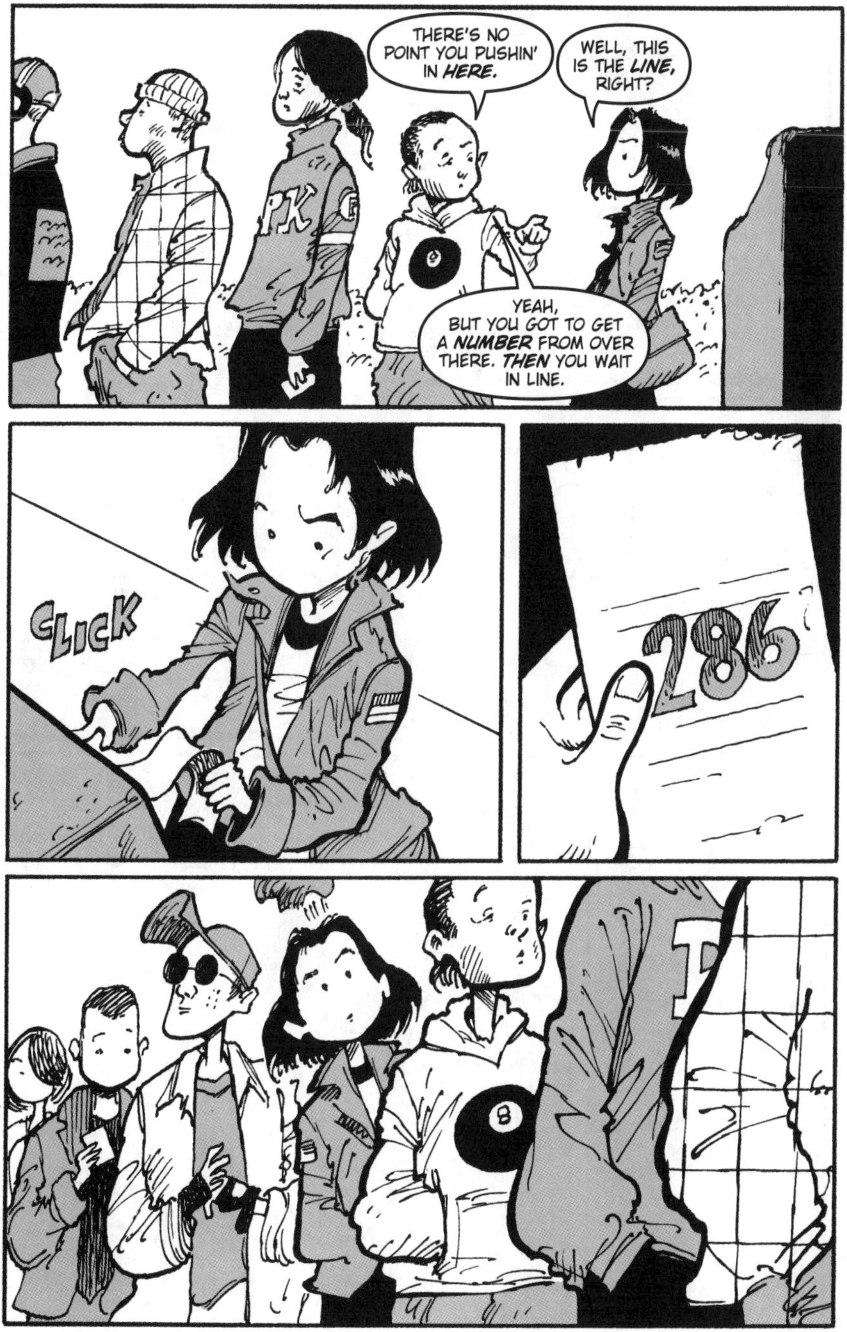
THERE'S NO POINT YOU PUSHIN' IN HERE.
WELL, THIS IS THE LINE, RIGHT?
YEAH, BUT YOU GOT TO GET A NUMBER FROM OVER THERE. THEN YOU WAIT IN LINE.
CLICK
286

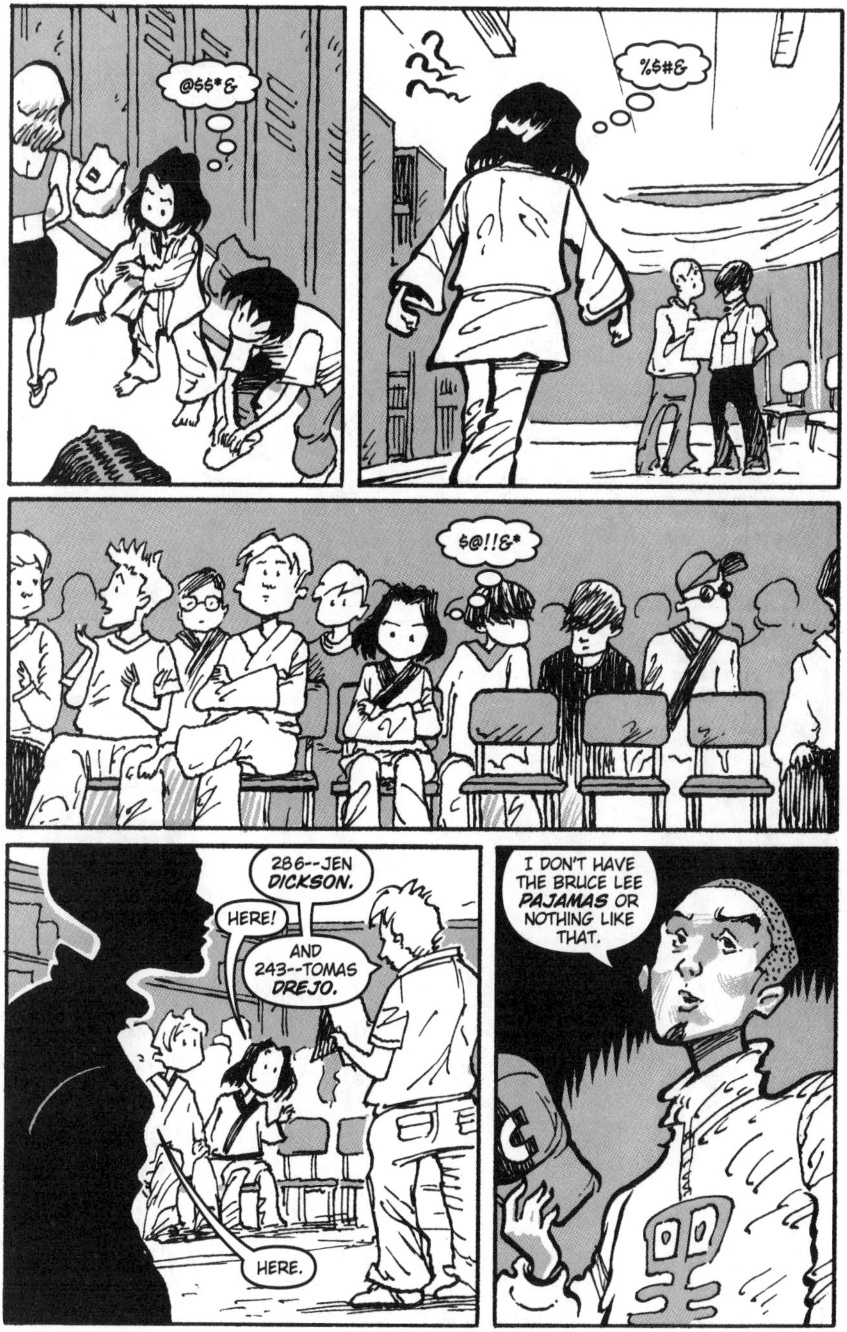
@$$*&
%$#&
$@!!&*
286--JEN DICKSON.
HERE!
AND 243--TOMAS DREJO.
HERE.
I DON'T HAVE THE BRUCE LEE PAJAMAS OR NOTHING LIKE THAT.

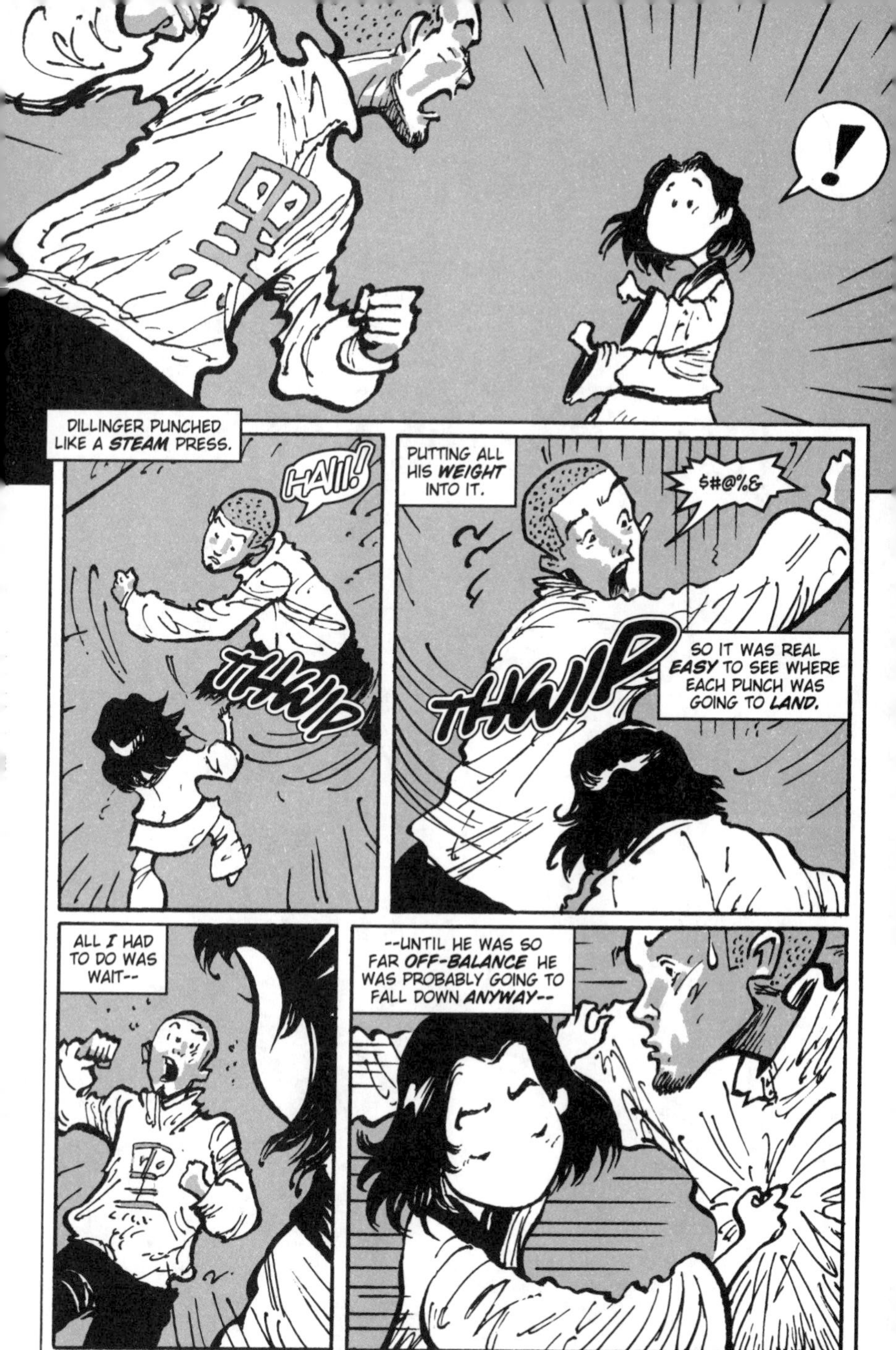
!
DILLINGER PUNCHED LIKE A STEAM PRESS.
HAIII!
THWIP
PUTTING ALL HIS WEIGHT INTO IT.
$#@%&
THWIP
SO IT WAS REAL EASY TO SEE WHERE EACH PUNCH WAS GOING TO LAND.
ALL I HAD TO DO WAS WAIT--
--UNTIL HE WAS SO FAR OFF-BALANCE HE WAS PROBABLY GOING TO FALL DOWN ANYWAY--

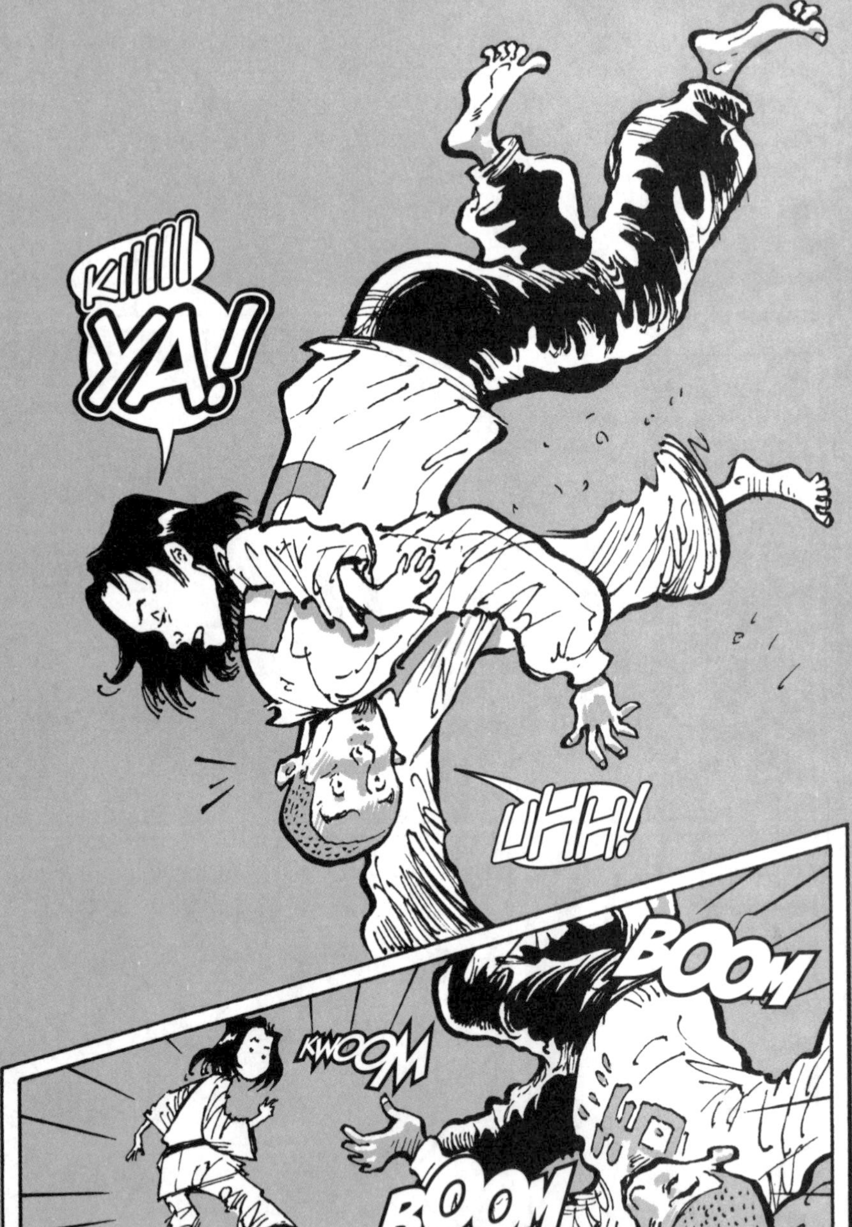
KIIIII
YA!
UHH!
BOOM
KWOOM
BOOM

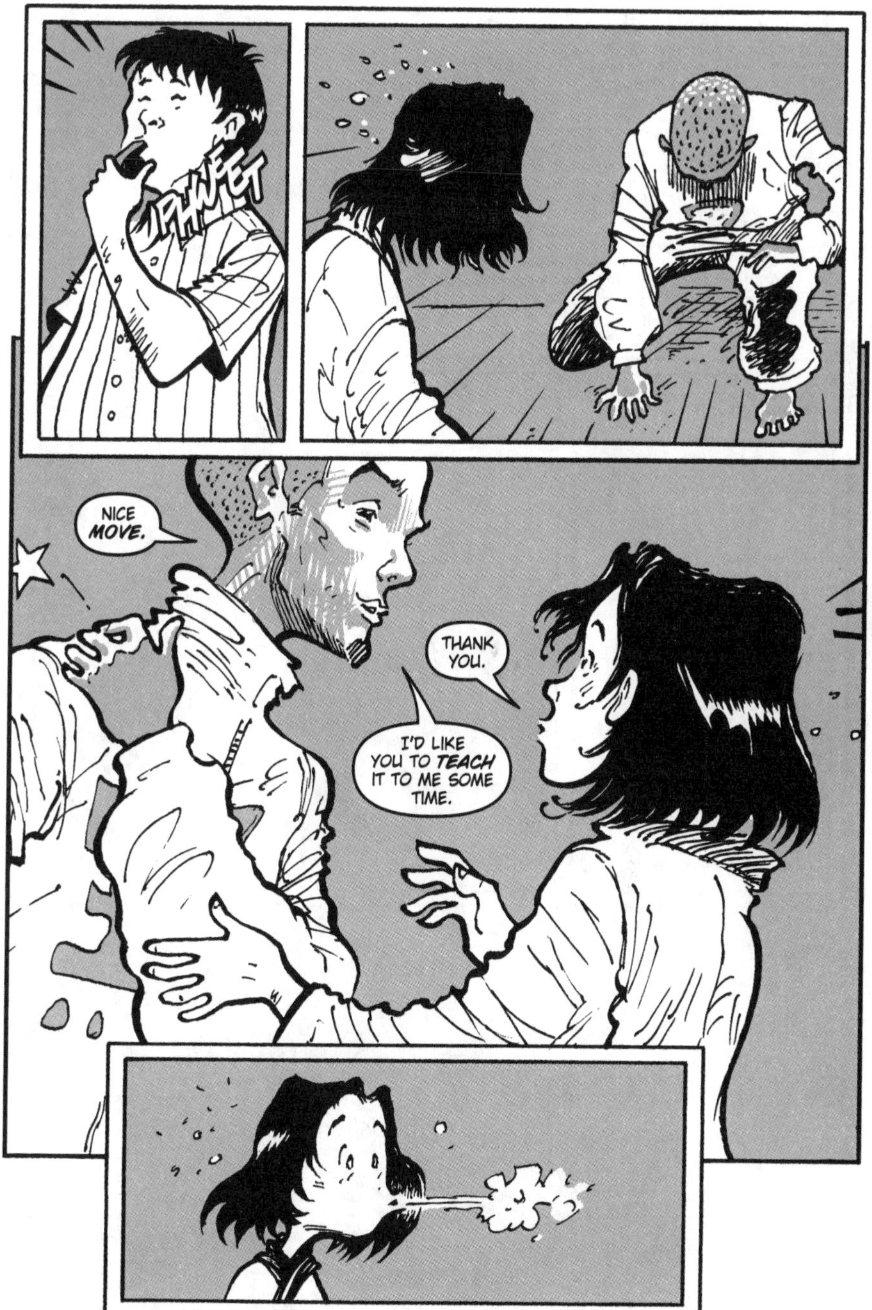
PHWEET
NICE MOVE.
THANK YOU.
I'D LIKE YOU TO TEACH IT TO ME SOME TIME.

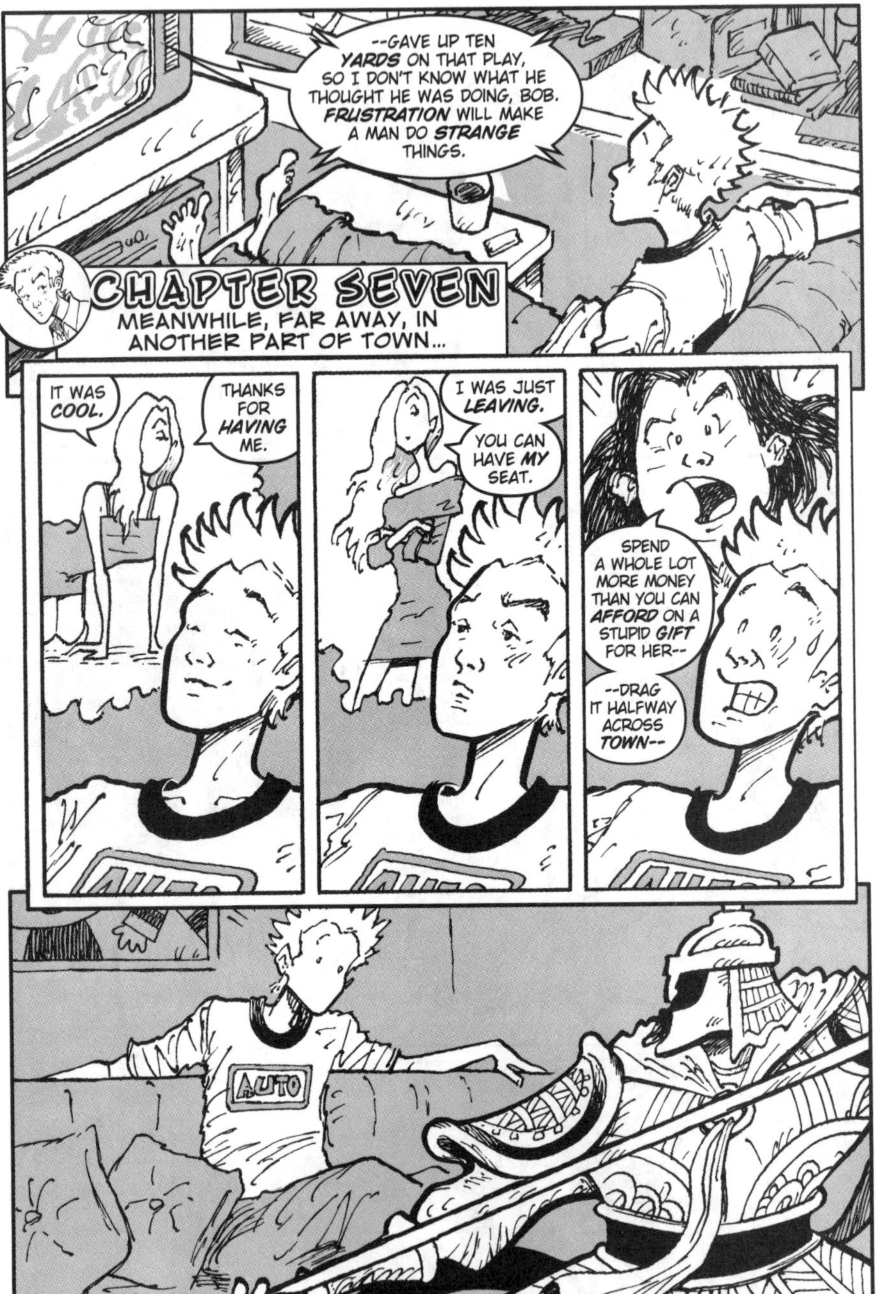
--GAVE UP TEN YARDS ON THAT PLAY, SO I DON'T KNOW WHAT HE THOUGHT HE WAS DOING, BOB. FRUSTRATION WILL MAKE A MAN DO STRANGE THINGS.
CHAPTER SEVEN
MEANWHILE, FAR AWAY, IN ANOTHER PART OF TOWN...
IT WAS COOL.
THANKS FOR HAVING ME.
I WAS JUST LEAVING.
YOU CAN HAVE MY SEAT.
SPEND A WHOLE LOT MORE MONEY THAN YOU CAN AFFORD ON A STUPID GIFT FOR HER--
--DRAG IT HALFWAY ACROSS TOWN--
AUTO

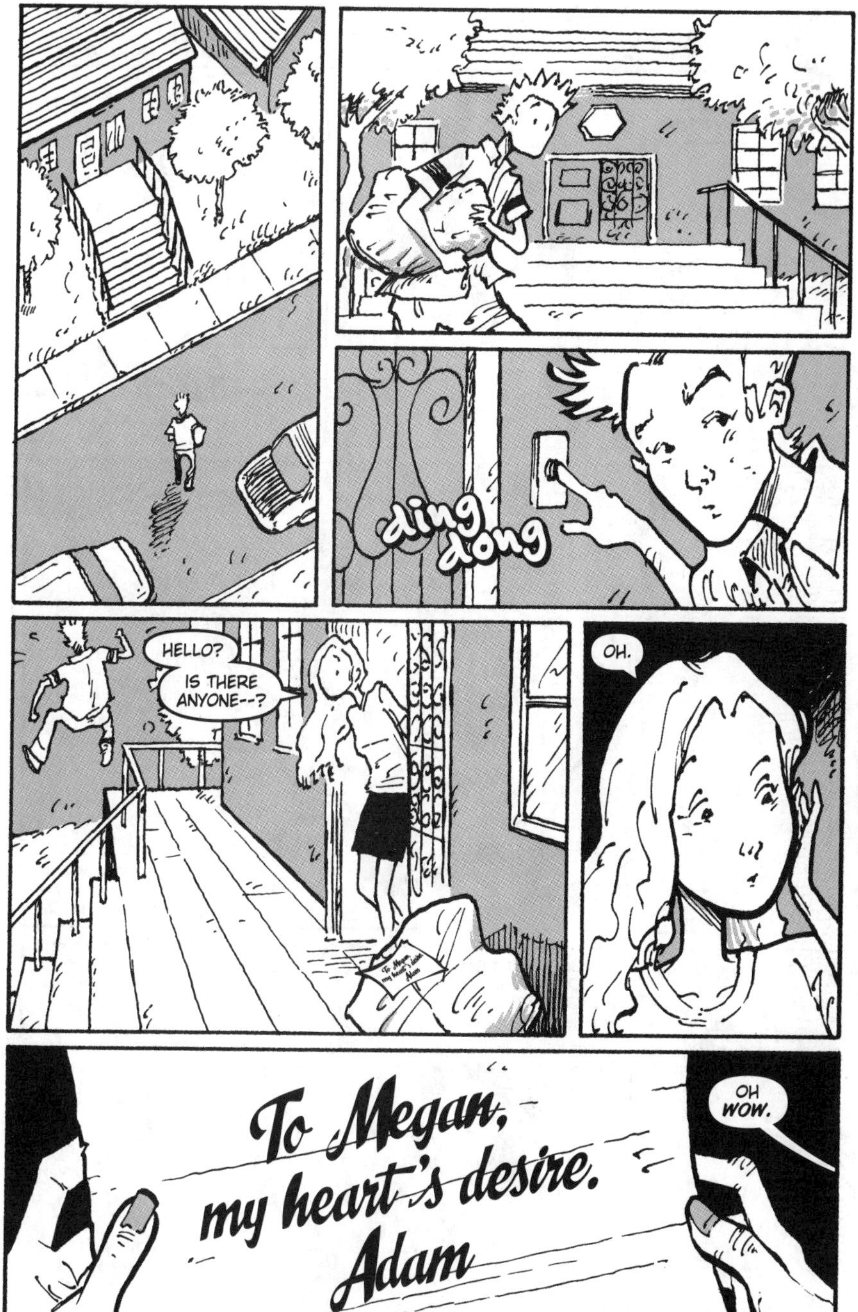
ding dong
HELLO?
IS THERE ANYONE--?
To Megan, my heart's desire. Adam
OH.
To Megan,
my heart's desire.
Adam
OH WOW.

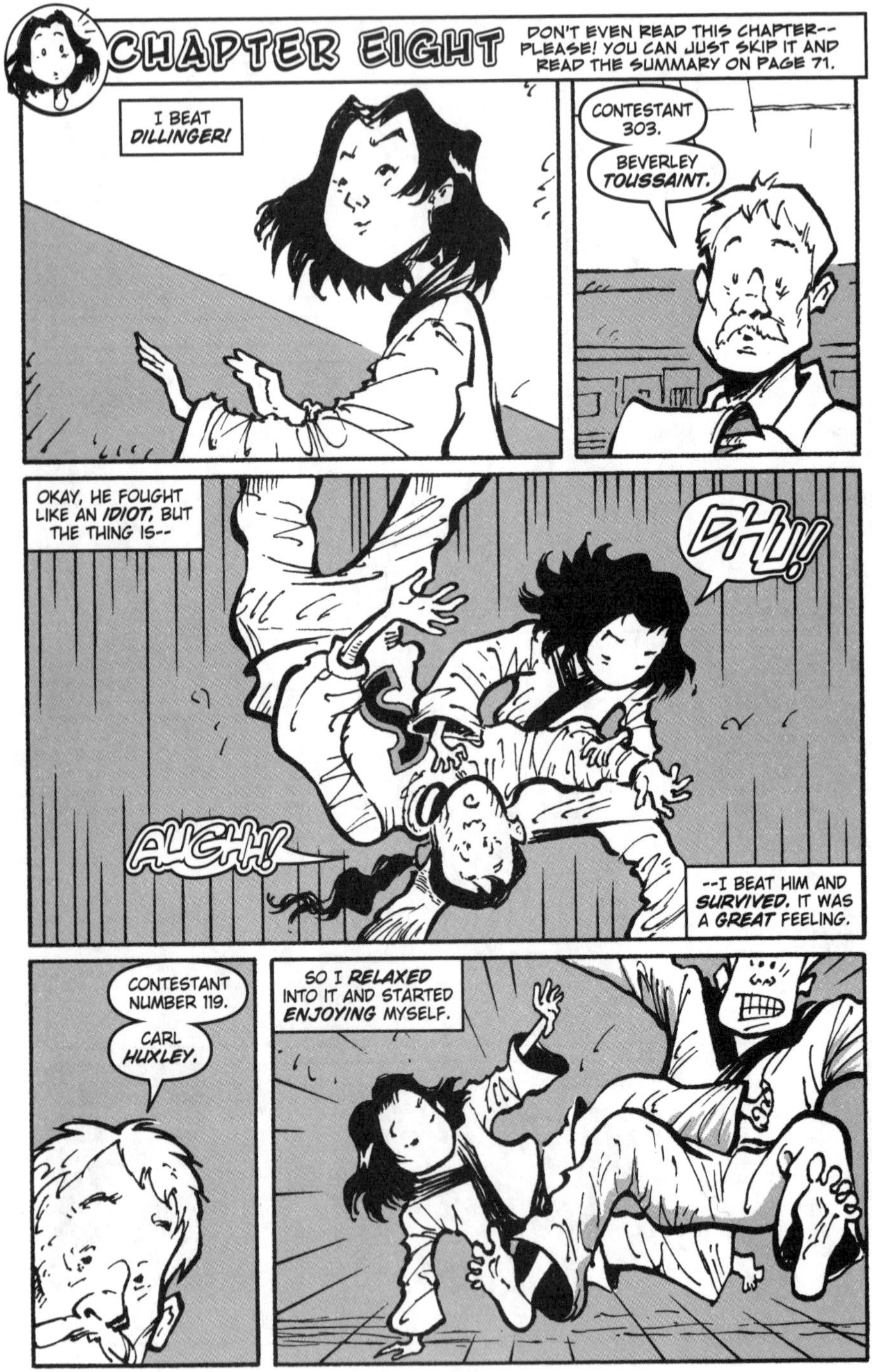
CHAPTER EIGHT
DON'T EVEN READ THIS CHAPTER-- PLEASE! YOU CAN JUST SKIP IT AND READ THE SUMMARY ON PAGE 71.
I BEAT DILLINGER!
CONTESTANT 303.
BEVERLEY TOUSSAINT.
OKAY, HE FOUGHT LIKE AN IDIOT, BUT THE THING IS--
DHU!!
AUGHH!
--I BEAT HIM AND SURVIVED. IT WAS A GREAT FEELING.
CONTESTANT NUMBER 119.
CARL HUXLEY.
SO I RELAXED INTO IT AND STARTED ENJOYING MYSELF.

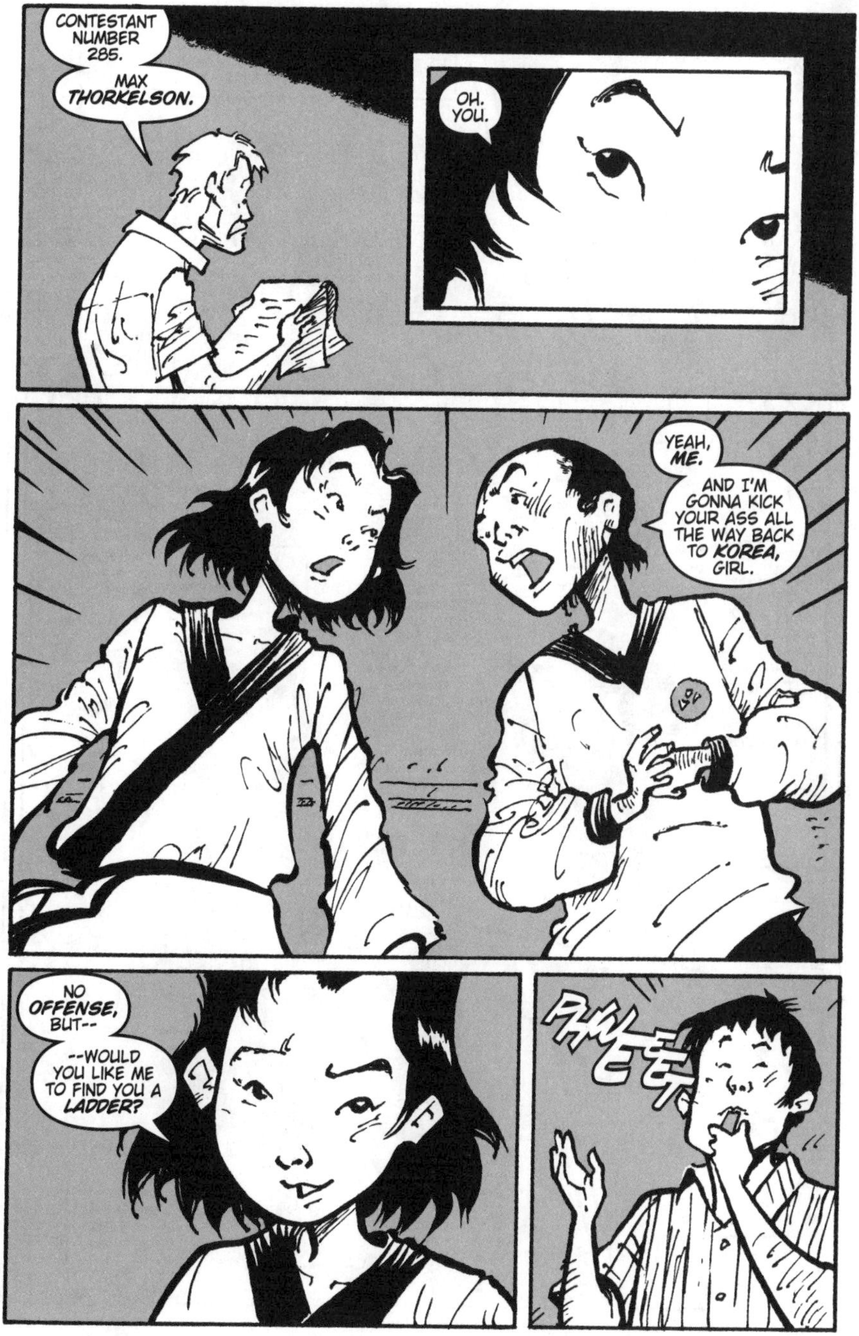
CONTESTANT NUMBER 285.
MAX THORKELSON.
OH. YOU.
YEAH, ME.
AND I'M GONNA KICK YOUR ASS ALL THE WAY BACK TO KOREA, GIRL.
NO OFFENSE, BUT--
--WOULD YOU LIKE ME TO FIND YOU A LADDER?
PHWEEET

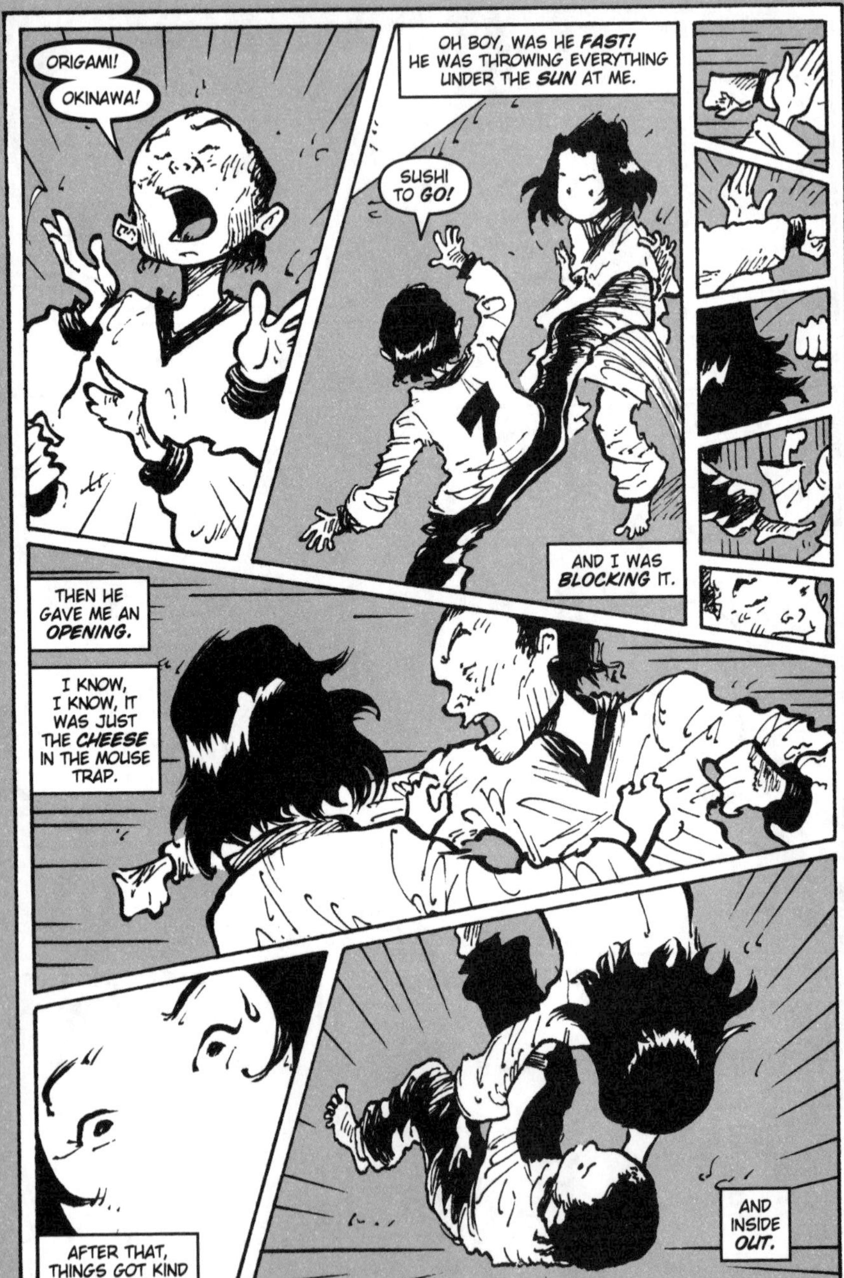
ORIGAMI!
OKINAWA!
OH BOY, WAS HE FAST! HE WAS THROWING EVERYTHING UNDER THE SUN AT ME.
SUSHI TO GO!
AND I WAS BLOCKING IT.
THEN HE GAVE ME AN OPENING.
I KNOW, I KNOW, IT WAS JUST THE CHEESE IN THE MOUSE TRAP.
AFTER THAT, THINGS GOT KIND OF MIXED UP.
AND INSIDE OUT.

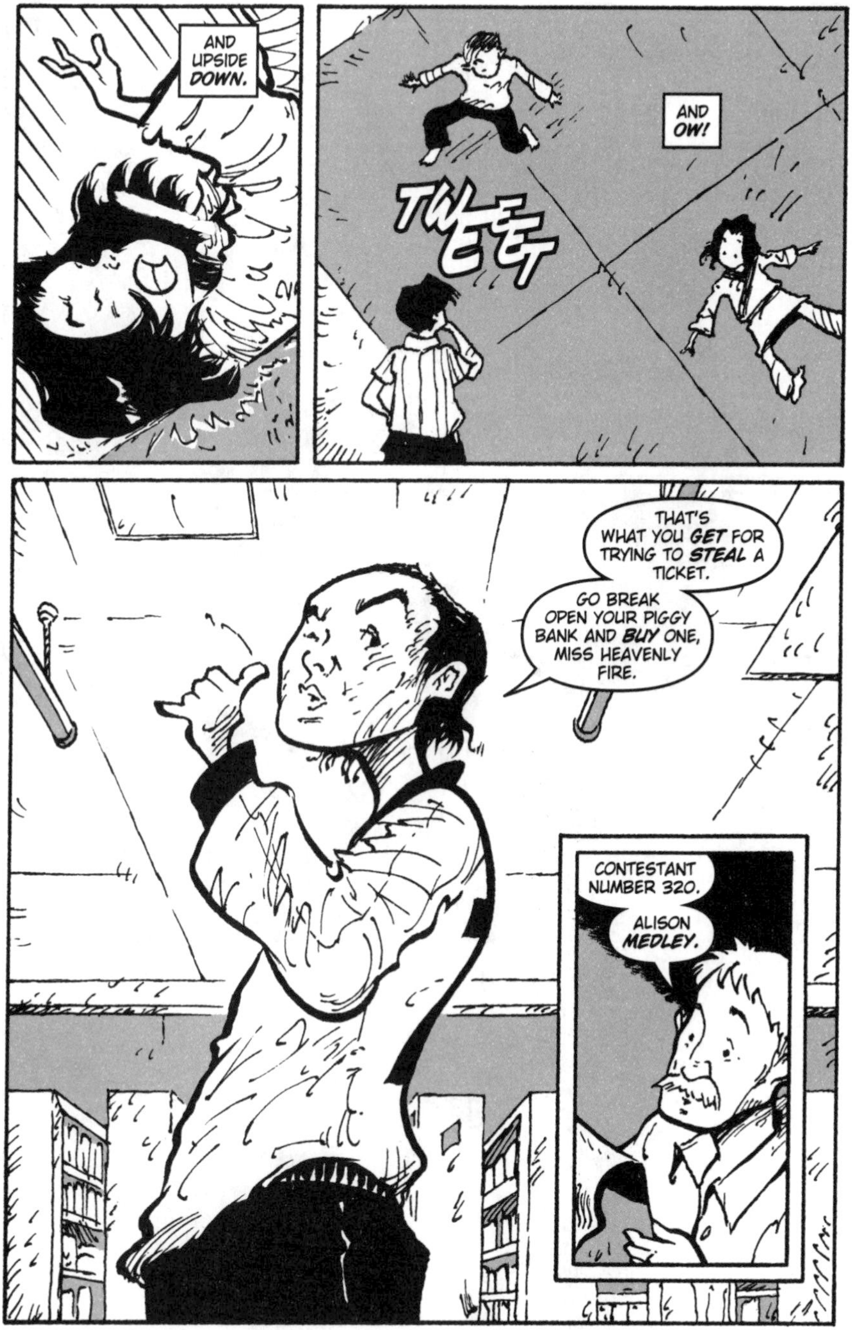
AND UPSIDE DOWN.
AND OW!
TWEET
THAT'S WHAT YOU GET FOR TRYING TO STEAL A TICKET.
GO BREAK OPEN YOUR PIGGY BANK AND BUY ONE, MISS HEAVENLY FIRE.
CONTESTANT NUMBER 320.
ALISON MEDLEY.

74

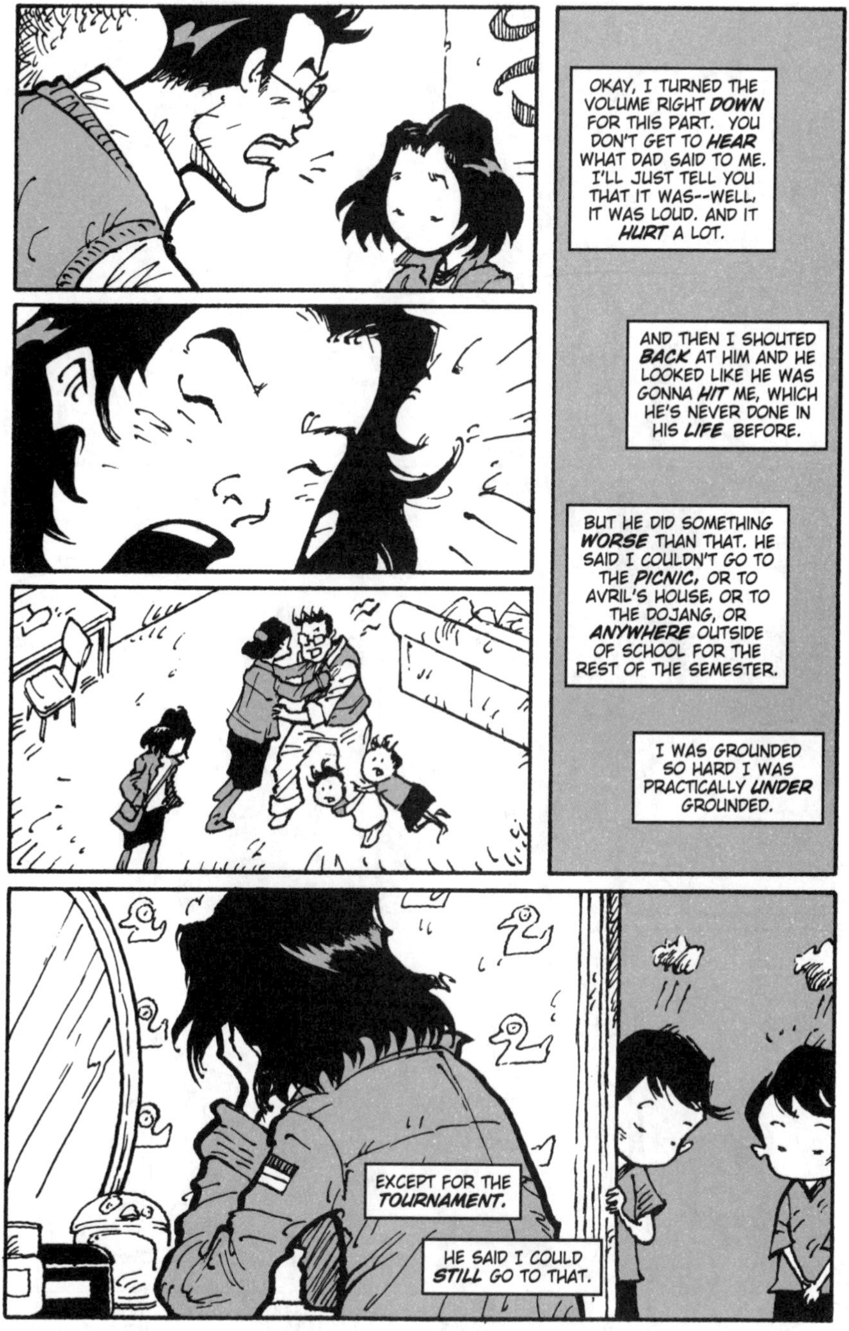
OKAY, I TURNED THE VOLUME RIGHT DOWN FOR THIS PART. YOU DON'T GET TO HEAR WHAT DAD SAID TO ME. I'LL JUST TELL YOU THAT IT WAS--WELL, IT WAS LOUD. AND IT HURT A LOT.
AND THEN I SHOUTED BACK AT HIM AND HE LOOKED LIKE HE WAS GONNA HIT ME, WHICH HE'S NEVER DONE IN HIS LIFE BEFORE.
BUT HE DID SOMETHING WORSE THAN THAT. HE SAID I COULDN'T GO TO THE PICNIC, OR TO AVRIL'S HOUSE, OR TO THE DOJANG, OR ANYWHERE OUTSIDE OF SCHOOL FOR THE REST OF THE SEMESTER.
I WAS GROUNDED SO HARD I WAS PRACTICALLY UNDER GROUNDED.
EXCEPT FOR THE TOURNAMENT.
HE SAID I COULD STILL GO TO THAT.

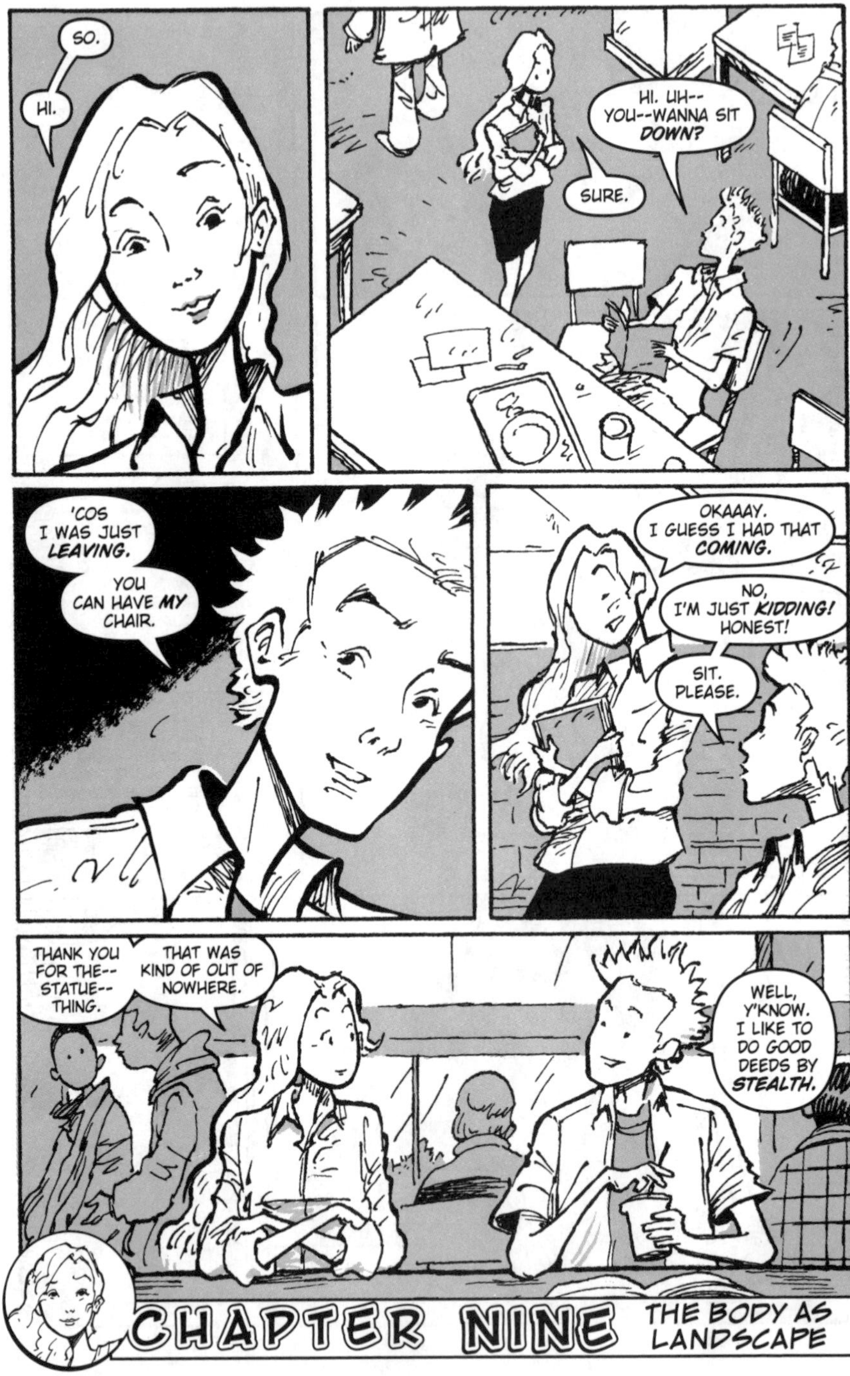
SO.
HI.
HI. UH--
YOU--WANNA SIT
DOWN?
SURE.
'COS
I WAS JUST
LEAVING.
YOU
CAN HAVE MY
CHAIR.
OKAAAY.
I GUESS I HAD THAT
COMING.
NO,
I'M JUST KIDDING!
HONEST!
SIT.
PLEASE.
THANK YOU
FOR THE--
STATUE--
THING.
THAT WAS
KIND OF OUT OF
NOWHERE.
WELL,
Y'KNOW.
I LIKE TO
DO GOOD
DEEDS BY
STEALTH.
CHAPTER NINE
THE BODY AS
LANDSCAPE

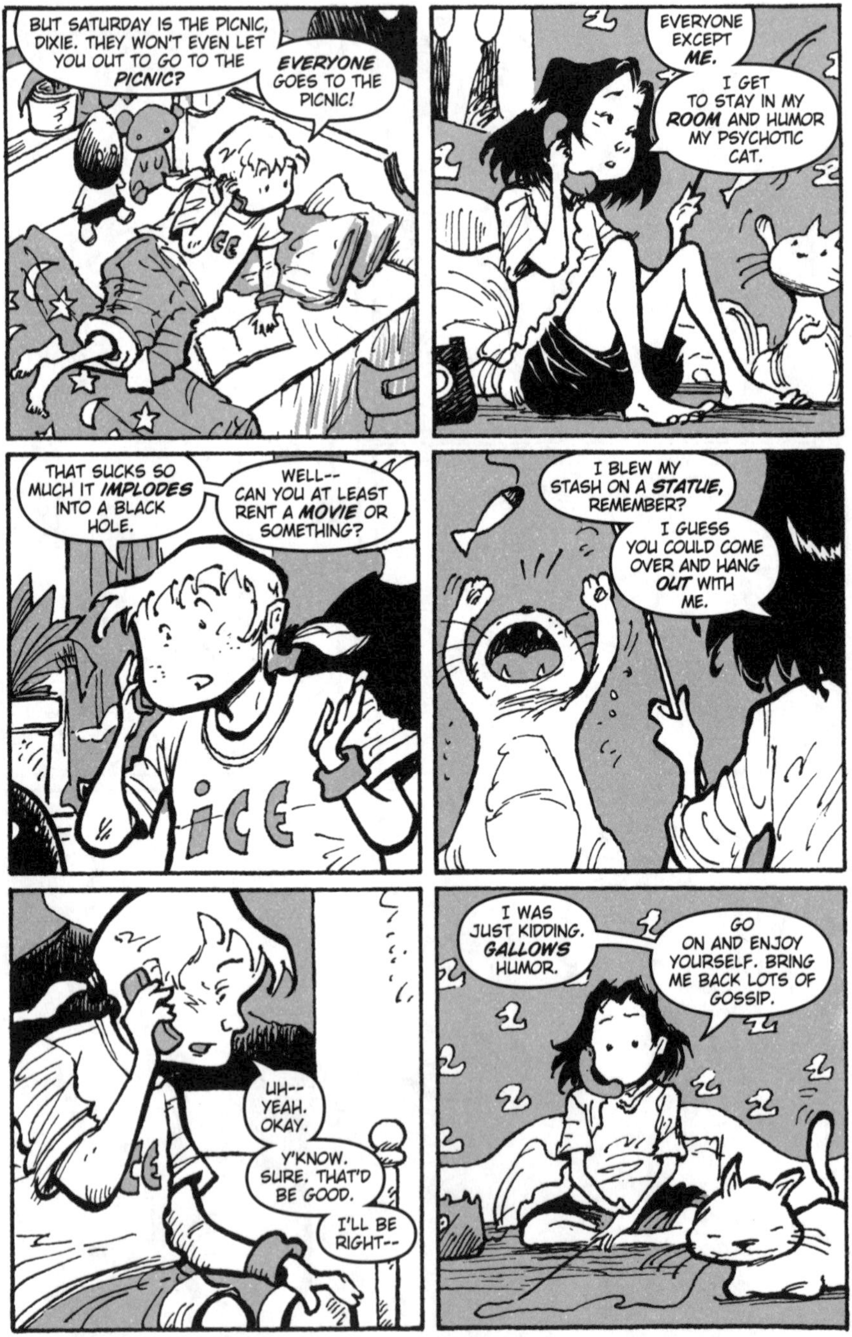
BUT SATURDAY IS THE PICNIC, DIXIE. THEY WON'T EVEN LET YOU OUT TO GO TO THE PICNIC?
EVERYONE GOES TO THE PICNIC!
EVERYONE EXCEPT ME.
I GET TO STAY IN MY ROOM AND HUMOR MY PSYCHOTIC CAT.
THAT SUCKS SO MUCH IT IMPLODES INTO A BLACK HOLE.
WELL-- CAN YOU AT LEAST RENT A MOVIE OR SOMETHING?
I BLEW MY STASH ON A STATUE, REMEMBER?
I GUESS YOU COULD COME OVER AND HANG OUT WITH ME.
UH-- YEAH. OKAY.
Y'KNOW. SURE. THAT'D BE GOOD.
I'LL BE RIGHT--
I WAS JUST KIDDING. GALLOWS HUMOR.
GO ON AND ENJOY YOURSELF. BRING ME BACK LOTS OF GOSSIP.

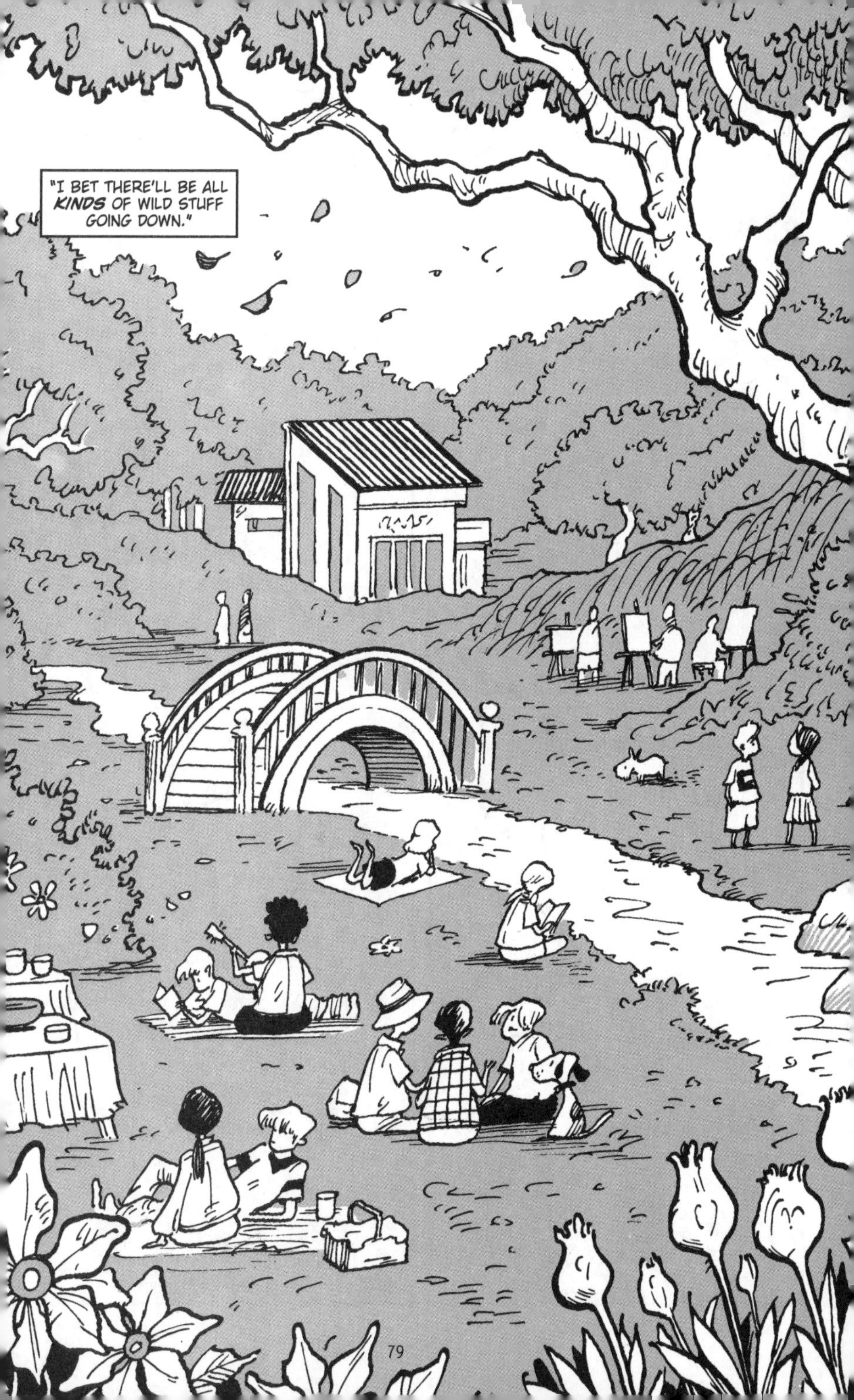
"I BET THERE'LL BE ALL *KINDS* OF WILD STUFF GOING DOWN."

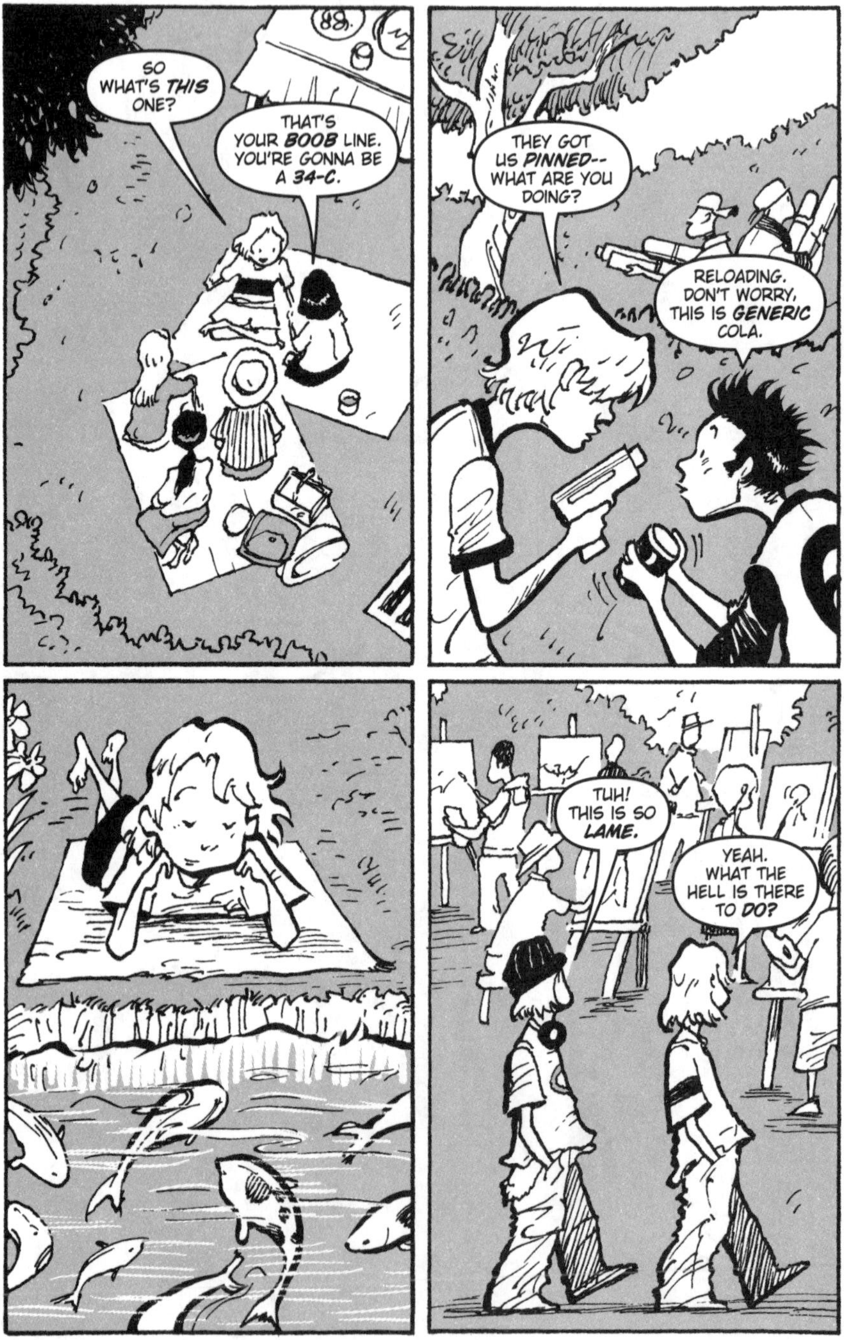
SO WHAT'S THIS ONE?
THAT'S YOUR BOOB LINE. YOU'RE GONNA BE A 34-C.
THEY GOT US PINNED-- WHAT ARE YOU DOING?
RELOADING. DON'T WORRY, THIS IS GENERIC COLA.
TUH! THIS IS SO LAME.
YEAH. WHAT THE HELL IS THERE TO DO?

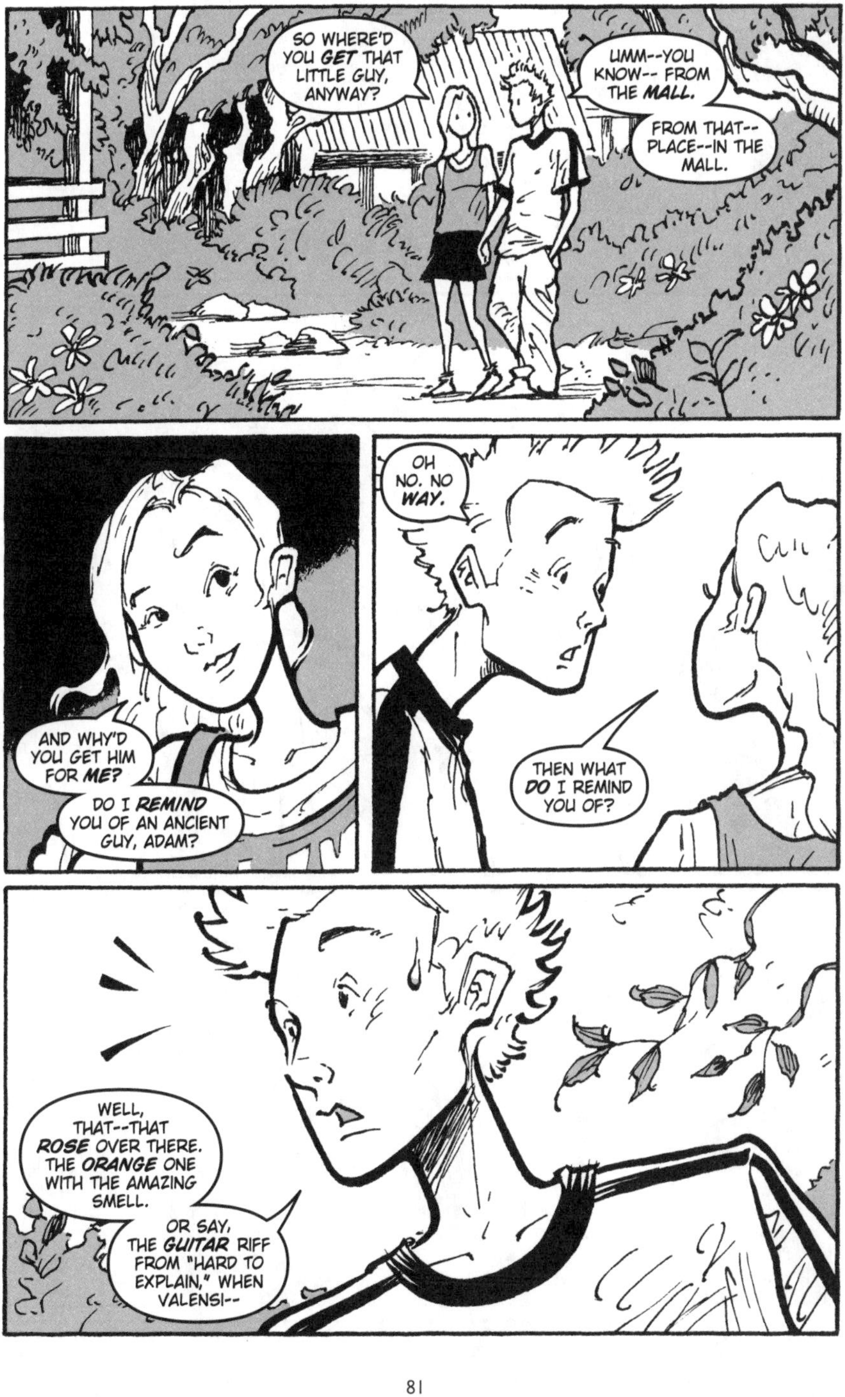
SO WHERE'D YOU GET THAT LITTLE GUY, ANYWAY?
UMM--YOU KNOW-- FROM THE MALL.
FROM THAT--PLACE--IN THE MALL.
AND WHY'D YOU GET HIM FOR ME?
DO I REMIND YOU OF AN ANCIENT GUY, ADAM?
OH NO. NO WAY.
THEN WHAT DO I REMIND YOU OF?
WELL, THAT--THAT ROSE OVER THERE. THE ORANGE ONE WITH THE AMAZING SMELL.
OR SAY, THE GUITAR RIFF FROM "HARD TO EXPLAIN," WHEN VALENSI--

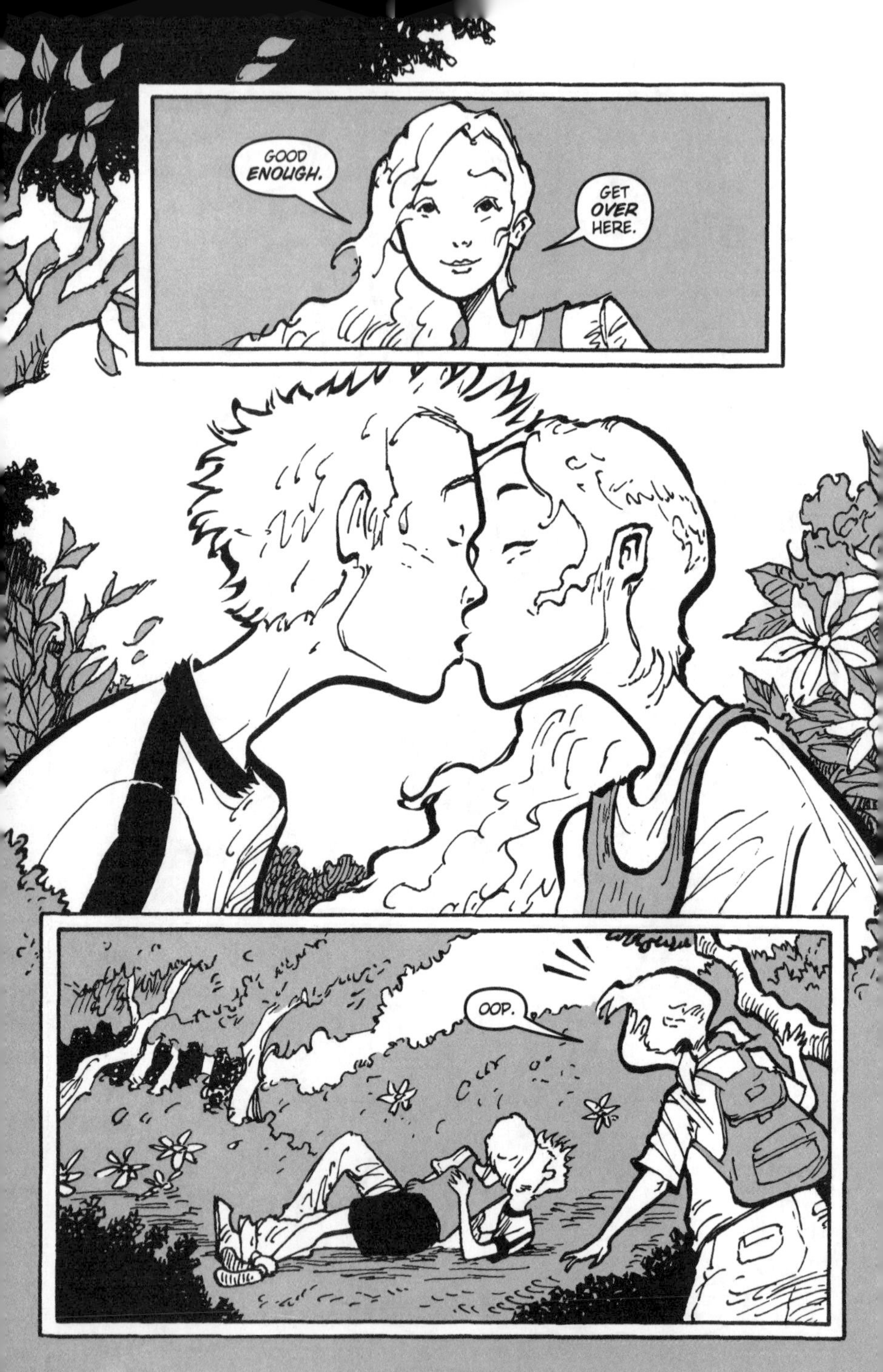
GOOD ENOUGH.
GET OVER HERE.
OOP.

83

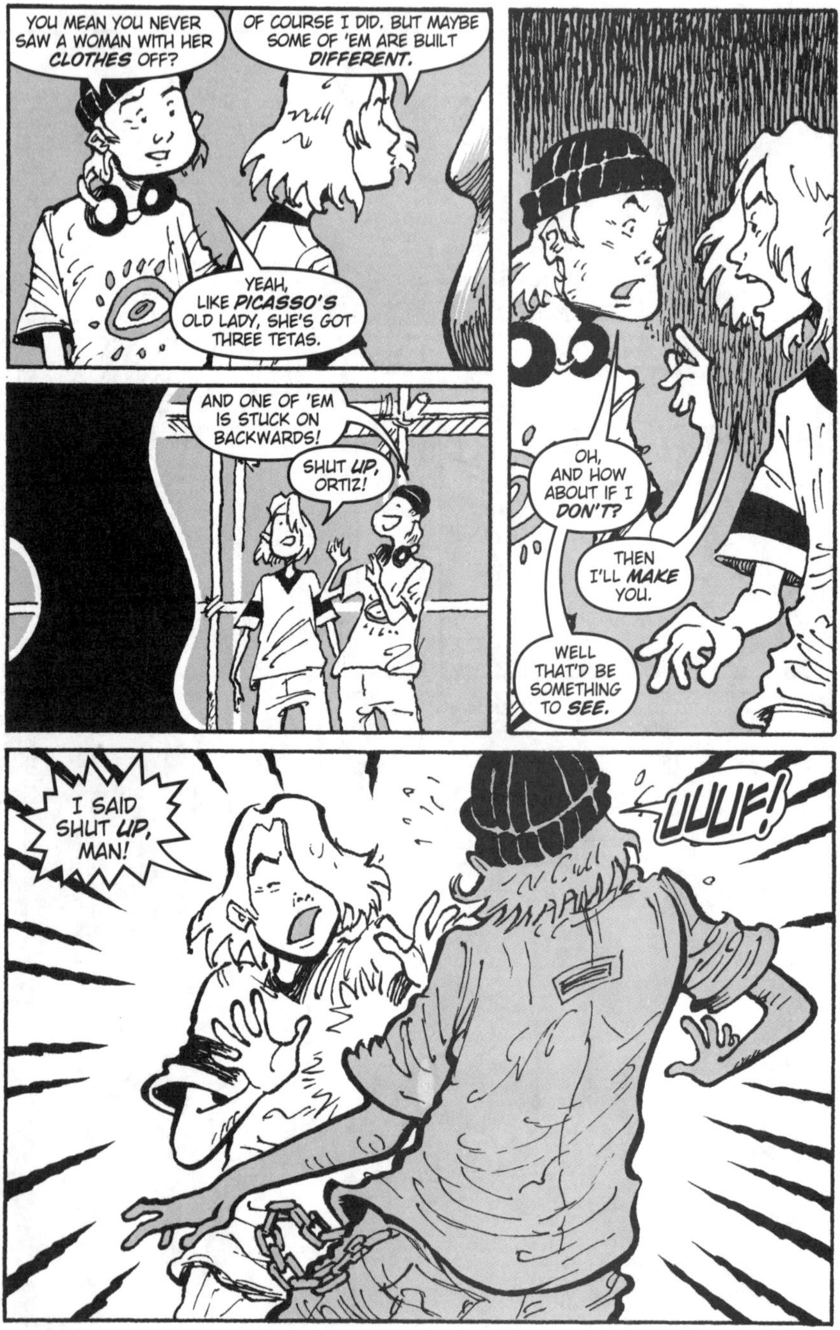

YOU MEAN YOU NEVER SAW A WOMAN WITH HER **CLOTHES** OFF?
OF COURSE I DID. BUT MAYBE SOME OF 'EM ARE BUILT **DIFFERENT.**
YEAH, LIKE **PICASSO'S** OLD LADY, SHE'S GOT THREE TETAS.
AND ONE OF 'EM IS STUCK ON BACKWARDS!
SHUT **UP,** ORTIZ!
OH, AND HOW ABOUT IF I **DON'T?**
THEN I'LL **MAKE** YOU.
WELL THAT'D BE SOMETHING TO **SEE.**
I SAID SHUT **UP,** MAN!
UUUF!

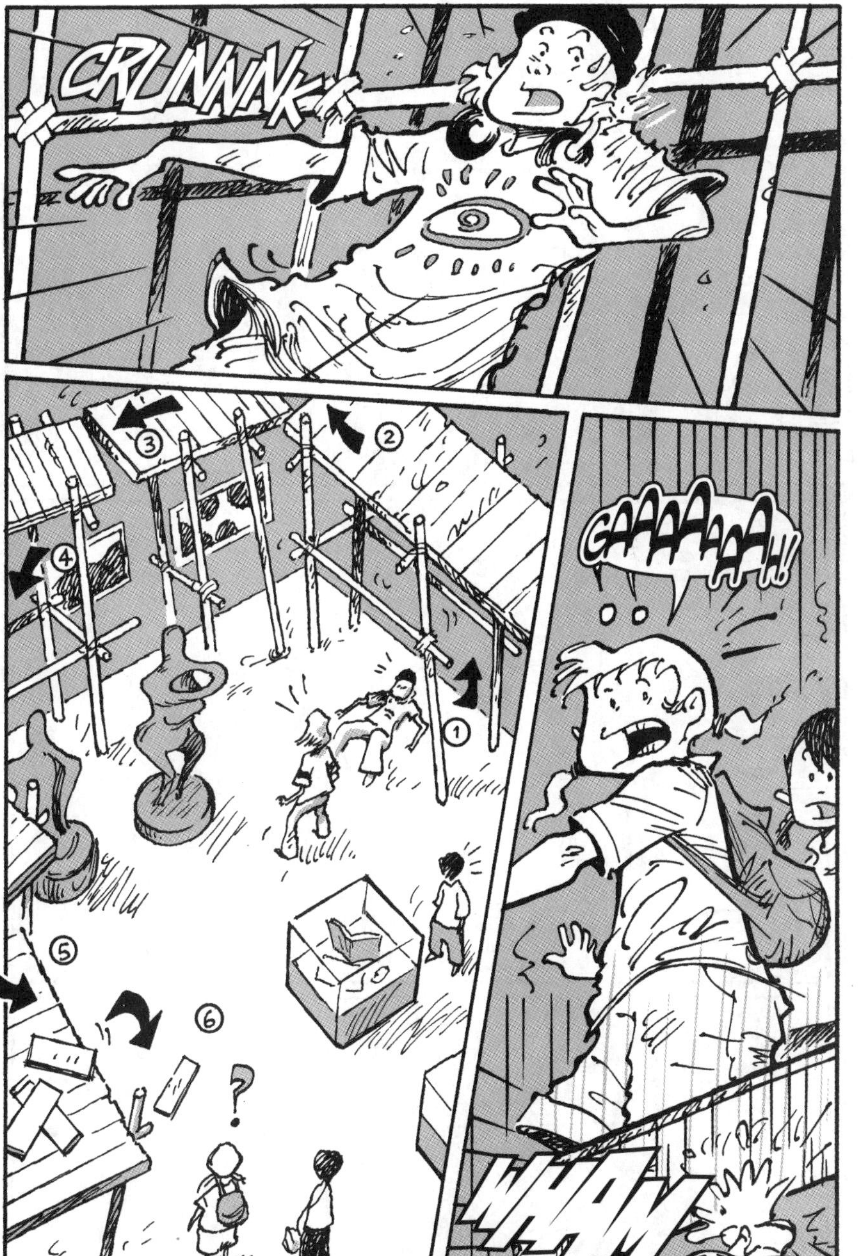
CRUNNNK
3
2
4
1
5
6
?
GAAAAAAAAH!!
WHAM

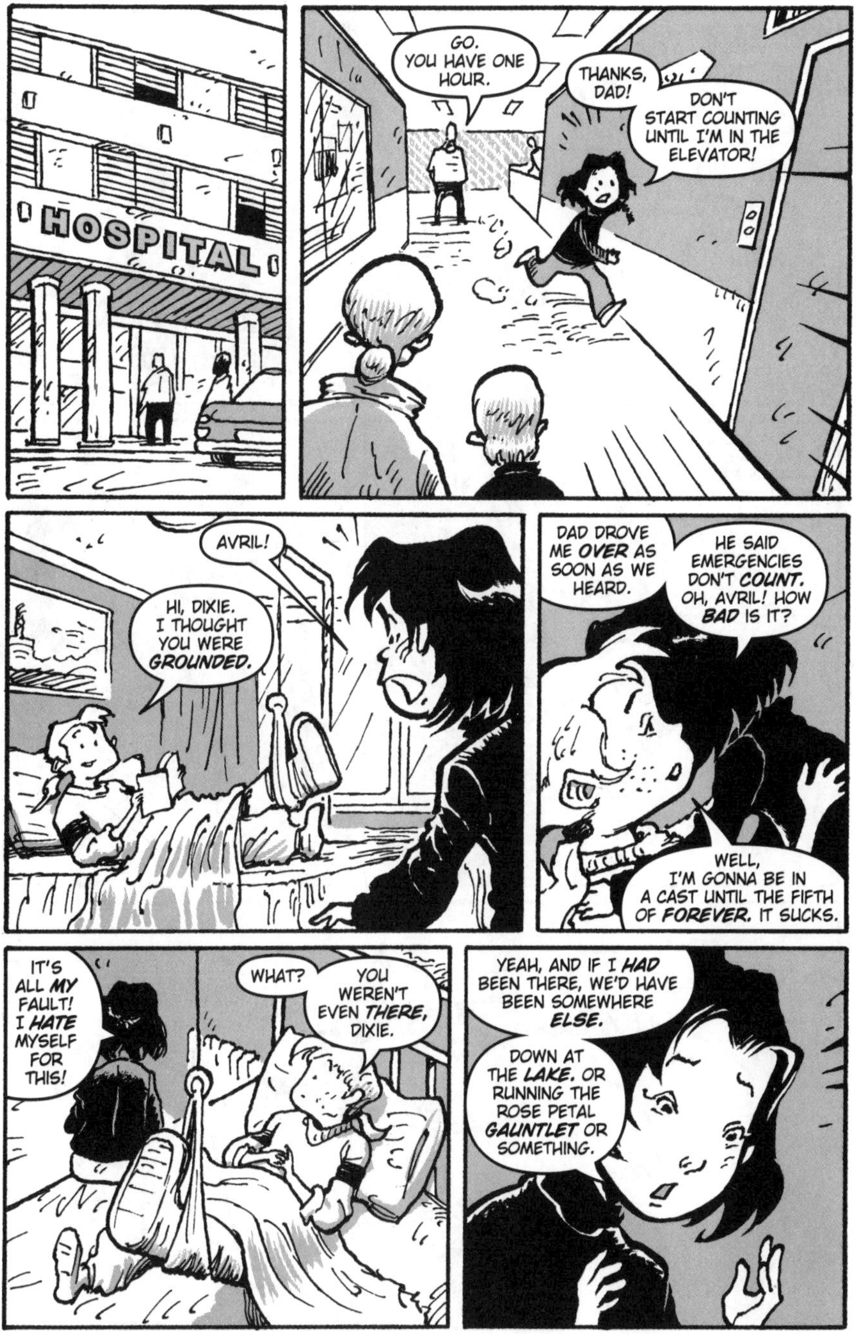
HOSPITAL
GO. YOU HAVE ONE HOUR.
THANKS, DAD!
DON'T START COUNTING UNTIL I'M IN THE ELEVATOR!
AVRIL!
HI, DIXIE. I THOUGHT YOU WERE GROUNDED.
DAD DROVE ME OVER AS SOON AS WE HEARD.
HE SAID EMERGENCIES DON'T COUNT. OH, AVRIL! HOW BAD IS IT?
WELL, I'M GONNA BE IN A CAST UNTIL THE FIFTH OF FOREVER. IT SUCKS.
IT'S ALL MY FAULT! I HATE MYSELF FOR THIS!
WHAT?
YOU WEREN'T EVEN THERE, DIXIE.
YEAH, AND IF I HAD BEEN THERE, WE'D HAVE BEEN SOMEWHERE ELSE.
DOWN AT THE LAKE. OR RUNNING THE ROSE PETAL GAUNTLET OR SOMETHING.

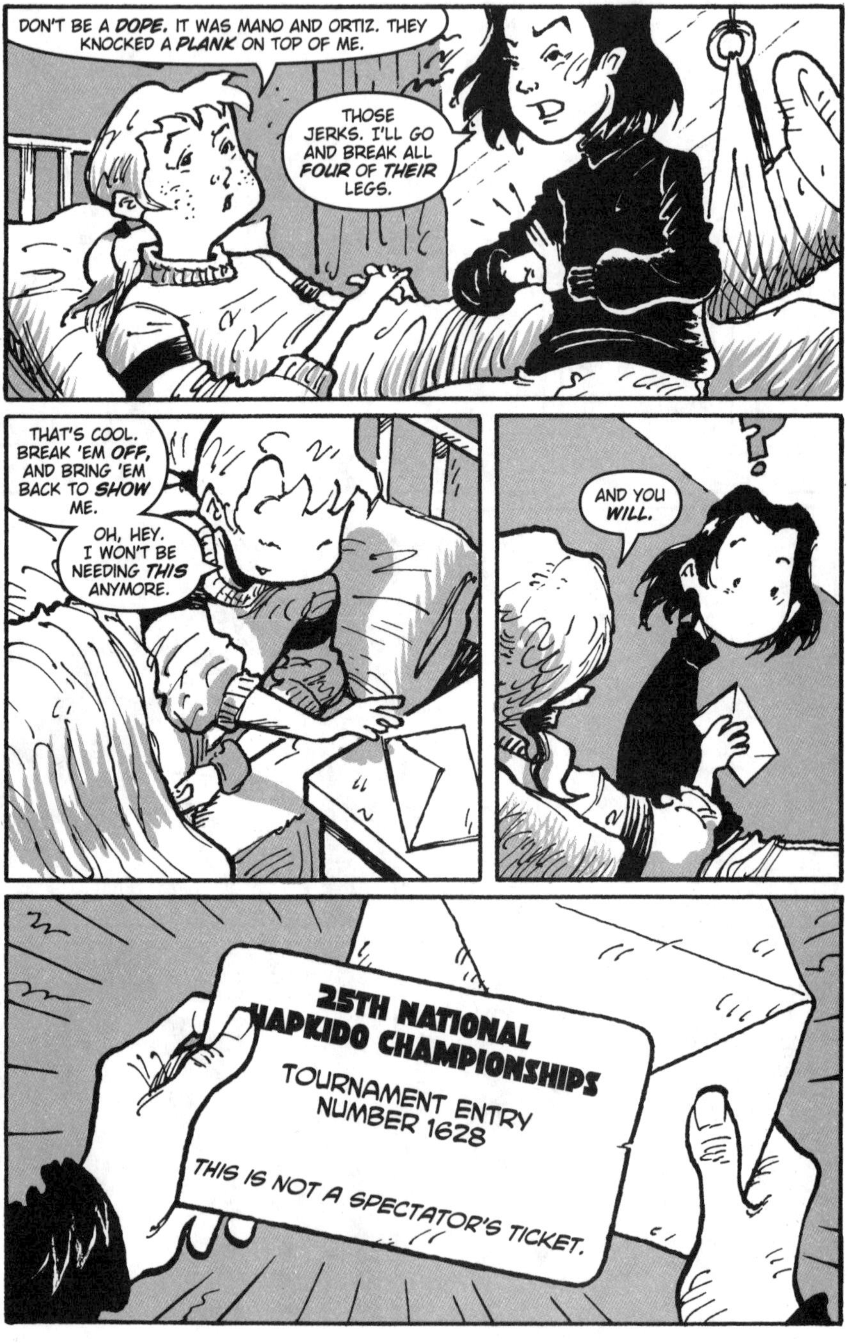
DON'T BE A DOPE. IT WAS MANO AND ORTIZ. THEY KNOCKED A PLANK ON TOP OF ME.
THOSE JERKS. I'LL GO AND BREAK ALL FOUR OF THEIR LEGS.
THAT'S COOL. BREAK 'EM OFF, AND BRING 'EM BACK TO SHOW ME.
OH, HEY. I WON'T BE NEEDING THIS ANYMORE.
?
AND YOU WILL.
25TH NATIONAL HAPKIDO CHAMPIONSHIPS
TOURNAMENT ENTRY NUMBER 1628
THIS IS NOT A SPECTATOR'S TICKET.

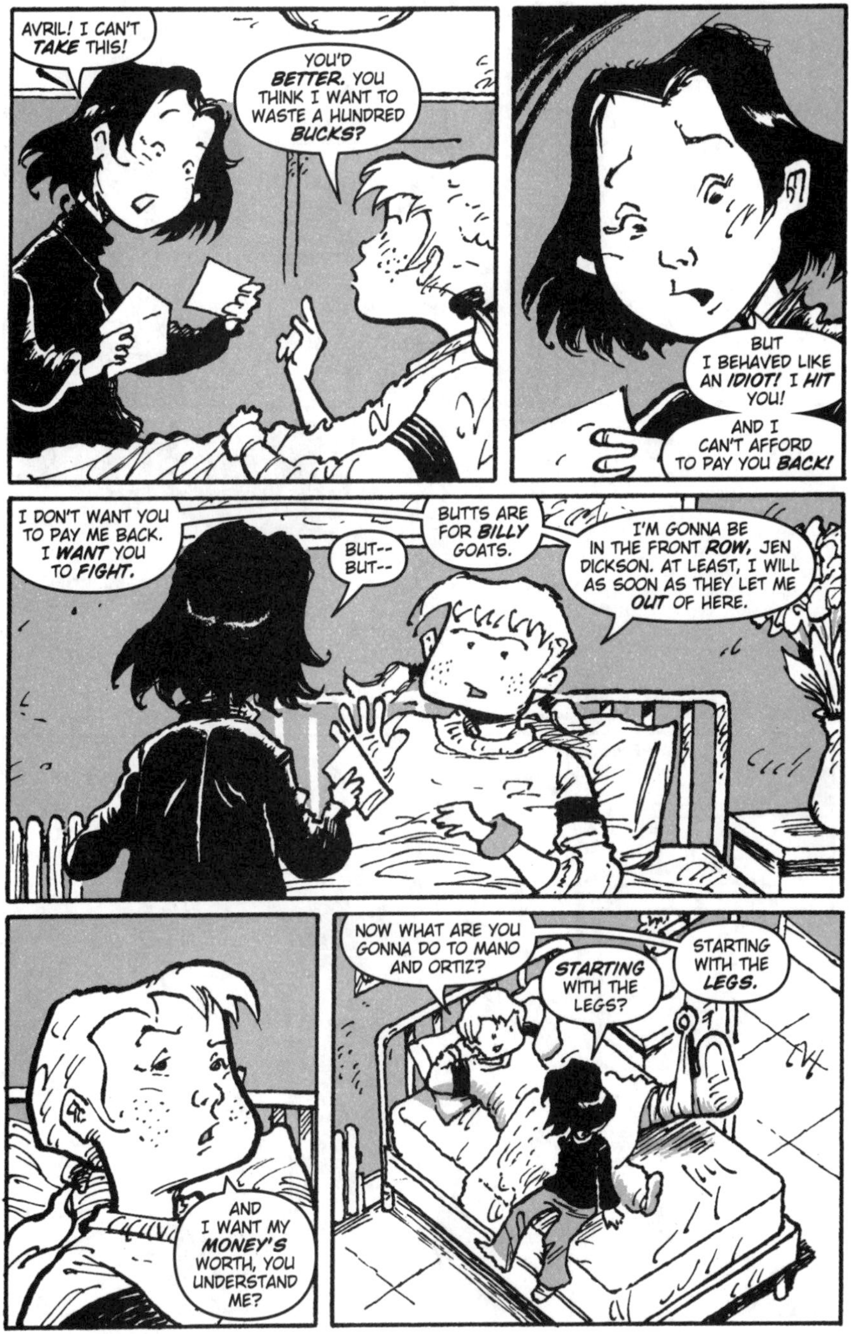
AVRIL! I CAN'T TAKE THIS!
YOU'D BETTER. YOU THINK I WANT TO WASTE A HUNDRED BUCKS?
BUT I BEHAVED LIKE AN IDIOT! I HIT YOU!
AND I CAN'T AFFORD TO PAY YOU BACK!
I DON'T WANT YOU TO PAY ME BACK. I WANT YOU TO FIGHT.
BUT-- BUT--
BUTTS ARE FOR BILLY GOATS.
I'M GONNA BE IN THE FRONT ROW, JEN DICKSON. AT LEAST, I WILL AS SOON AS THEY LET ME OUT OF HERE.
AND I WANT MY MONEY'S WORTH, YOU UNDERSTAND ME?
NOW WHAT ARE YOU GONNA DO TO MANO AND ORTIZ?
STARTING WITH THE LEGS.
STARTING WITH THE LEGS?

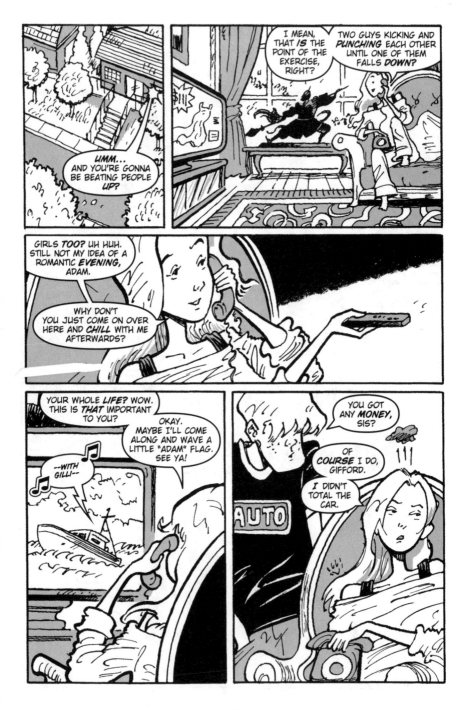

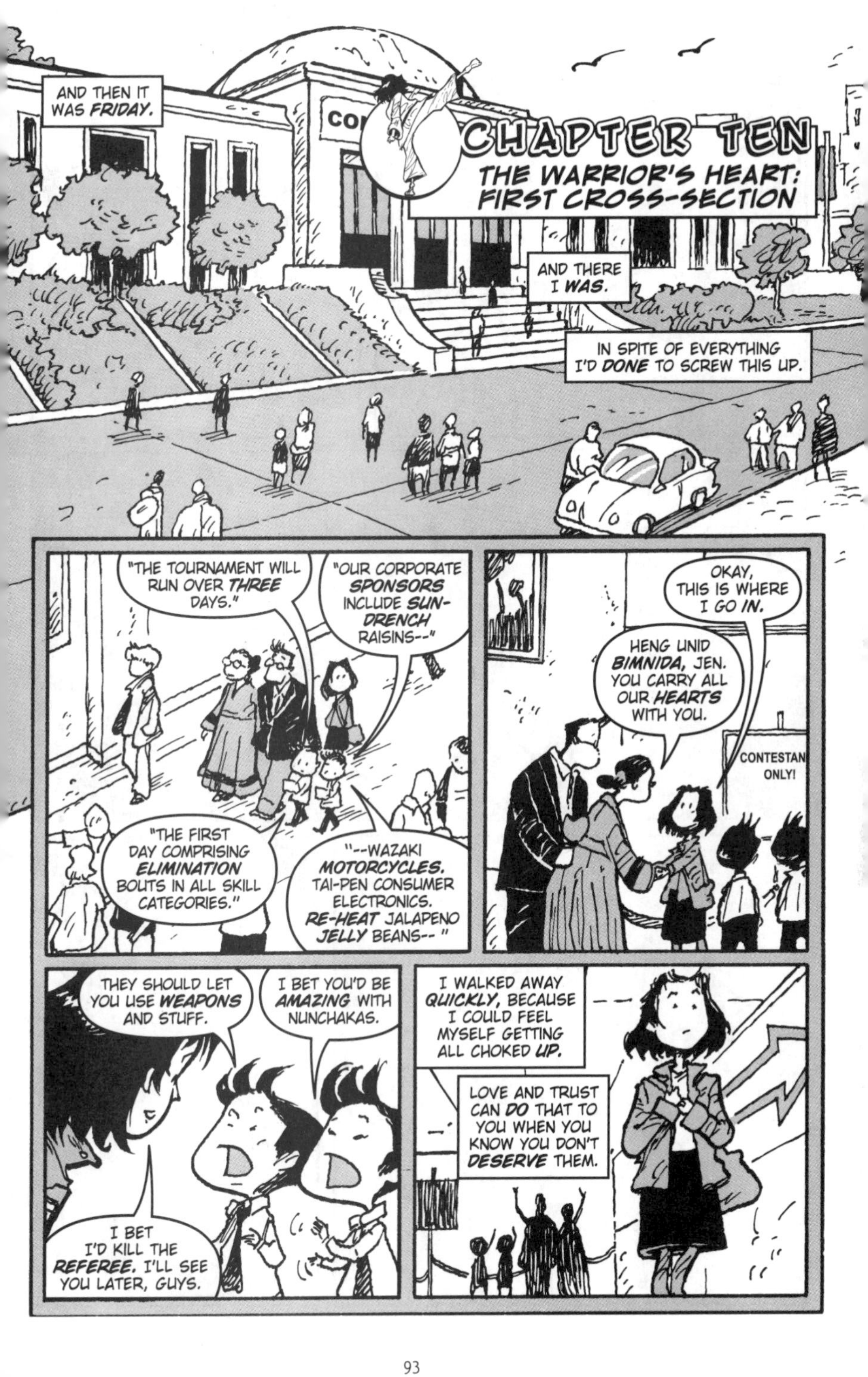
AND THEN IT WAS FRIDAY.
CHAPTER TEN
THE WARRIOR'S HEART: FIRST CROSS-SECTION
AND THERE I WAS.
IN SPITE OF EVERYTHING I'D DONE TO SCREW THIS UP.
"THE TOURNAMENT WILL RUN OVER THREE DAYS."
"OUR CORPORATE SPONSORS INCLUDE SUN-DRENCH RAISINS--"
"THE FIRST DAY COMPRISING ELIMINATION BOUTS IN ALL SKILL CATEGORIES."
"--WAZAKI MOTORCYCLES. TAI-PEN CONSUMER ELECTRONICS. RE-HEAT JALAPENO JELLY BEANS-- "
OKAY, THIS IS WHERE I GO IN.
HENG UNID BIMNIDA, JEN. YOU CARRY ALL OUR HEARTS WITH YOU.
CONTESTAN ONLY!
THEY SHOULD LET YOU USE WEAPONS AND STUFF.
I BET YOU'D BE AMAZING WITH NUNCHAKAS.
I BET I'D KILL THE REFEREE. I'LL SEE YOU LATER, GUYS.
I WALKED AWAY QUICKLY, BECAUSE I COULD FEEL MYSELF GETTING ALL CHOKED UP.
LOVE AND TRUST CAN DO THAT TO YOU WHEN YOU KNOW YOU DON'T DESERVE THEM.

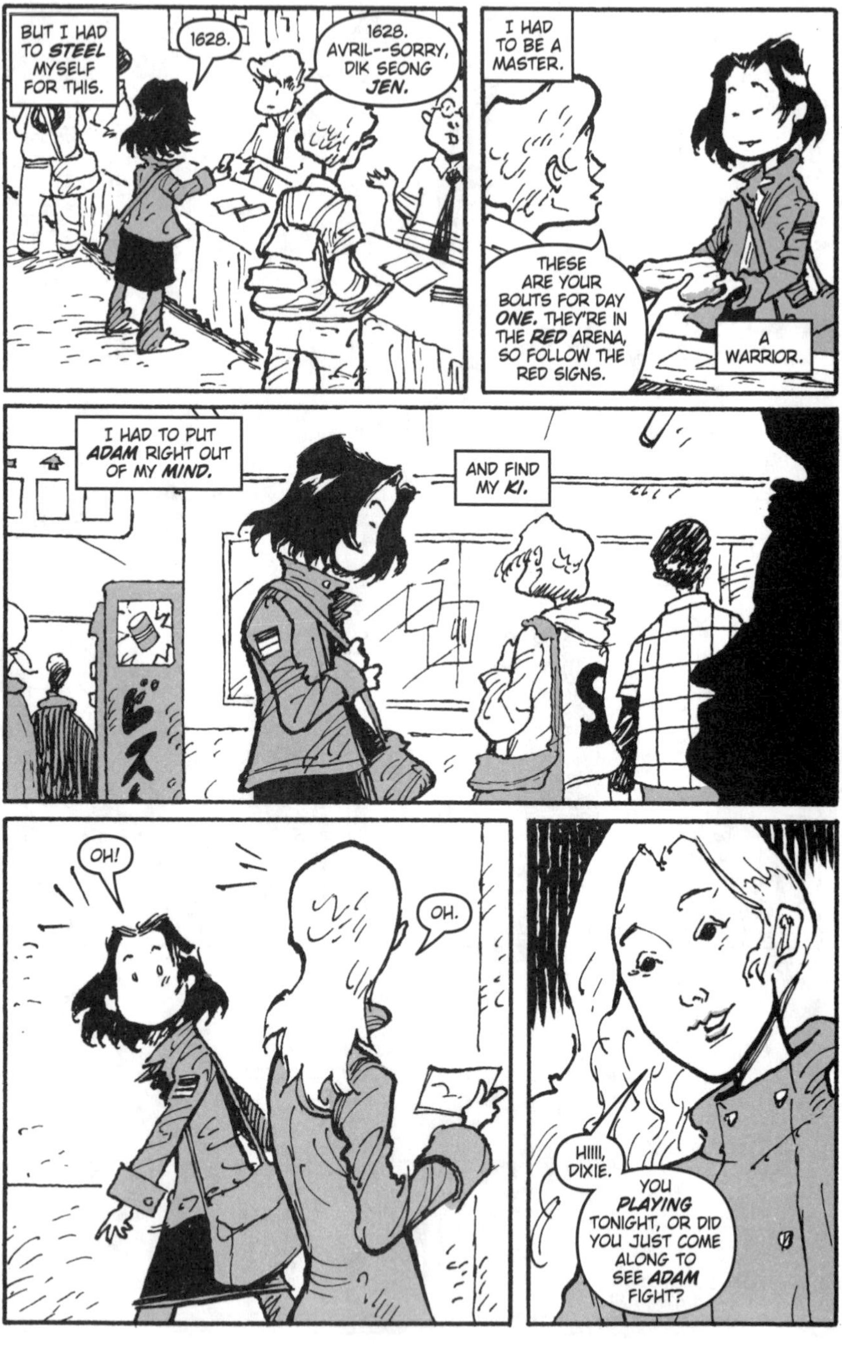
BUT I HAD TO STEEL MYSELF FOR THIS.
1628.
1628. AVRIL--SORRY, DIK SEONG JEN.
I HAD TO BE A MASTER.
THESE ARE YOUR BOUTS FOR DAY ONE. THEY'RE IN THE RED ARENA, SO FOLLOW THE RED SIGNS.
A WARRIOR.
I HAD TO PUT ADAM RIGHT OUT OF MY MIND.
AND FIND MY KI.
OH!
OH.
HIIII, DIXIE.
YOU PLAYING TONIGHT, OR DID YOU JUST COME ALONG TO SEE ADAM FIGHT?

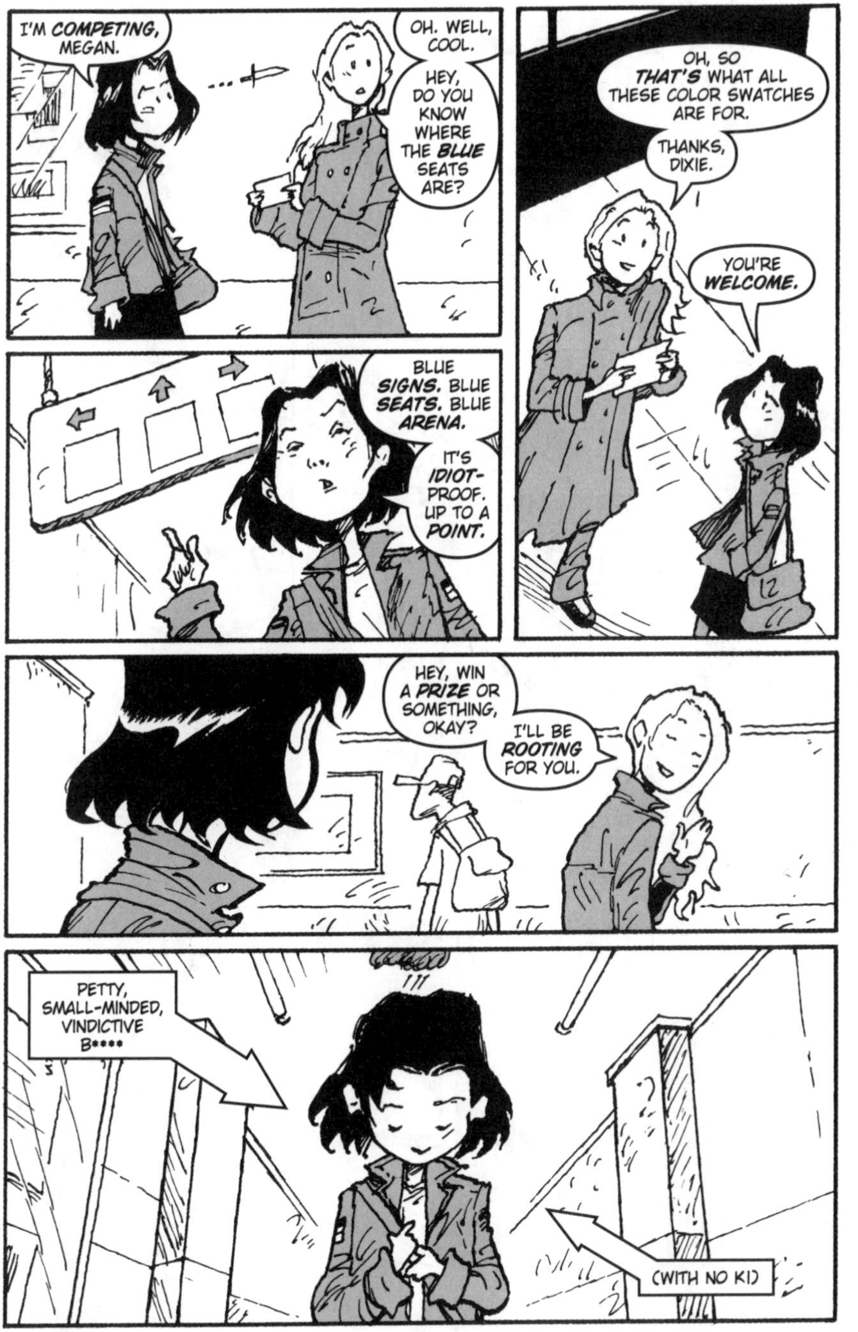
I'M COMPETING, MEGAN.
OH. WELL, COOL.
HEY, DO YOU KNOW WHERE THE BLUE SEATS ARE?
OH, SO THAT'S WHAT ALL THESE COLOR SWATCHES ARE FOR.
THANKS, DIXIE.
YOU'RE WELCOME.
BLUE SIGNS. BLUE SEATS. BLUE ARENA.
IT'S IDIOT-PROOF. UP TO A POINT.
HEY, WIN A PRIZE OR SOMETHING, OKAY?
I'LL BE ROOTING FOR YOU.
PETTY, SMALL-MINDED, VINDICTIVE B****
(WITH NO KI)

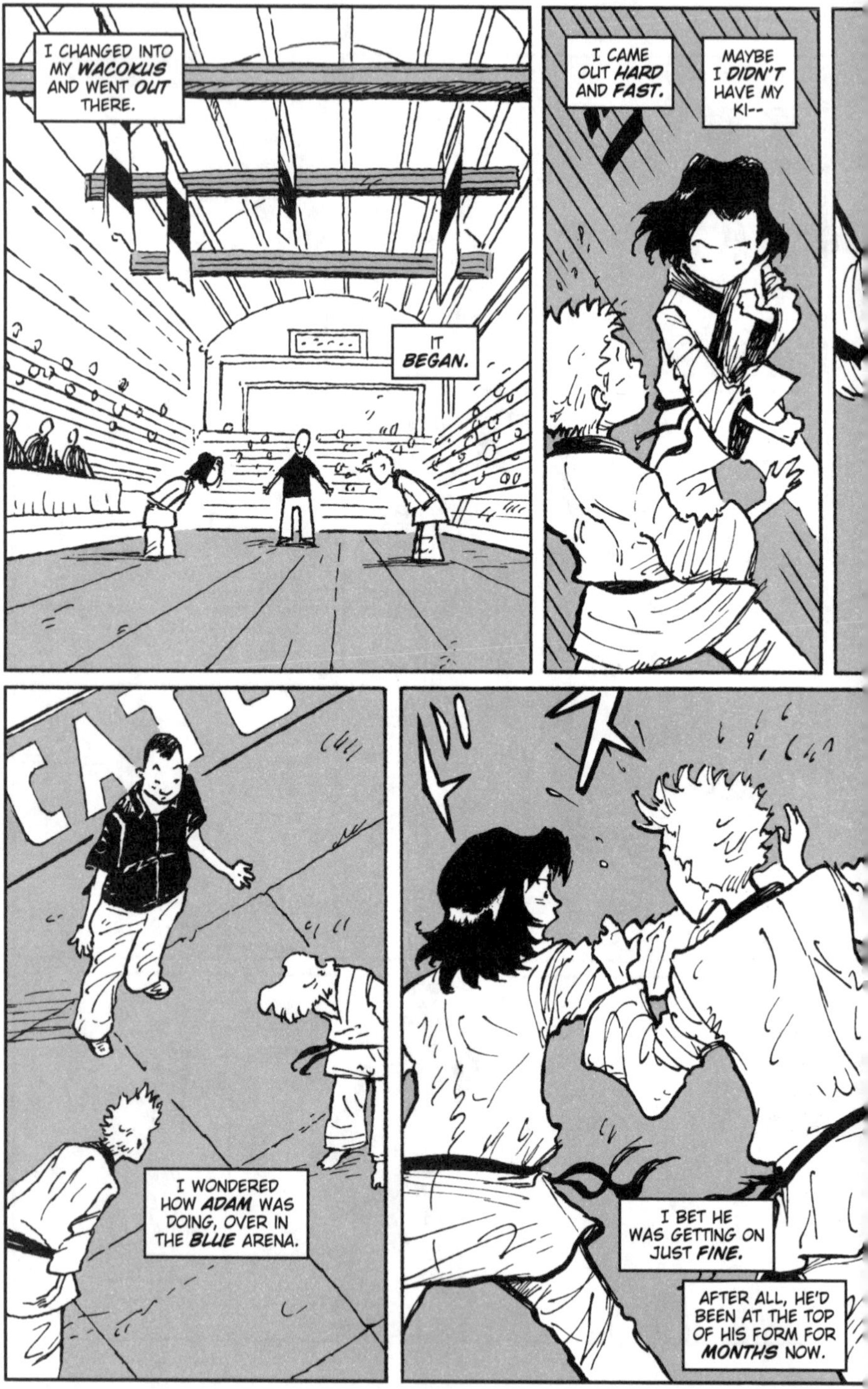
I CHANGED INTO MY WACOKUS AND WENT OUT THERE.
IT BEGAN.
I CAME OUT HARD AND FAST.
MAYBE I DIDN'T HAVE MY KI--
I WONDERED HOW ADAM WAS DOING, OVER IN THE BLUE ARENA.
I BET HE WAS GETTING ON JUST FINE.
AFTER ALL, HE'D BEEN AT THE TOP OF HIS FORM FOR MONTHS NOW.

97

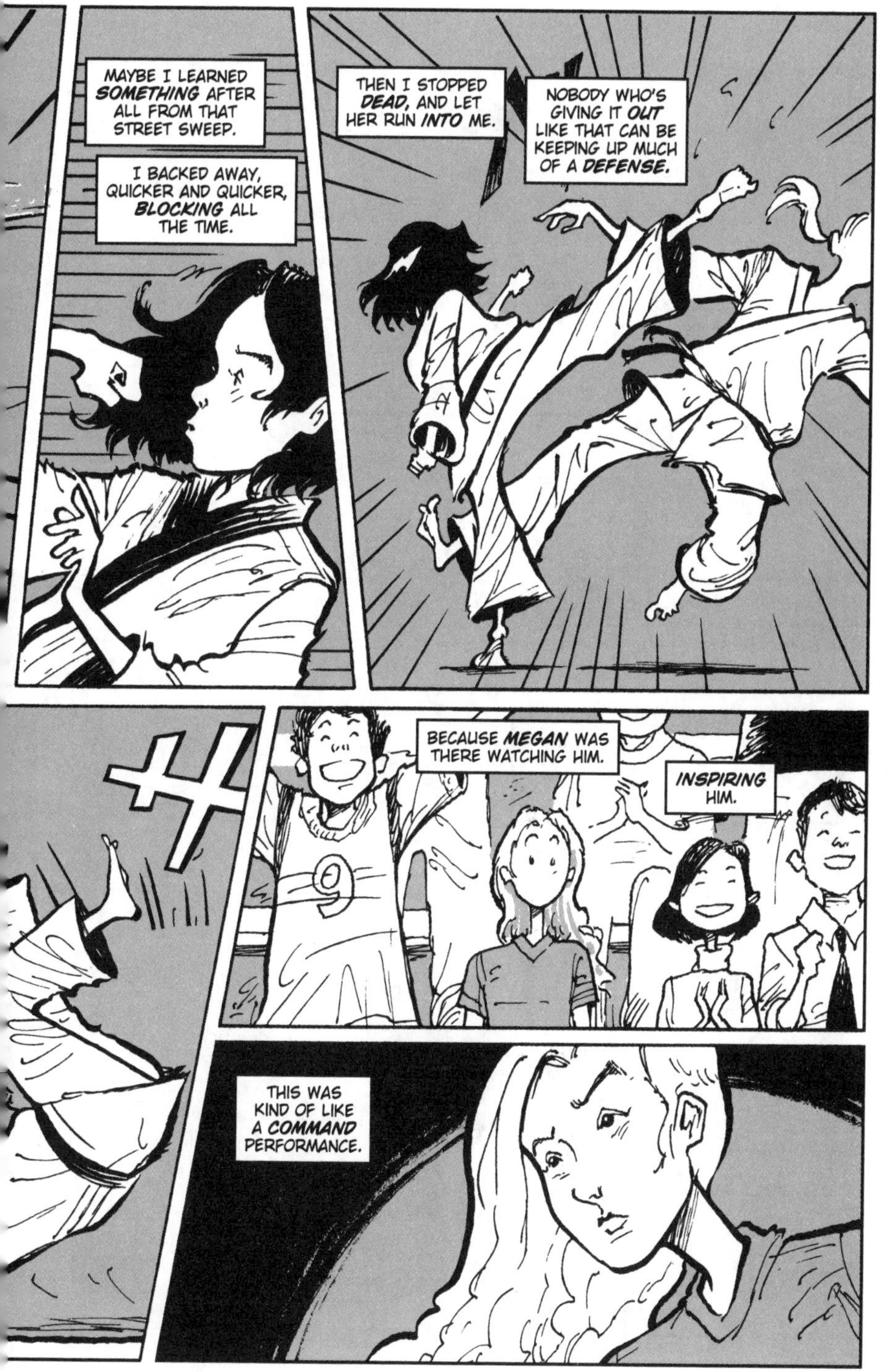
MAYBE I LEARNED SOMETHING AFTER ALL FROM THAT STREET SWEEP.
I BACKED AWAY, QUICKER AND QUICKER, BLOCKING ALL THE TIME.
THEN I STOPPED DEAD, AND LET HER RUN INTO ME.
NOBODY WHO'S GIVING IT OUT LIKE THAT CAN BE KEEPING UP MUCH OF A DEFENSE.
BECAUSE MEGAN WAS THERE WATCHING HIM.
INSPIRING HIM.
THIS WAS KIND OF LIKE A COMMAND PERFORMANCE.

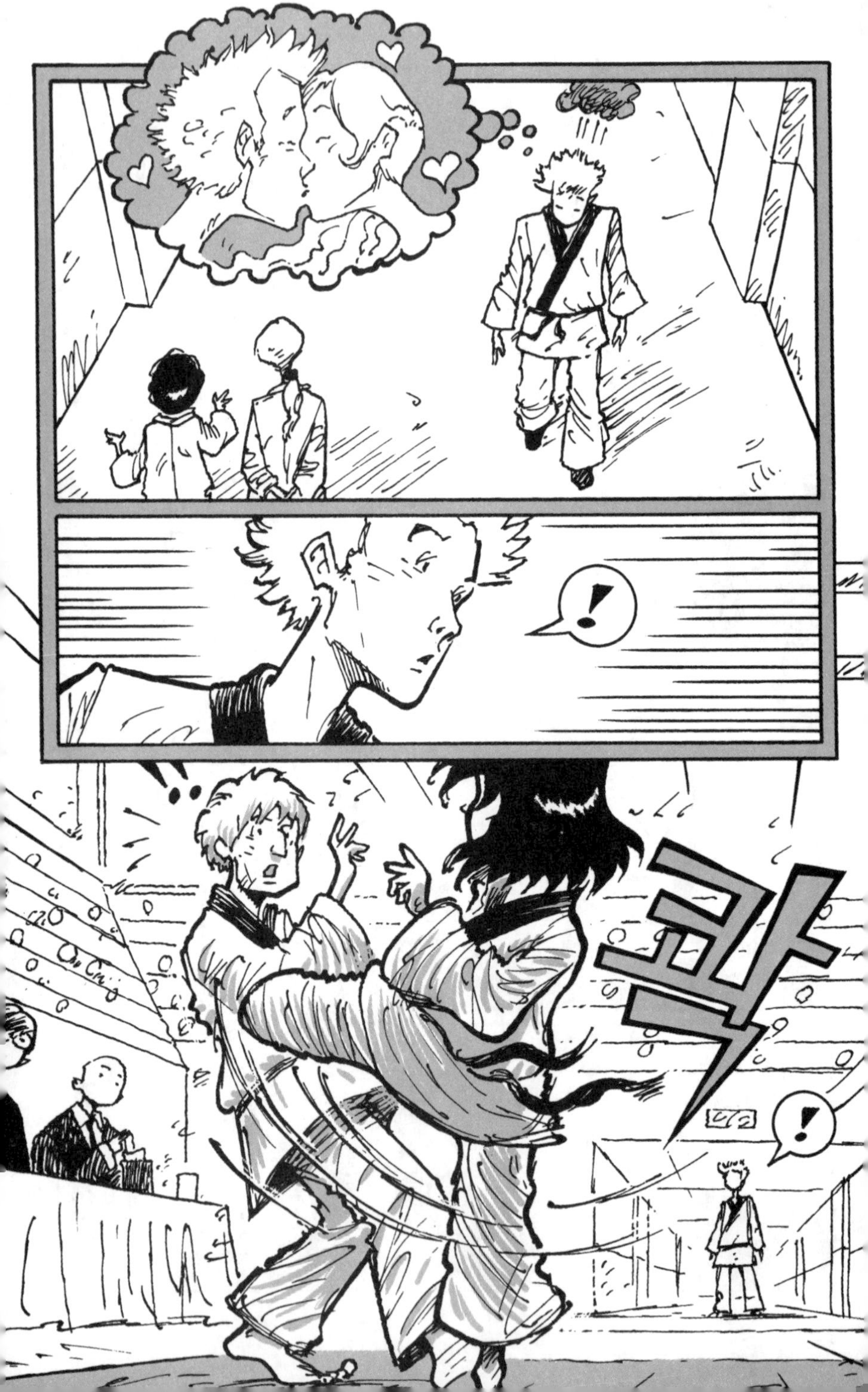
!
!!
!

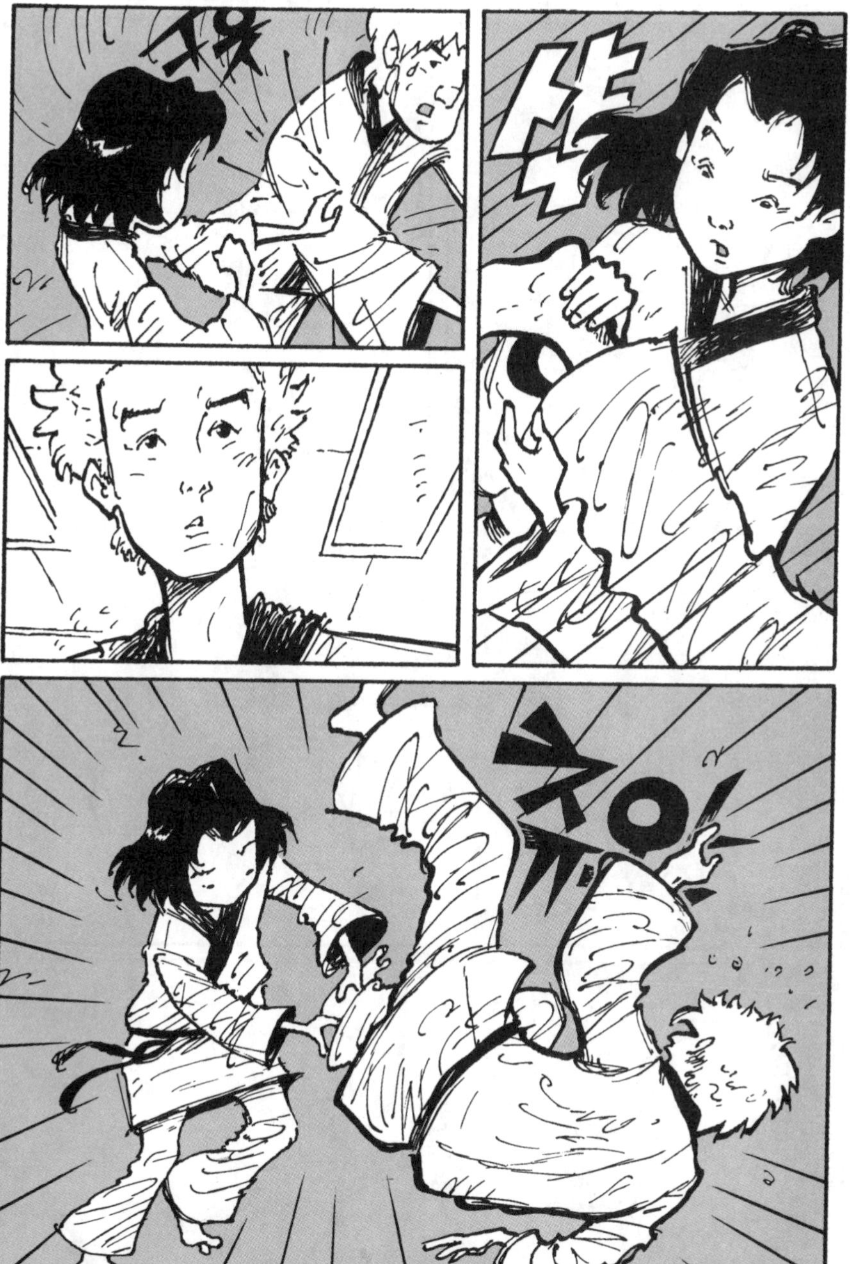

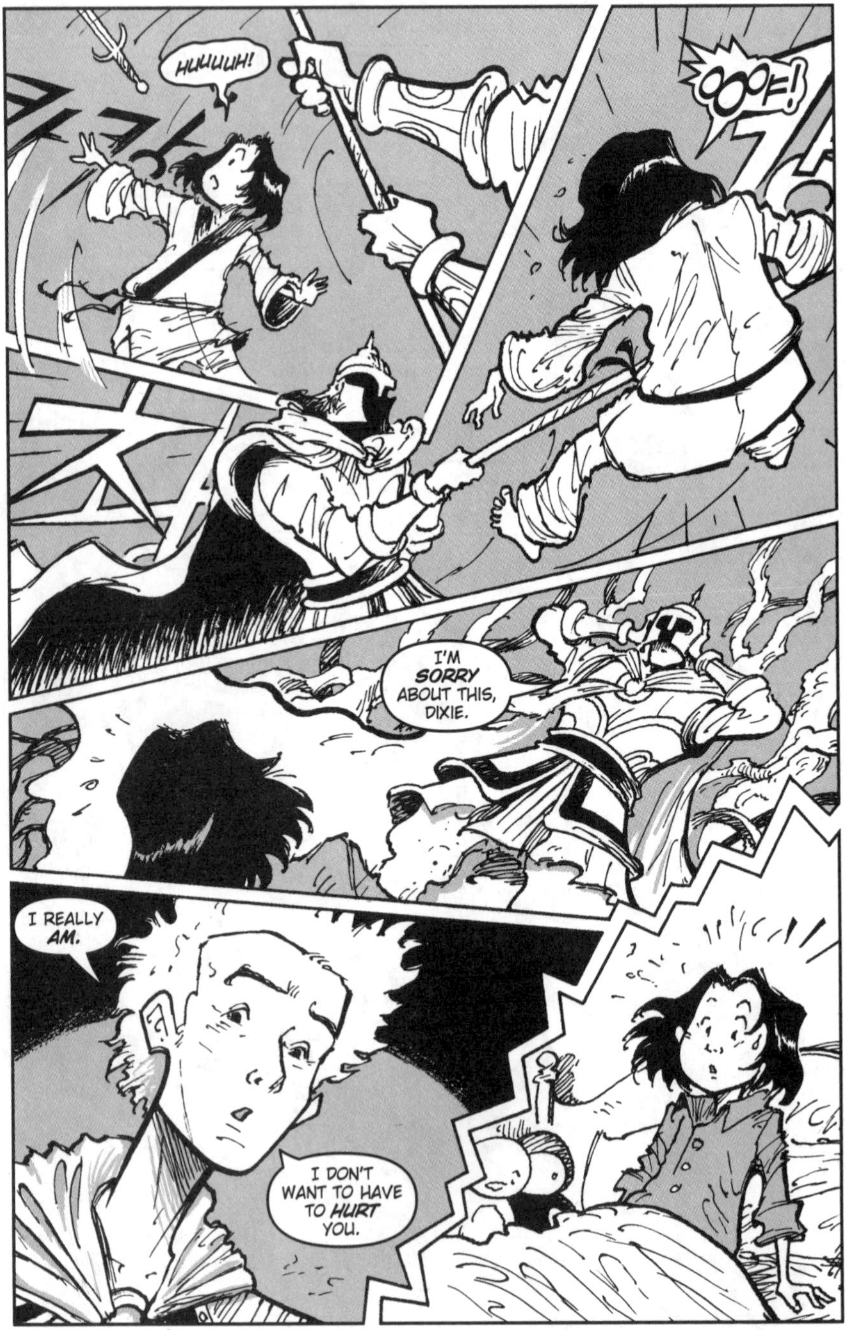
HUUUUH!
OOOF!
I'M SORRY ABOUT THIS, DIXIE.
I REALLY AM.
I DON'T WANT TO HAVE TO HURT YOU.

109

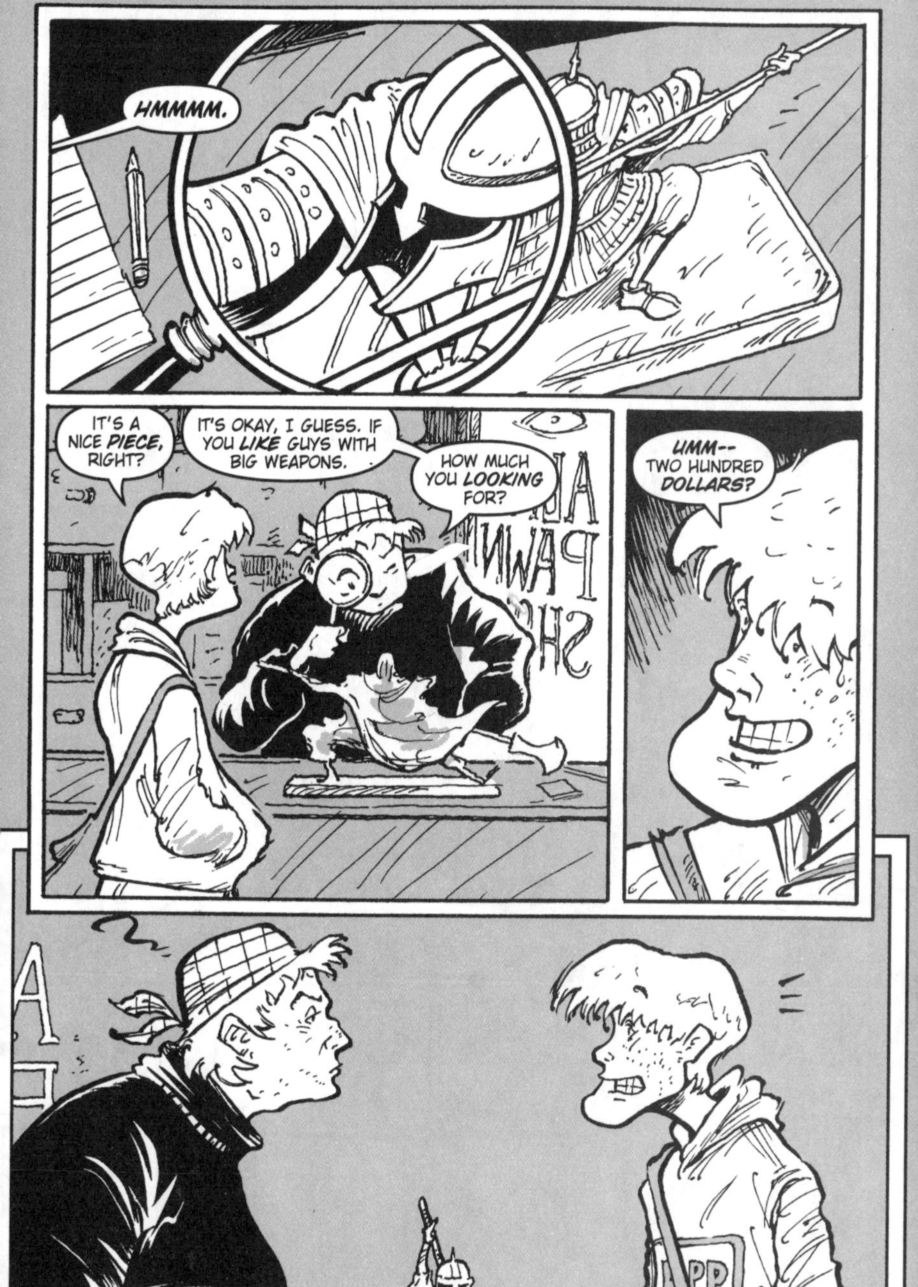
HMMMM.
IT'S A NICE PIECE, RIGHT?
IT'S OKAY, I GUESS. IF YOU LIKE GUYS WITH BIG WEAPONS.
HOW MUCH YOU LOOKING FOR?
PAWN
UMM-- TWO HUNDRED DOLLARS?

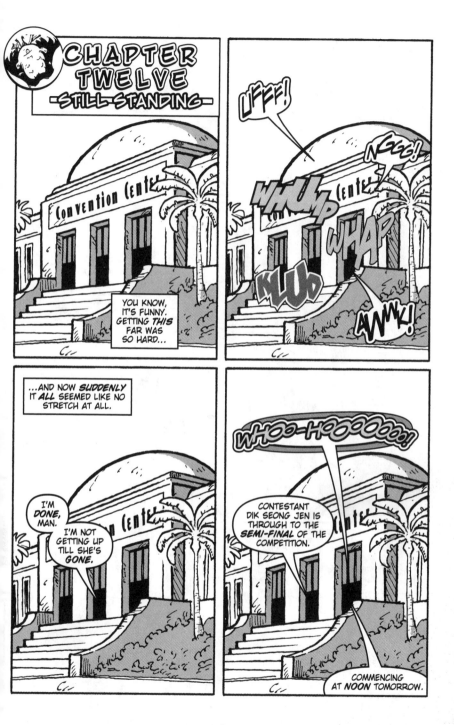

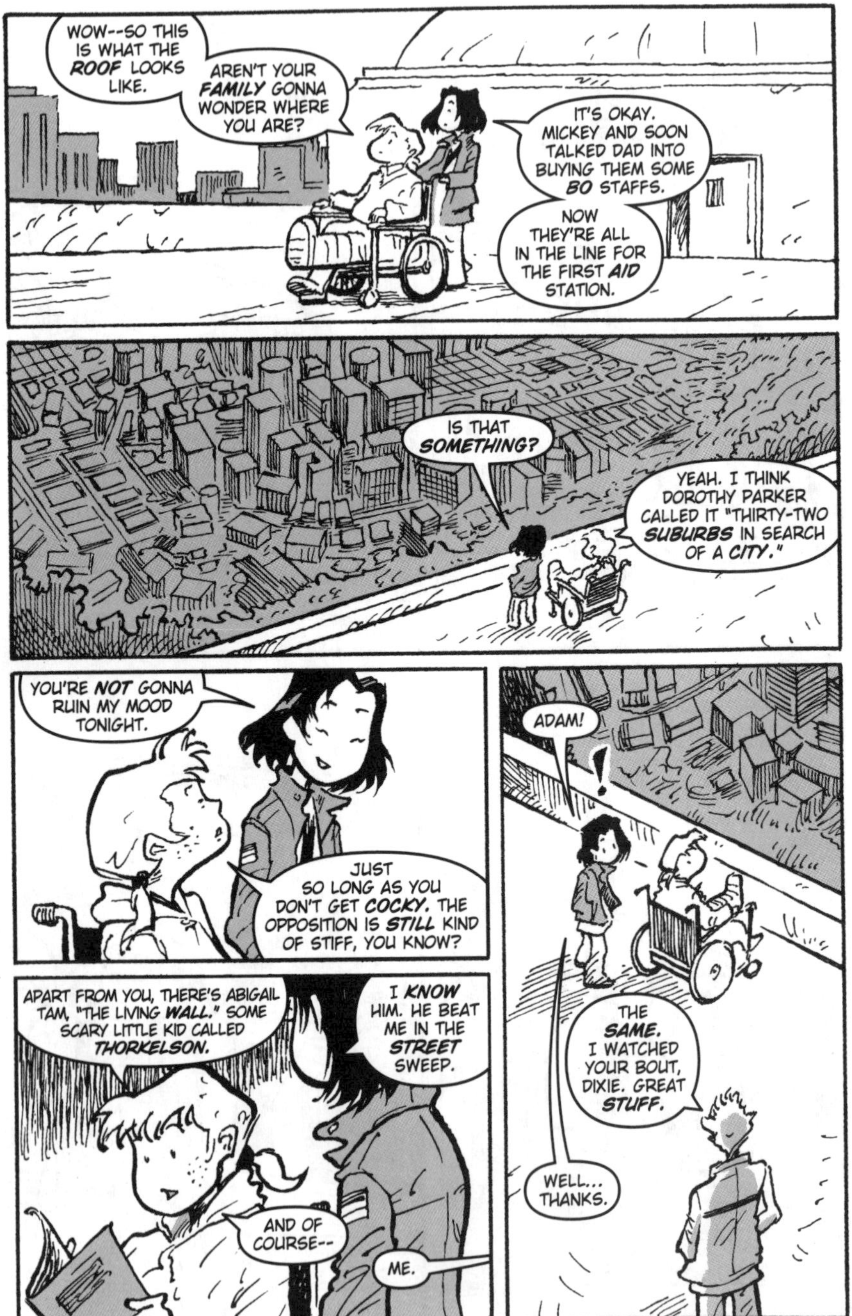

WOW--SO THIS IS WHAT THE ROOF LOOKS LIKE.
AREN'T YOUR FAMILY GONNA WONDER WHERE YOU ARE?
IT'S OKAY. MICKEY AND SOON TALKED DAD INTO BUYING THEM SOME BO STAFFS.
NOW THEY'RE ALL IN THE LINE FOR THE FIRST AID STATION.
IS THAT SOMETHING?
YEAH. I THINK DOROTHY PARKER CALLED IT "THIRTY-TWO SUBURBS IN SEARCH OF A CITY."
YOU'RE NOT GONNA RUIN MY MOOD TONIGHT.
JUST SO LONG AS YOU DON'T GET COCKY. THE OPPOSITION IS STILL KIND OF STIFF, YOU KNOW?
APART FROM YOU, THERE'S ABIGAIL TAM, "THE LIVING WALL." SOME SCARY LITTLE KID CALLED THORKELSON.
I KNOW HIM. HE BEAT ME IN THE STREET SWEEP.
AND OF COURSE--
ME.
ADAM!
!
THE SAME. I WATCHED YOUR BOUT, DIXIE. GREAT STUFF.
WELL... THANKS.

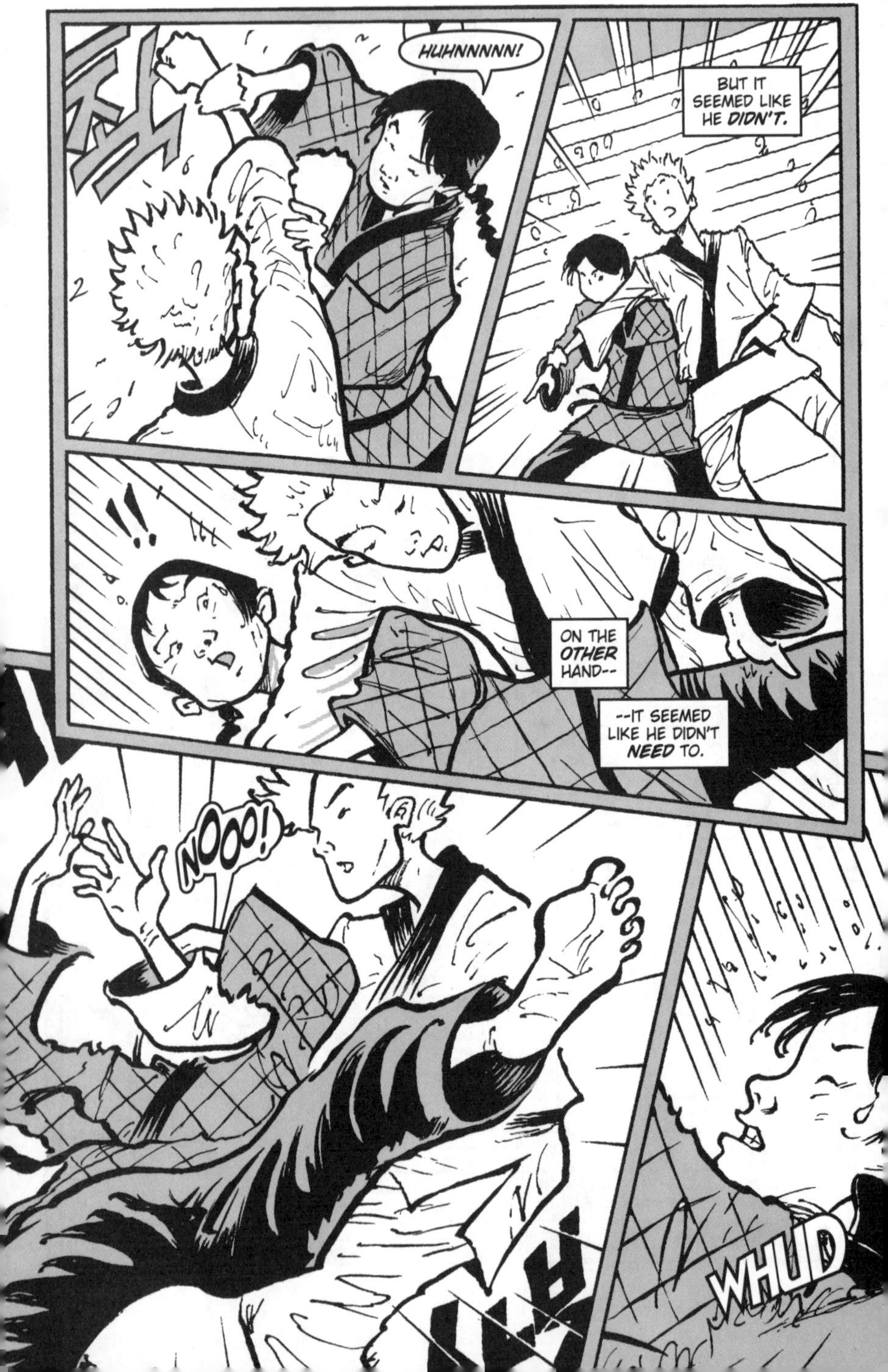
HUHNNNNN!
BUT IT SEEMED LIKE HE DIDN'T.
!!
ON THE OTHER HAND--
--IT SEEMED LIKE HE DIDN'T NEED TO.
NOOO!
WHUD

130

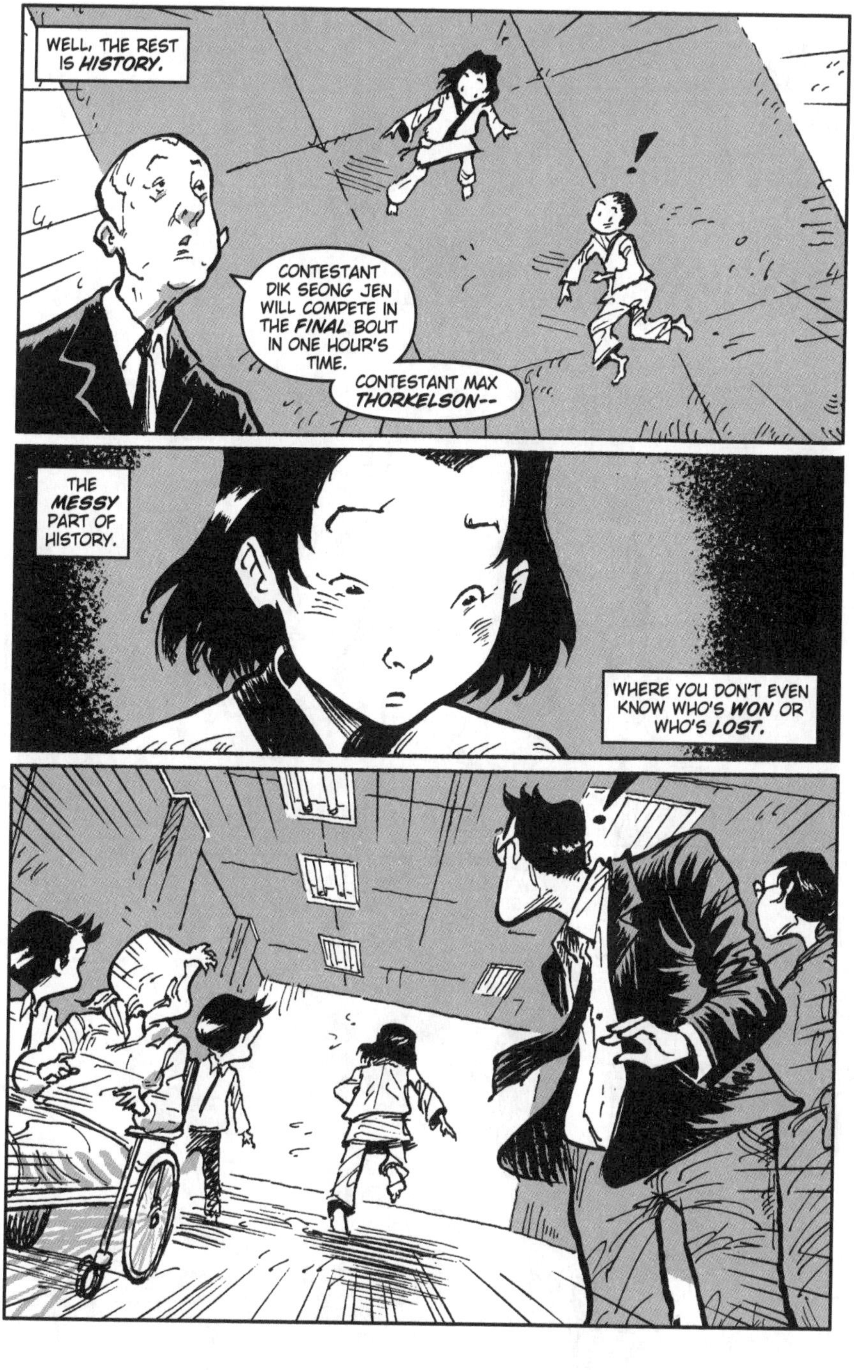
WELL, THE REST IS *HISTORY.*
!
CONTESTANT DIK SEONG JEN WILL COMPETE IN THE *FINAL* BOUT IN ONE HOUR'S TIME.
CONTESTANT MAX *THORKELSON--*
THE *MESSY* PART OF HISTORY.
WHERE YOU DON'T EVEN KNOW WHO'S *WON* OR WHO'S *LOST.*
!

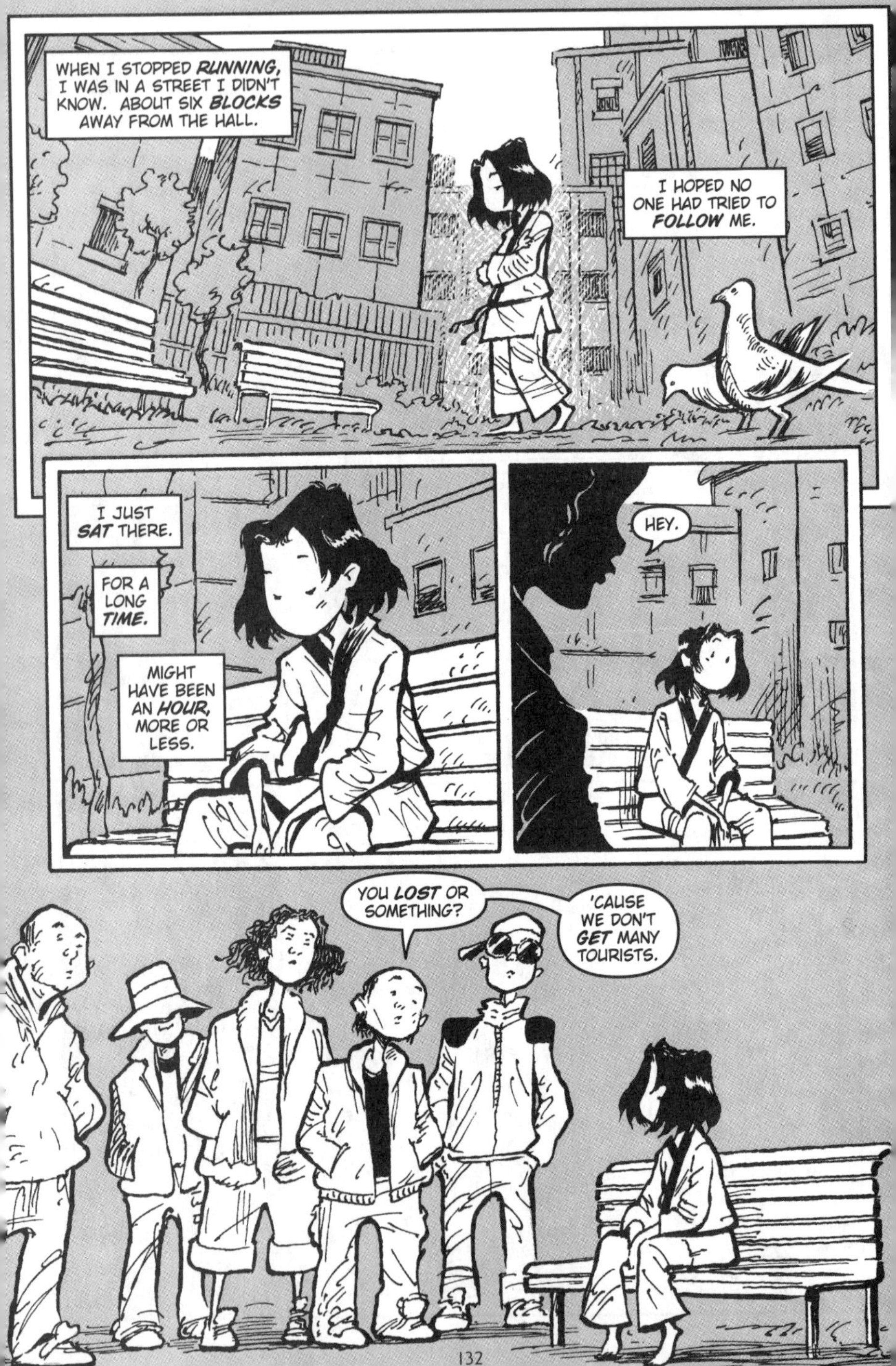
WHEN I STOPPED RUNNING, I WAS IN A STREET I DIDN'T KNOW. ABOUT SIX BLOCKS AWAY FROM THE HALL.
I HOPED NO ONE HAD TRIED TO FOLLOW ME.
I JUST SAT THERE.
FOR A LONG TIME.
MIGHT HAVE BEEN AN HOUR, MORE OR LESS.
HEY.
YOU LOST OR SOMETHING?
'CAUSE WE DON'T GET MANY TOURISTS.

134

138

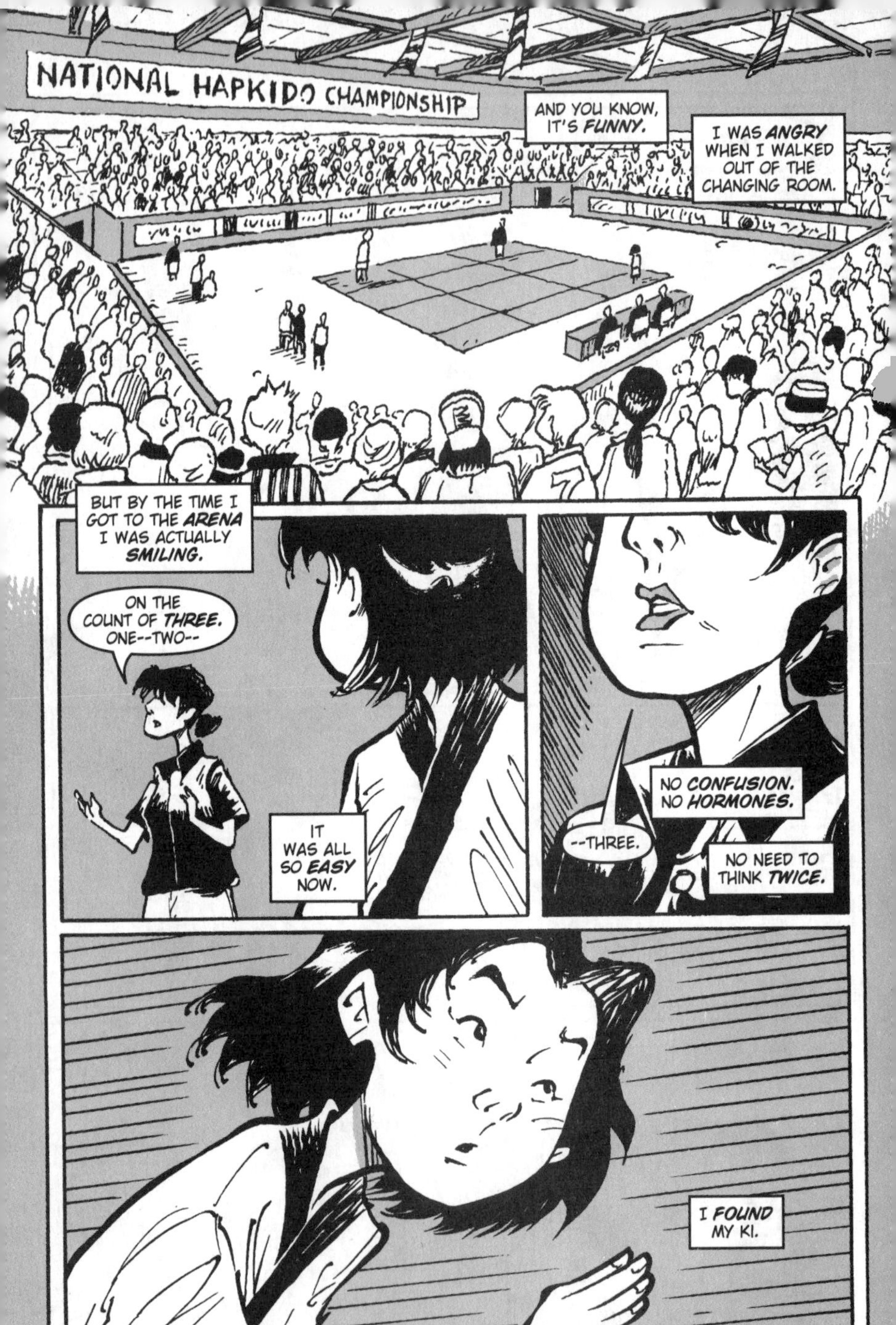
NATIONAL HAPKIDO CHAMPIONSHIP
AND YOU KNOW, IT'S FUNNY.
I WAS ANGRY WHEN I WALKED OUT OF THE CHANGING ROOM.
BUT BY THE TIME I GOT TO THE ARENA I WAS ACTUALLY SMILING.
ON THE COUNT OF THREE. ONE--TWO--
IT WAS ALL SO EASY NOW.
NO CONFUSION. NO HORMONES.
--THREE.
NO NEED TO THINK TWICE.
I FOUND MY KI.

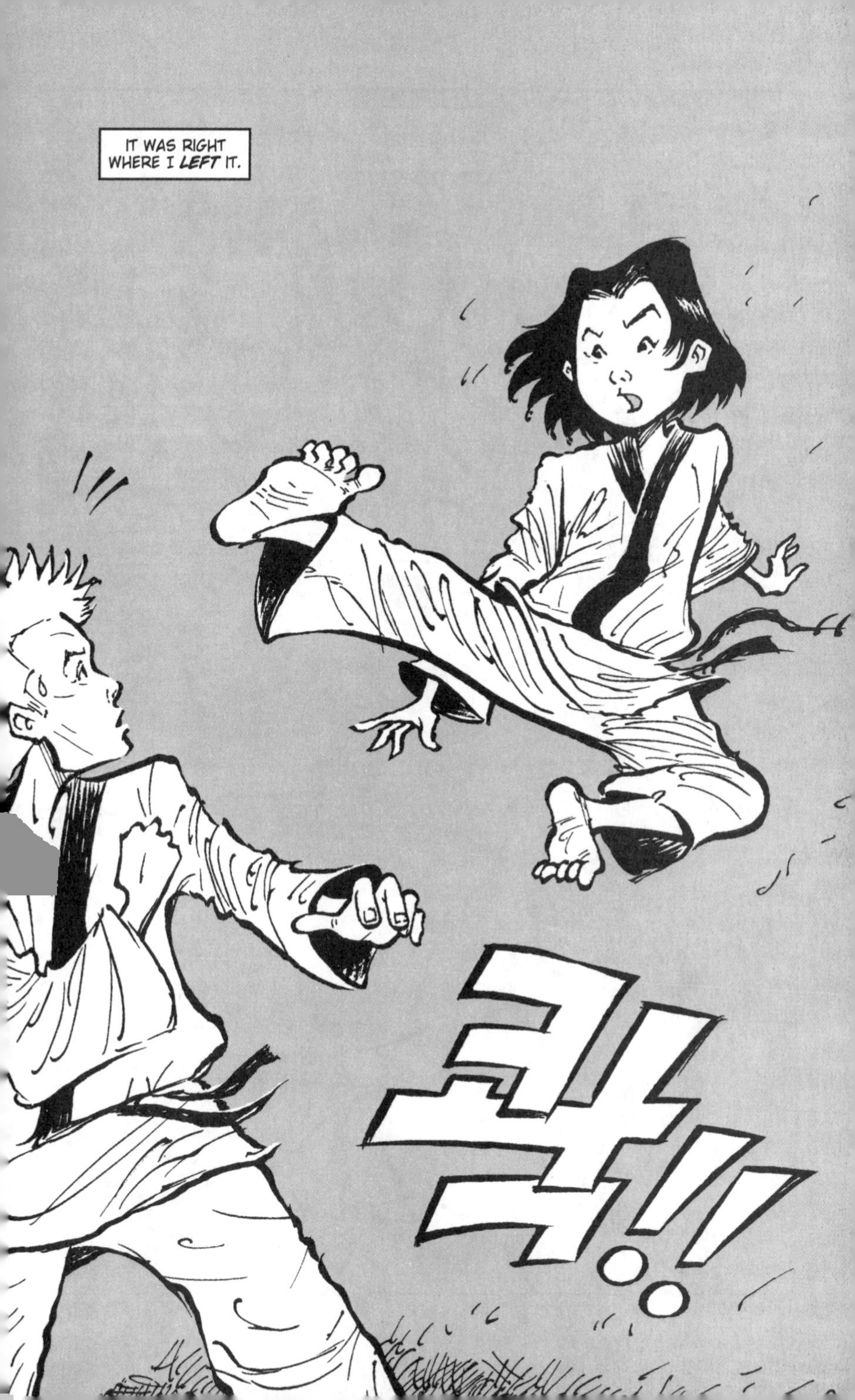
IT WAS RIGHT WHERE I *LEFT* IT.

MIKE CAREY

Mike is a comics writer, novelist and screenwriter who lives
and works in London and is best known for his VERTIGO
work on the multiple Eisner-nominated LUCIFER series and
MY FAITH IN FRANKIE. His screenplay *Frost Flowers* will be
a feature film starring Holly Hunter and James McEvoy.
He wants it known that the human body has 206 bones.
In researching the hapkido moves in RE-GIFTERS, Mike broke
all but three of them. Next Up: Co-writing the MINX book
CONFESSIONS OF A BLABBERMOUTH with his daughter,
Louise — should he survive the experience.

SONNY LIEW

Sonny is an illustrator currently residing in Singapore. His
work includes MY FAITH IN FRANKIE, *Malinky Robot* and
contributions to the *Flight* and *24Seven* anthologies. Currently
working on the series *Wonderland* for Slave Labor Graphics
and Disney, Sonny has been nominated for an Eisner Award
and can been reached at sonnyliew.com.

MARC HEMPEL

Originally from Chicago, Marc now lives in Baltimore,
Maryland, where he enjoys relative fame as "America's Most
Beloved Semi-Obscure Cartoonist." He is best known for
his collaboration with Neil Gaiman on THE SANDMAN:
THE KINDLY ONES and is a regular contributor to
MAD Magazine.

SPECIAL BACKSTAGE PASS:

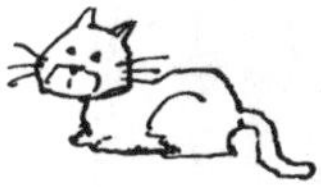

If you liked the story you've just read, fear not: Other MINX books will be available in the months to come. MINX is a line of books that's designed especially for you — someone who's a bit bored with straight fiction and ready for stories that are visually exciting beyond words — literally. In fact, we thought you might like to get in on a secret, behind-the-scenes look at a few of the new MINX titles that will aid in your escape to cool places during the long, hot summer. So hurry up and turn the page already!

And be sure to check out other exclusive material at

minxbooks.net

By the highly acclaimed author of *Boy Proof* and *The Queen of Cool*

THE PLAIN JANES

CECIL CASTELLUCCI
and JIM RUGG

Four girls named Jane are anything but ordinary once they form a

secret art gang and take on Suburbia by painting the town P.L.A.I.N. —

People Loving Art In Neighborhoods.

OUT NOW!

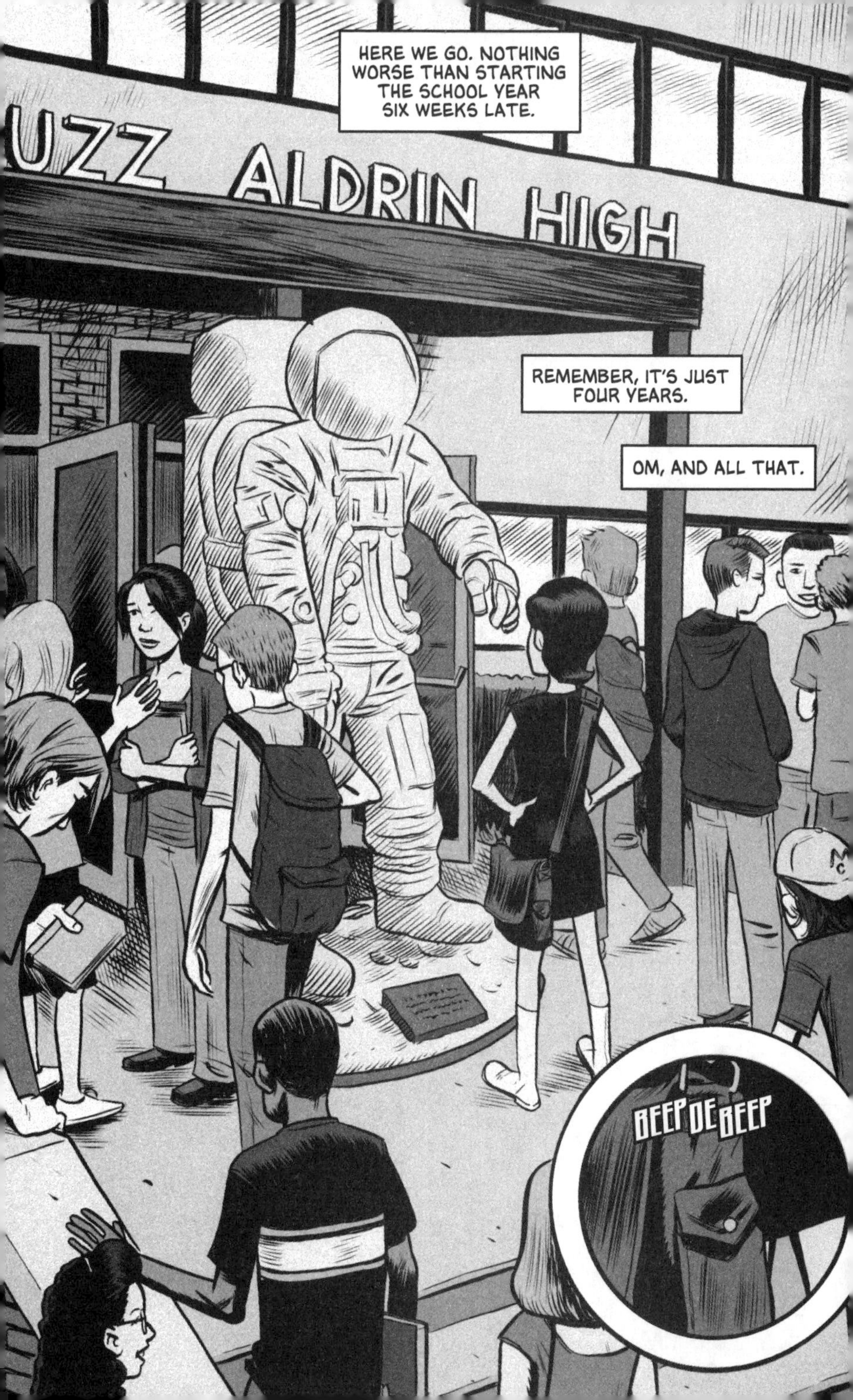
HERE WE GO. NOTHING WORSE THAN STARTING THE SCHOOL YEAR SIX WEEKS LATE.
UZZ ALDRIN HIGH
REMEMBER, IT'S JUST FOUR YEARS.
OM, AND ALL THAT.
BEEP DE BEEP

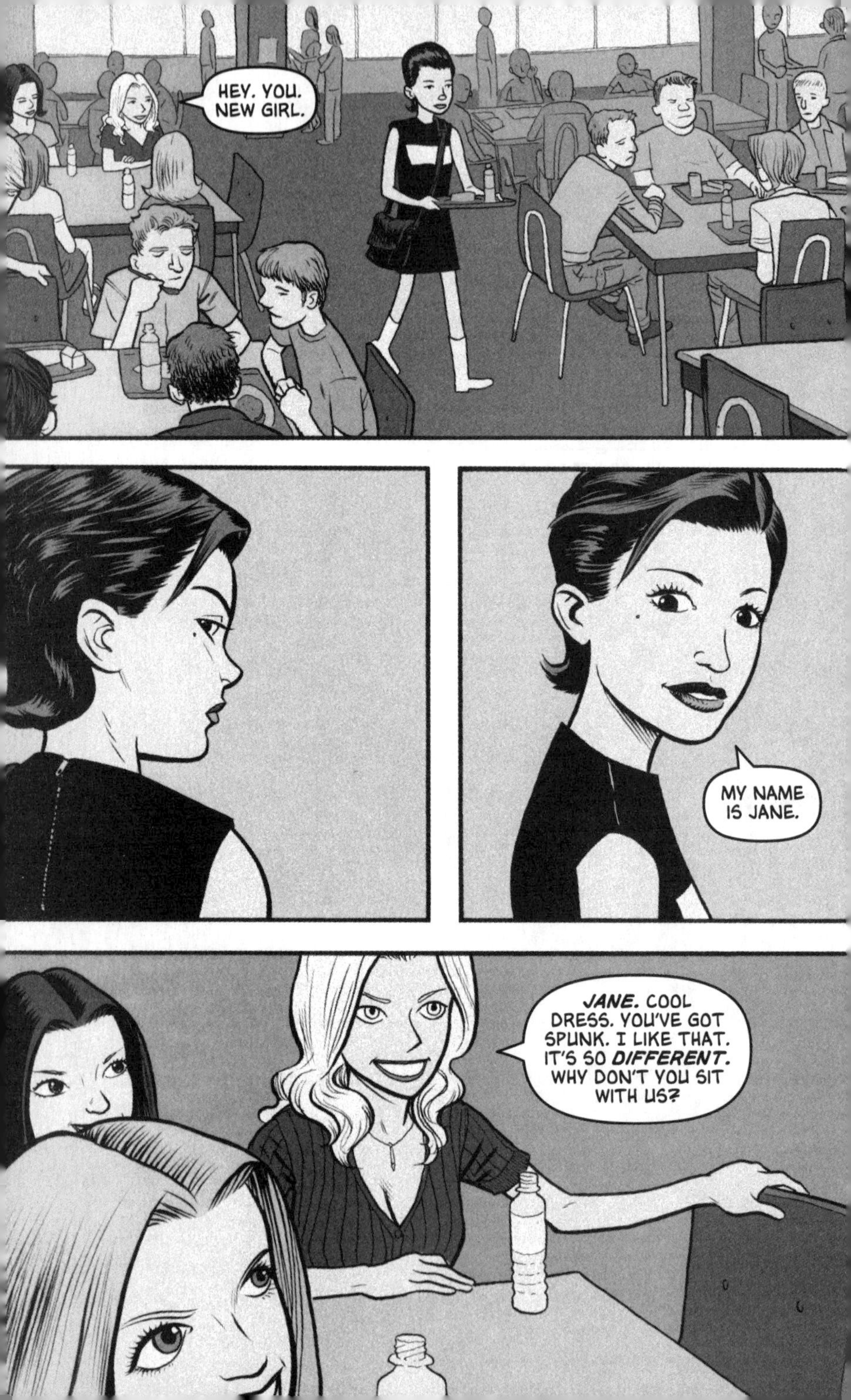
HEY. YOU. NEW GIRL.
MY NAME IS JANE.
JANE. COOL DRESS. YOU'VE GOT SPUNK. I LIKE THAT. IT'S SO *DIFFERENT.* WHY DON'T YOU SIT WITH US?

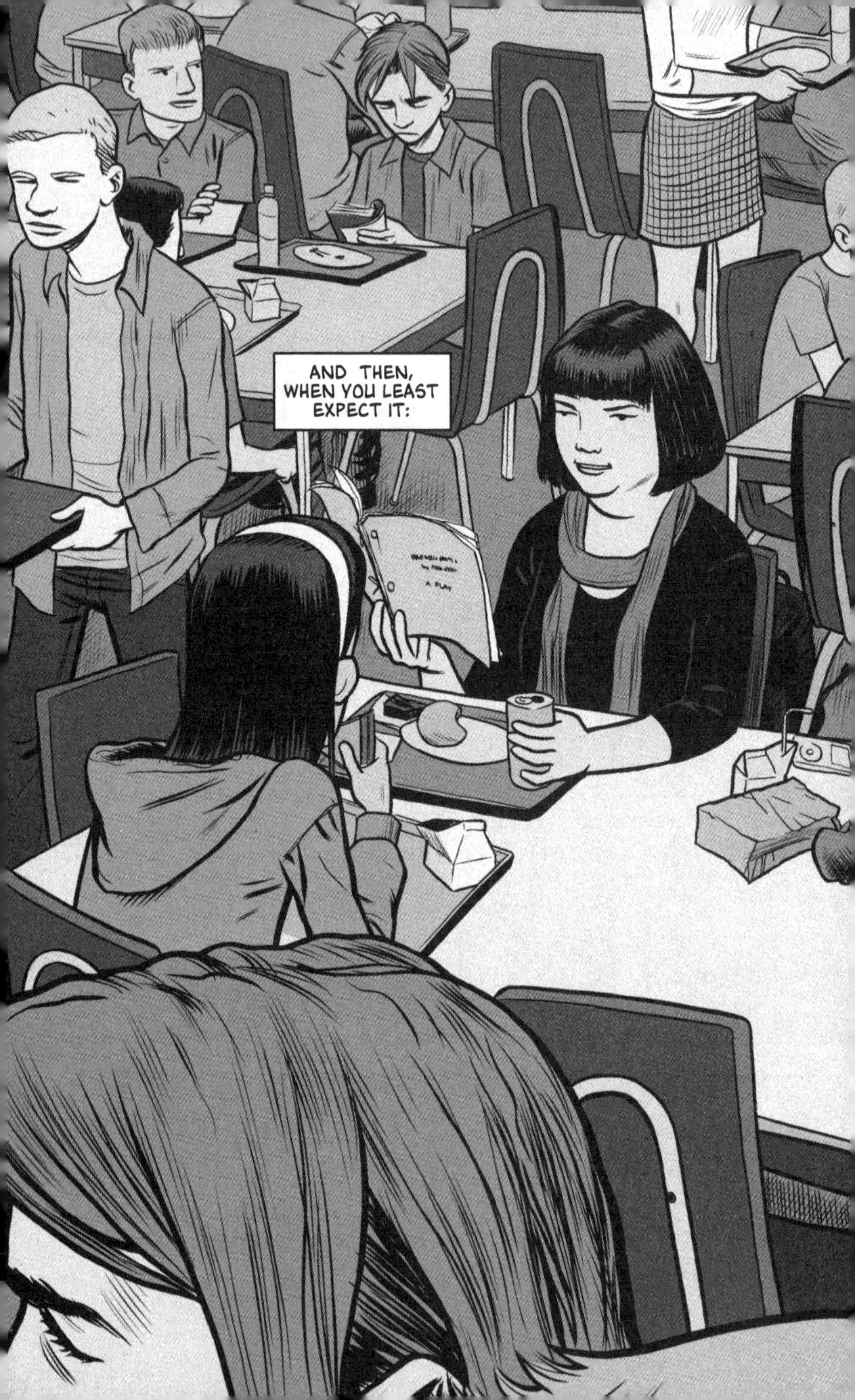
AND THEN, WHEN YOU LEAST EXPECT IT:

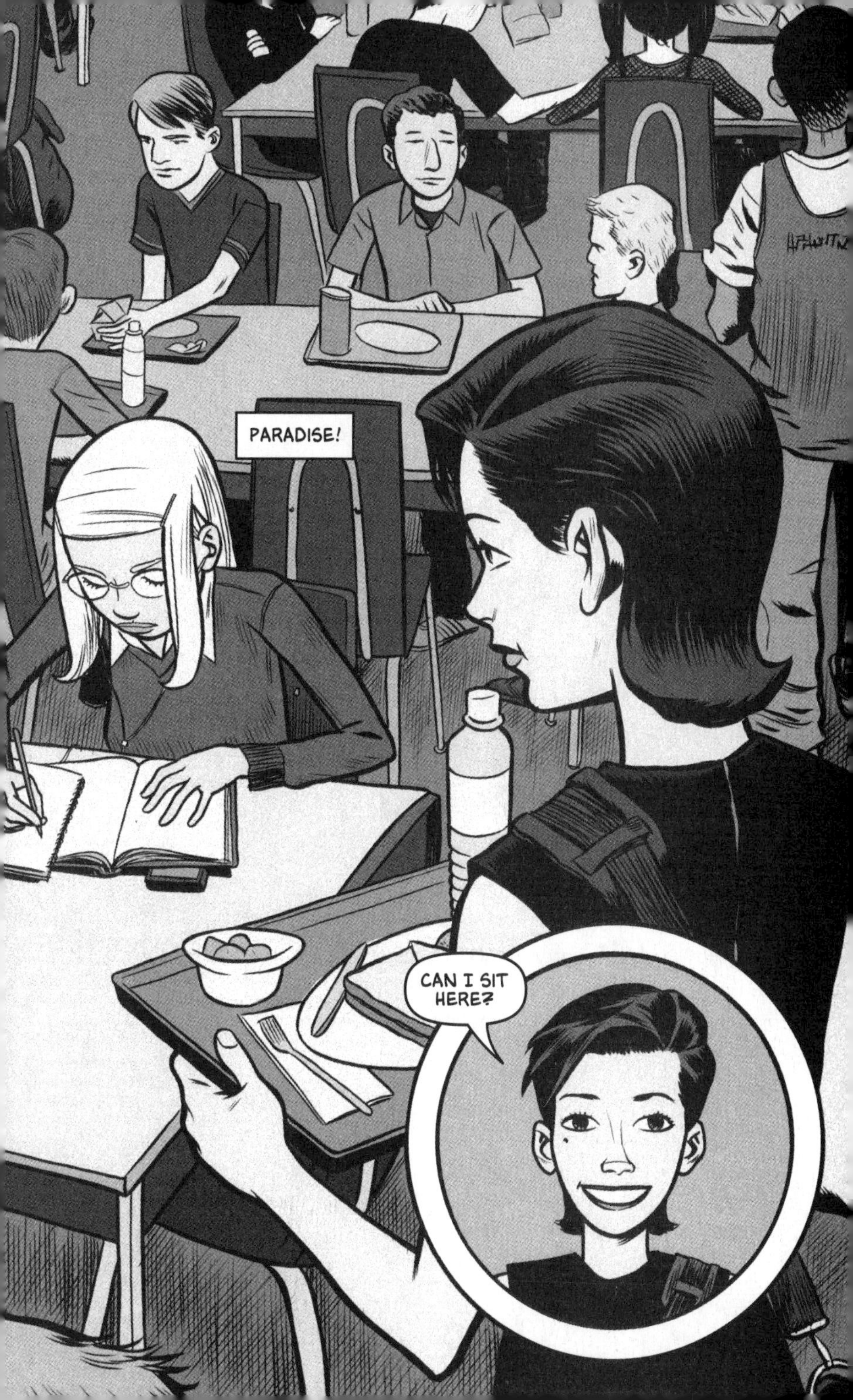
PARADISE!
CAN I SIT HERE?

A spoiled, rebellious London teenager conquers

the stuffy English countryside when she solves a

murder mystery on the 19th hole of her grandparents'

golf course.

COMING IN JULY 2007 ■ Read on.

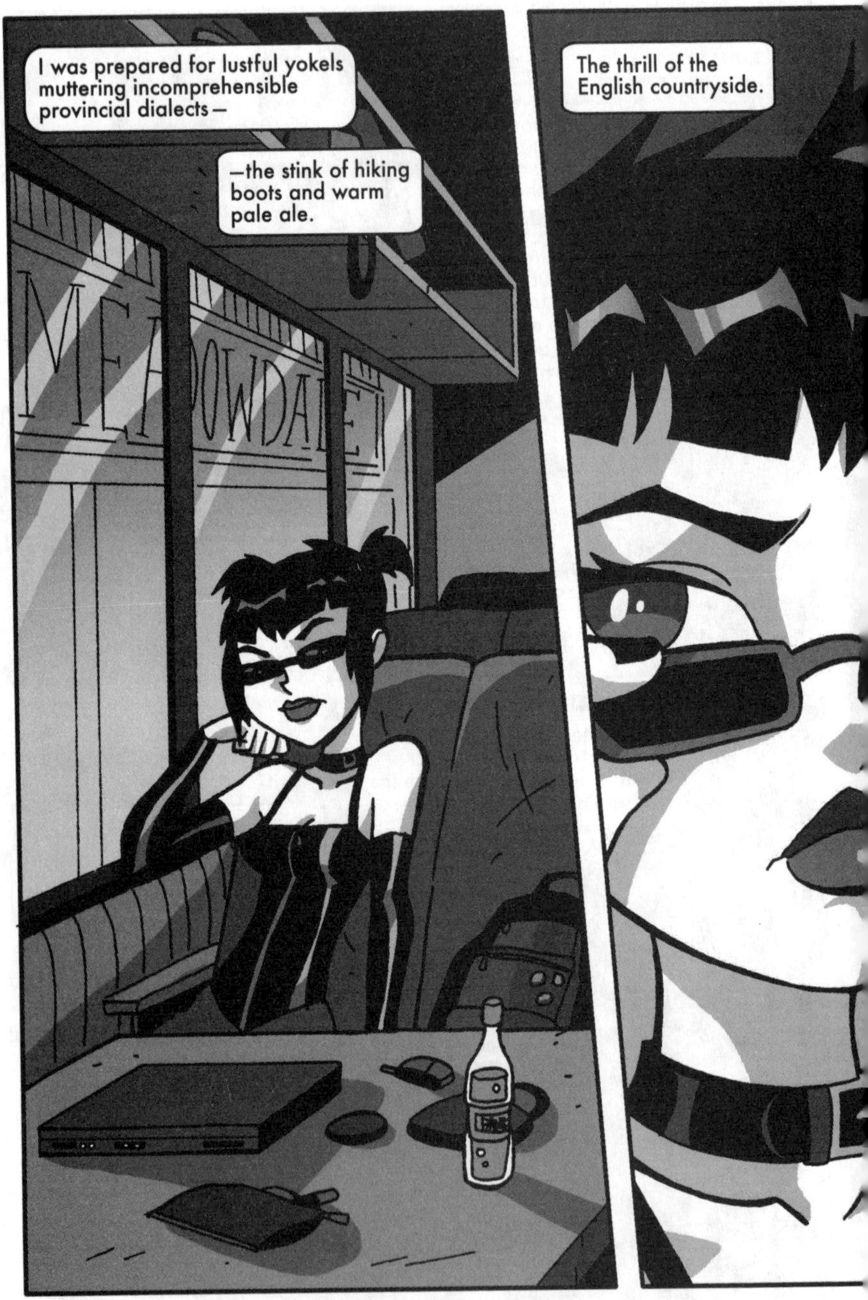

I was prepared for lustful yokels muttering incomprehensible provincial dialects—
—the stink of hiking boots and warm pale ale.
MEADOWDALE
The thrill of the English countryside.

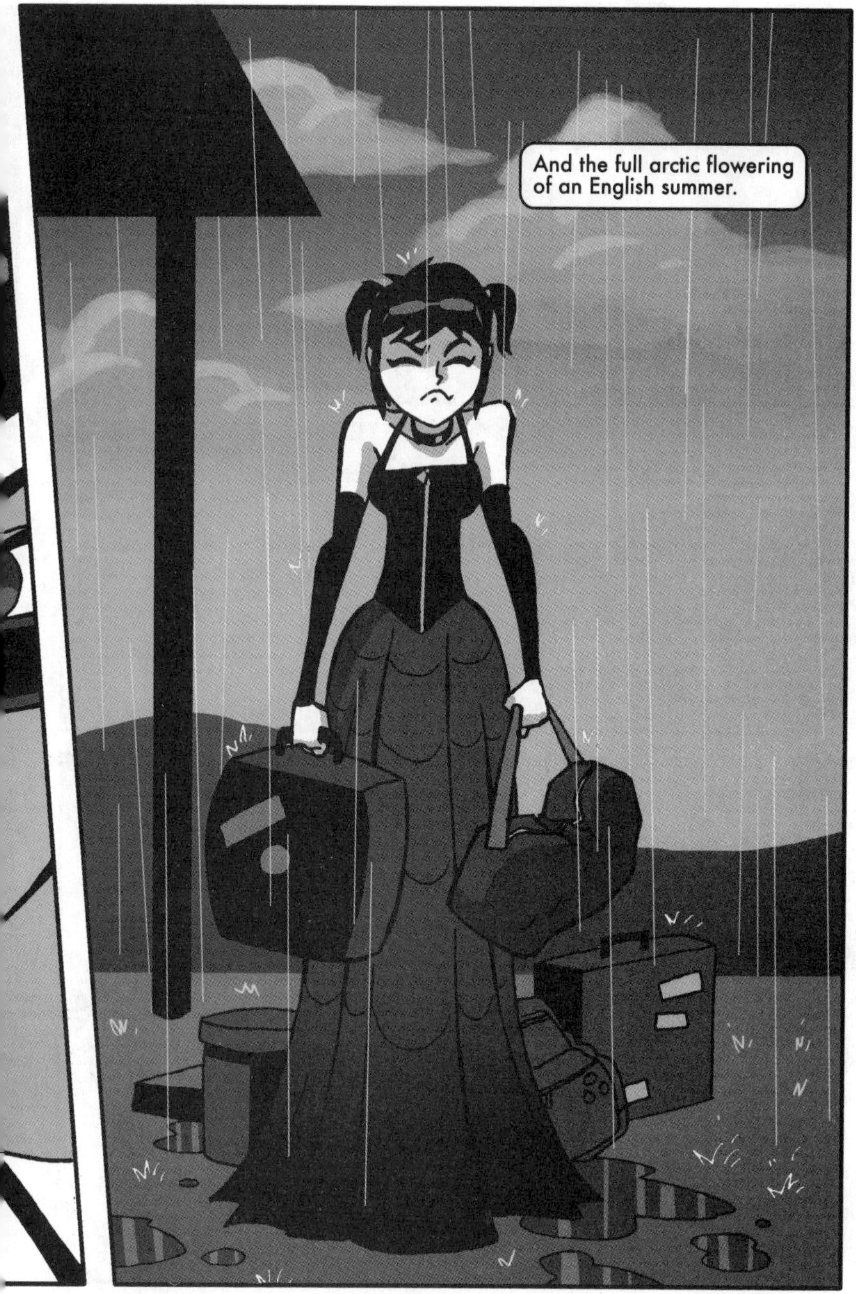
And the full arctic flowering of an English summer.

Derek Kirk Kim & Jesse Hamm

Good As Lily

What would you do if versions of yourself at ages 6, 29 and 70

suddenly became part of your already complicated high school life?

COMING IN AUGUST 2007 ■ Read on,
but please note: the following pages are not sequential.

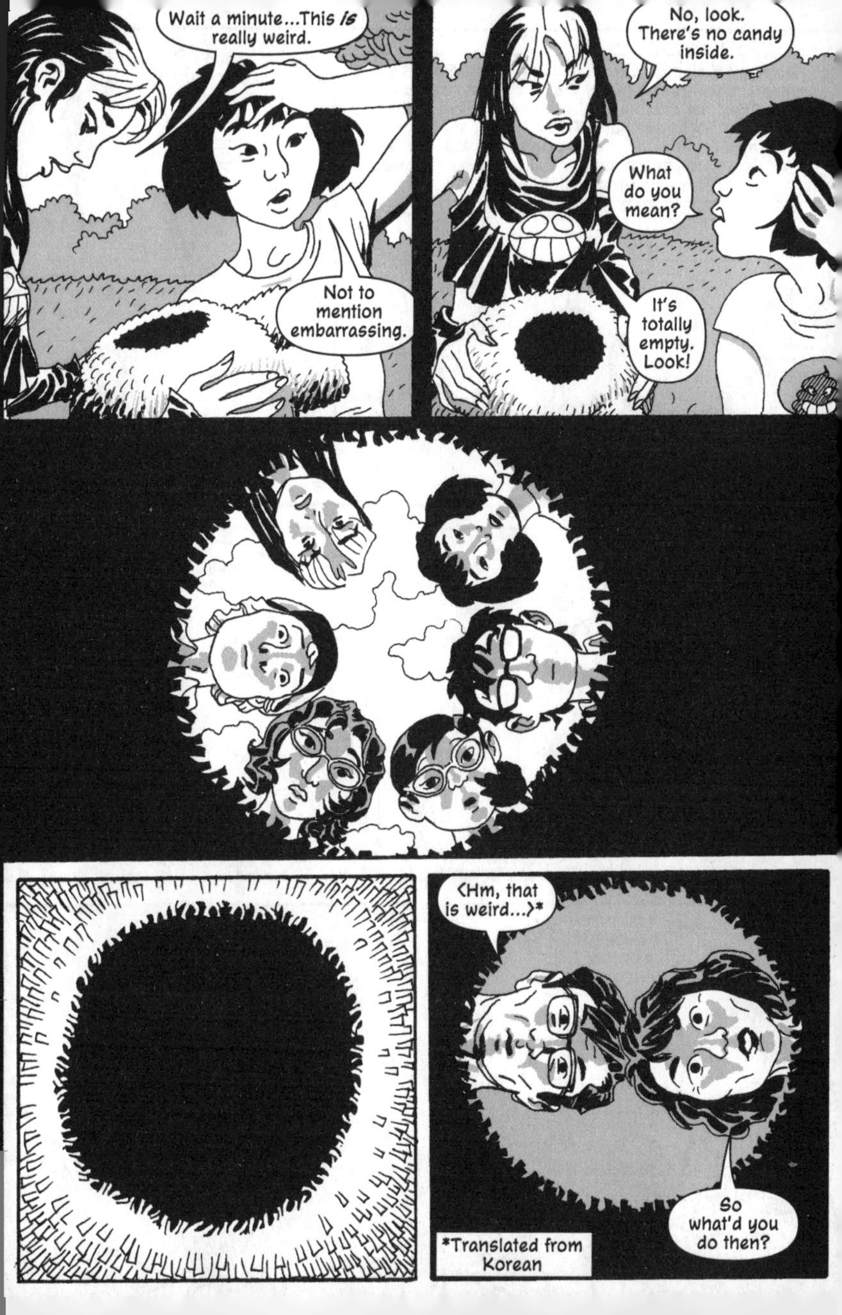
Wait a minute...This *is* really weird.
Not to mention embarrassing.
No, look. There's no candy inside.
What do you mean?
It's totally empty. Look!
<Hm, that is weird...>*
So what'd you do then?
*Translated from Korean

Go to
minxbooks.net
for exclusive interviews
and bonus artwork!

The Face of Modern Fiction